"What does the doctrine of adoption ha[v] [...] [t]ic, deistic' teenager? How does the Reforme[d] [...] [et]er-score human freedom? Are we getting too [...] [nal] ministry'? Can we talk about a relationsh[ip] [...] [i]nto sentimentalism? How does Christ's work [...] by his Word and Spirit? Only after reading t[hi]s [...] [...] .ted are all of these themes. And the integrating framework is union with Christ. In this fresh, winsome, learned yet down-to-earth exploration, Billings displays the research of a scholar and the heart of a pastor. This is one of the best books available on the heart of the gospel and its relevance for our lives."

—**Michael Horton**, Westminster Seminary California

"The beautiful, mystical, and biblical idea of Christ's union with the body of Christ—considered both ecclesially and individually—had nearly evaporated from the religious consciousness of evangelical and Reformed Christians for a while. That is no longer the case with Billings's new book. The doctrines of adoption and incarnation receive a fresh treatment in this book to open up the wide vista of application for the Christian life. Billings has done a wonderful job of weaving together a robust presentation of the heart of the gospel and the corresponding ecclesial praxis."

—**Paul C. H. Lim**, Vanderbilt University

"Drawing upon the likes of Augustine, Calvin, Bavinck, and others, Todd Billings ably demonstrates why the biblical truth of union and communion with God has had such historical and theological significance. Thankfully, he doesn't leave us out of the story. Along the way he highlights why union with Christ continues to matter for our understanding of the Christian life, making insightful connections between adoption and participation, incomprehensibility and accommodation, justice and Eucharist, grace and action. Let Billings take you into a deeper appreciation of what it means to be united to Christ—you won't regret it."

—**Kelly M. Kapic**, Covenant College

"Billings has been at the forefront of academic debates over the concept of union with Christ. With this book he shows all of us why union with Christ matters for our Christian lives and ministries and worship. Drawing on contexts as diverse as sixteenth-century Europe and contemporary Africa, Billings explores a theme that takes us to the heart of the gospel in a way that enriches and corrects our faith, our understanding, and our practices."

—**Suzanne McDonald**, Calvin College

"In *Union with Christ*, Todd Billings expounds upon an important New Testament doctrine by exploring its contemporary ramifications in light of careful historical and exegetical reflection. This is a thought-provoking book that will ignite fresh conversations about the nature of our participation in Christ."

—**Trevin Wax**, coauthor of *Counterfeit Gospels* and *Holy Subversion*

To my students
at Western Theological Seminary,
who helped show me the life-changing nature
of union with Christ

Contents

Acknowledgments

I t would be ironic for a book about union with Christ to be the product of a solitary individual. For in union with Christ, we are united not only to Jesus Christ but to his body, a community of faith brought into fellowship by the Spirit. While I hold final responsibility for the material in this book, it reflects many gifts of fellowship—the wise input of many friends and interlocutors over the course of several years.

Numerous scholars, pastors, and students gave me helpful feedback on earlier drafts of chapters. Special thanks for providing specific feedback goes to Drs. John Bolt, James Brownson, Jason Byassee, R. Scott Clark, Matt Floding, Michael Horton, Kristen Johnson, Trygve Johnson, Kelly Kapic, Suzanne McDonald, Richard Muller, and John Witvliet. I also received helpful input on chapter material from pastors and students, including Jill Carattini, Dan Claus, Ann Conklin, Brannon Ellis, Travis Else, David Feiser, Brian Keepers, Dustyn Keepers, Stephen Schaffer, Chris Theule-Van Dam, and Tim Truesdell. At each stage of the writing process, I have received exceptionally competent help from my research assistant, Andrew Mead. To all of these conversation partners, I am deeply grateful.

In addition to these specific readers, others offered assistance that helped make this book possible. I am grateful to the Templeton Foundation and the University of Heidelberg for providing the Templeton Award for Theological Promise. After my first book won this award in 2009, funding was provided for further lectures; those lectures served as the initial raw material that was expanded into this book.

Thus I am grateful to the schools that hosted these Templeton lectures and the audiences who offered valuable feedback on earlier drafts of these chapters. My thanks goes to Dirkie Smit and the faculty at the University of Stellenbosch and to Ernst M. Conradie and the faculty at the University of West Cape for their feedback on my lecture on the Lord's Supper and justice, which was revised and expanded into chapter 4. For their insightful input on chapter 3, I am grateful to John Webster and the faculty at the University of Aberdeen; Paul Nimmo and the faculty at the University of Edinburgh; Alan Torrance, Steve Holmes, and Julie Canlis at the University of St. Andrews; and Scott Manetsch and the faculty at Trinity Evangelical Divinity School. At all of these schools, I benefited greatly from the opportunity to present earlier drafts of the material in this book to faculty and students.

In addition, I am thankful for the invitation to give a series of three lectures on the contemporary significance of Reformed theology at Western Theological Seminary—an event that was enhanced by respondents from Hope College, Calvin College, and Calvin Theological Seminary. The series, in honor of Eugene Osterhaven, served as an opportunity to put together lectures in coherent form, which contributed significantly to the development of this book. I am grateful to more people than can be named for participating in that event and for bringing salient insights that I hope are reflected at points throughout.

It has been a pleasure to work with the editors at Baker Academic, including Bob Hosack and Arika Theule-Van Dam. I appreciate their enthusiasm and flexibility, as some of the planning for this book was completed transcontinentally while my wife and I were teaching in Ethiopia for five months.

I am also grateful to various groups for providing copyright permissions for this book. For permission to reprint the contemporary English translation of the Belhar Confession, available as an appendix at the end of chapter 4, I am grateful to the Office of the General Assembly of the Presbyterian Church (USA), as well as the Publication Committee of the Uniting Reformed Church in Southern Africa. In a few places I use a very small amount of material from my previous two books. I am grateful to Oxford University Press for their permission to use revised material from pages 10, 13–14, and 52–53 in *Calvin, Participation, and the Gift: The Activity of Believers in Union with*

Christ (Oxford: Oxford University Press, 2007). I am also grateful to Eerdmans for permission to include two paragraphs of modified material from *The Word of God for the People of God: An Entryway to the Theological Interpretation of Scripture* (Grand Rapids: Eerdmans, 2010). In addition, I am grateful for permission to use a small amount of material adapted from my article "Incarnational Ministry and the Unique, Incarnate Christ" (*Modern Reformation*, March/April 2009, 19–22).

Finally, my thanks goes to the communities that make my overall work possible: my colleagues at Western Theological Seminary, as well as friends at Hope College; my church family, First Reformed Church in Holland, Michigan; and most of all, my luminous wife, Rachel, and our dear children, Neti and Nathaniel.

This book is dedicated to my students at Western Theological Seminary in Holland, Michigan. It is with thanks to God that I offer this as a gift to them.

Abbreviations

Comm.   Commentary

CTS   John Calvin, *Calvin's Commentaries*, trans. Calvin
            Translation Society, ed. John King, 22 vols. (1845–56;
            repr., Grand Rapids: Baker, 1981)

CC   D. W. Torrance and T. F. Torrance, eds., *Calvin's
            Commentaries*, 12 vols. (Grand Rapids: Eerdmans,
            1960–72)

CD   Karl Barth, *Church Dogmatics*, 4 vols. in 13 parts
            (Edinburgh: T&T Clark, 1956–69)

HC Comm. Zacharias Ursinus, *The Commentary of Dr. Zacha-
            rias Ursinus on the Heidelberg Catechism*, trans.
            G. W. Williard (Grand Rapids: Eerdmans, 1954)

Inst.   John Calvin, *Institutes of the Christian Religion*,
            1559, ed. J. T. McNeill, trans. F. L. Båttles, 2 vols.
            (Philadelphia: Westminster, 1960)

Introduction

Union with Christ is a central New Testament description of Christian identity, the life of salvation in Christ. It entails the giving of a new identity such that in Christ, forgiveness and new life are received through the Spirit. Union with Christ involves abiding in Christ the Vine. It means that through the Spirit, sinners are adopted into the household of God as co-heirs with Christ. It means that God's Spirit is poured out to make the life and teaching of Jesus real to us. It implicates our worship, our vocation in the world, and our witness as the church. Union with Christ is theological shorthand for the gospel itself—a key image that pulls together numerous motifs in the biblical witness.[1] As one biblical scholar exclaims, in the course of biblical commentary, "Being 'in Christ' is the essence of Christian proclamation and experience. One may discuss legalism, nomism, and even justification by faith, but without treating the 'in Christ' motif we miss the heart of the Christian message."[2]

1. In the words of John Calvin, "the sum of the gospel" is the "newness of life and free reconciliation—[which] are conferred on us by Christ," in union with Christ as believers "possess" Christ by faith. *Institutes of the Christian Religion*, 1559, ed. J. T. McNeill and F. L. Battles (Philadelphia: Westminster, 1967), 3.3.1.

2. Richard N. Longenecker, *Galatians*, Word Biblical Commentary 41 (Dallas: Word, 2002), 159. While I would prefer not to use the term "essence" as this quotation does, Longenecker and many other recent biblical scholars have been emphatic about the significance of the notion of union with Christ in the New Testament.

In recent decades, the theme of union with Christ has become known in popular theological circles through controversies: a number of conferences and books have explored the notion of union with Christ in Calvin and Luther and in New Testament studies, often with a concern for ongoing debates about justification.[3]

This book is not a contribution to those debates. Instead, it emerges from the experience of teaching and lecturing on union with Christ and seeing how the theme challenges, nurtures, and enlivens hearers.[4] Many have testified that this doctrine has revolutionized the way they approach the Christian life and ministry. It reframes parts of our theology that make God too small and predictable, too close, or too distant. It gives a portrait of Christian identity that displaces the ever-fascinating self, replacing it with a God-given identity received from the Father through the Spirit in Christ. It makes us reconsider old theological debates in new ways, and calls us to lives of worship, justice, and service with a new sense of gratitude. My experience of teaching and dialoguing about this topic with various conversation partners has forced me to take seriously a question that has shaped the writing of this book: what is so amazing about God's action in uniting believers to Christ?

In addressing this question, I weave together scripture, doctrinal theology, and analysis of contemporary Western Christianity in a series of thematic essays. My previous writing on the subject has been primarily in the area of historical theology. While I seek to make a responsible use of historical sources, my work here is best seen as part of a theology of retrieval: hearing the voices of the past in such a way that they are allowed to exceed and overcome the chatter of the present.[5] In

---

3. A small sampling of this literature includes the following: Mark A. Garcia, *Life in Christ: Union with Christ and the Twofold Grace in Calvin's Theology* (Eugene, OR: Wipf & Stock, 2008); Carl Braaten and Robert Jenson, *Union with Christ: The New Finnish Interpretation of Luther* (Grand Rapids: Eerdmans, 1998); N. T. Wright, *Justification: God's Plan and Paul's Vision* (Downers Grove, IL: InterVarsity Academic, 2009); Stephen Westerholm, *Perspectives Old and New on Paul: The "Lutheran" Paul and His Critics* (Grand Rapids: Eerdmans, 2004); Bruce McCormack, ed., *Justification in Perspective: Historical Developments and Contemporary Challenges* (Grand Rapids: Baker Academic, 2006); Mark Husbands and Daniel J. Treier, eds., *Justification: What's at Stake in the Current Debates* (Downers Grove, IL: InterVarsity, 2004).

4. As noted in the acknowledgments above, in addition to emerging from my teaching on the subject at a seminary level, these chapters were originally based on a series of lectures given through the Templeton Award for Theological Promise and the Eugene Osterhaven Lectures at Western Theological Seminary in Holland, Michigan.

5. For an overview of theologies of retrieval as a contemporary approach to theology, see John Webster, "Theologies of Retrieval," in *Oxford Handbook of*

particular, this book seeks to highlight key present-day implications of a Reformational doctrine of union with Christ—implications that are often startling and thought-altering, as well as edifying. While this book contains fresh historical inquiries, it also builds upon and extends my earlier, more detailed historical-theological work on union with Christ.[6] In this way, I seek to help us hear the voices of the past in a way that illuminates scripture's witness to the reality of our union with Christ, giving us insights for theology, life, and ministry today.

Before giving an overview of the chapters and beginning the journey in this book, it is worth pondering the book's method in more depth. Why "retrieval"? And why, specifically, retrieval of Reformational accounts of the biblical theme of union with Christ?

Seeing with New Eyes

All Christians approach their faith from within a particular cultural context. This fact is inescapable. Yet one of the peculiar things about culture is that it involves many assumptions that we didn't recognize we had—until we encounter something different. For those who have traveled and seen cultures that are quite different from their own, there is one word that describes the day-by-day, if not minute-by-minute, experience: surprise! We have all sorts of assumptions about, for example, how to eat, how to interact, and how to perform certain tasks, and we take these to be "common sense." But in cross-cultural encounters we see that not everyone does things according to our assumptions. What we thought was simply "the way things are done" is now recognized as "the way *we* do things."

Some may be tempted to despair of discovering theological truth when they recognize the reality that truth is always perceived from a

---

Systematic Theology, ed. John Webster, Kathryn Tanner, and Iain Torrance (Oxford: Oxford University Press, 2007), 583–99.

6. See J. Todd Billings, *Calvin, Participation, and the Gift: The Activity of Believers in Union with Christ*, Changing Paradigms in Historical and Systematic Theology (Oxford: Oxford University Press, 2007); "John Calvin's Soteriology: Key Issues in Interpretation and Retrieval," *International Journal of Systematic Theology* 11, no. 4 (October 2009): 428–47; "United to God through Christ: Calvin on the Question of Deification," *Harvard Theological Review* 98, no. 3 (July 2005): 315–34; "John Calvin's Theology of Union with Christ, and Its Early Retrieval," in *Calvin's Theology and Its Reception: Disputes, Developments, and New Possibilities*, ed. J. Todd Billings and I. John Hesselink (Louisville: Westminster John Knox, 2012).

particular perspective shaped by many social, historical, and cultural factors. But it is better to recognize that our different perspectives provide both distinctive gifts and distinctive blind spots in our interpretation of the Bible and our articulation of theology. In terms of the distinctive gifts, for example, chapter 4 explores how the Reformed Christians in South Africa who penned the Belhar Confession have some valuable insights that come from a long struggle to overcome apartheid and its heritage. Likewise, as Philip Jenkins has explored, the Global South brings special gifts to the church at large by its engagement with themes such as poverty and healing in scripture.[7] Learning about the biblical interpretation and theology of different cultures can be an illuminating enterprise, for it can both reveal our blind spots and point the way toward a more faithful approach to receiving and living the gospel that scripture testifies to. Reading the Belhar Confession can both unveil our own sinful attitudes and open us in a deeper way to the Bible's message of unity, reconciliation, and justice. Reading theology from the Global South can help reveal the materialistic and gnostic tendencies in contemporary Western Christianity that make us read scripture as a story about "souls" rather than real bodies, a story about the real temptation of wealth and the real hardship of poverty. At the same time, interpretations of scripture from the Global South can open Western readers to a more holistic sense in which the gospel is "good news."

In a similar way, a theology of retrieval—reading scripture along with Christians of ages past—can have particular value. Consider three prominent virtues to this approach: First, it possesses the advantages of reading scripture along with persons of another culture, as discussed above, for there are vast differences in culture as one looks to theologians in the church's history. Second, particular biblical and theological issues are often explored in great depth during specific historical periods. For example, those interested in refining their theology of the Trinity would do well to read the Bible along with the writers in the church of the fourth century. The way that the Bible's teaching relates to the Trinity was explored in great detail by numerous authors during that century. A theologian of retrieval will explore these texts not as "history" alone but also as conversation partners, thus allowing their thinking to go beyond the ordinary ways

---

7. See Philip Jenkins, *The New Faces of Christianity: Believing the Bible in the Global South* (New York: Oxford University Press, 2006).

of thinking in the twenty-first century. Precisely because these thinkers can exceed the possibility of the present—challenging twenty-first-century categories—their work is worth engaging.

This leads to the third virtue of a retrieval approach: having listened receptively to the theologians of the past, we can assess whether the new exegetical and theological possibilities discovered from this engagement with the past are valid or in error. For example, in his book *Reading the Bible with the Dead*, John L. Thompson surveys the premodern biblical interpretation of difficult texts of scripture—biblical texts that appear to marginalize women, promote hatred of one's enemies, or advocate violence.[8] Thompson shows that reading the Bible with premodern theologians can yield remarkable and helpful insights but that there are also claims that contemporary readers are right to reject. For example, while a prominent stream of premodern interpretation gives a sympathetic and theologically insightful account of Jephthah's daughter (Judg. 11), others fill in the gaps of the biblical narrative with reflections that would justify Jephthah's abusive act.[9] Theologians of retrieval can benefit from a historical distance that allows them to see the idolatries of another age and better discern what to accept or reject from biblical interpreters and theologians in earlier eras of history.

What new possibilities are opened up by a theological method of retrieval? Essentially, it is a possibility of seeing scripture, theology, and the world itself with "new eyes." Passages of scripture that we have read many times before can be seen with new insight, new possibilities. This involves simultaneously critiquing our ordinary ways of seeing things and gaining new ways to understand scripture and theology.

Cross-cultural encounters provide a useful analogy for this process. I recall when I first arrived in a rural area of Uganda to learn the language and participate in community development work. When I looked around the village, there was much that was different from the West, but much seemed the same as well. There were obvious differences: the houses were made out of mud and grass; many of the households had one man with multiple wives; nearly everyone in the village was a farmer, at least for part of their occupation. Yet when I saw people interacting with each other—laughing, talking,

---

8. John L. Thompson, *Reading the Bible with the Dead: What You Can Learn from the History of Exegesis That You Can't Learn from Exegesis Alone* (Grand Rapids: Eerdmans, 2007).

9. See ibid., 33–47.

sharing, debating—it seemed just like such interactions in the West. But I was wrong.

In a sense, everything was different, even though there were similarities. I soon found that there was an underlying kinship structure that shaped the countless social interactions in the village. I discovered that an unmarried male would not speak more than a few words to an unmarried woman—unless they were about to get married. Yet some of the young, unmarried people I knew spent a great deal of time with young people of the opposite sex. How could that be? I learned that it was because they were part of the same "family" or "kin" group. They would refer to each other as "brother" and "sister," even though they may have been, at most, distant cousins. Yet there was a great deal of closeness and flexibility allowed in these relationships since they would not consider marrying their "brother" or "sister." There was a complex network of relationships underlying all the interactions that I was seeing on the surface. Kinship was central to the identity of the people in my village.

As I came to know members of the church in Uganda better, I began to see that my blindness to the power of kinship structures in their culture was related to another blindness: my inability to see the power and extent of kinship structures in the Bible. In one move of "seeing with new eyes," I both encountered the cultural limitation absorbed from my individualistic Western culture and began to see the power of biblical images in new ways: sons and daughters of Israel, God of your ancestors, children of Abraham, co-heirs with Christ, "brothers and sisters" in Christ, adopted by God, a new humanity, son of God, firstborn. These were no longer archaic biblical ways of speaking but powerful ways of speaking about issues at the core of identity.

A theology of retrieval works in a way that is similar to this example. With the new eyes that a theology of retrieval makes possible, the Western cultural captivity of the gospel can be broken through in a small but significant way, as it was in my own cross-cultural encounter; in this process, the Spirit brings new life and insight through illuminating God's word. This kind of insight is part of the feeding and nourishment that comes through receiving God's word. It is a moment of discomfort and yet new assurance, a taste of repentance and new life—a movement of transformation into the image of Christ.

If this is indeed what a theology of retrieval makes possible, then why have I chosen to retrieve this particular biblical and theological theme from this particular historical era? In other words, why should one think that there is much for twenty-first-century Christians to learn from a Reformational rendering of the biblical theme of union with Christ?

Union with Christ: Retrieving a Biblical Motif from the Reformation

Just as the fourth century is an appropriate period from which to retrieve theologies of the Trinity, so also the sixteenth-century era of Reformation and counter-Reformation is an appropriate period from which to retrieve theologies of union with Christ. Central in the debates at this time was the meaning of Paul's term "justification," a term that fits within Paul's larger theology of union with Christ. Thus, the cardinal Reformational doctrine of justification by faith presupposes and advances a particular theology of union with Christ—and is countered at the Council of Trent by a contrasting Roman Catholic doctrine of union with Christ. The debates between the two sides often involved close exegesis of biblical texts, a rereading of the church fathers, and careful theological reflection on union with Christ.

But union with Christ was not just a subject of polemical debate in this period; it was also a key theme in thinking through such varied topics as divine and human agency, prayer, the Christian life, and the sacraments. For example, in Calvin's *Institutes*, some material on justification is polemical, seeking to articulate a doctrinally precise position in contrast to views that he saw as aberrant, such as that of Andreas Osiander and of the Council of Trent. But as I have explored elsewhere, Calvin's theology of justification fit within his theology of union with Christ, which he used to speak about the nature of prayer and the Christian life. His reflections on these topics—informed by the same doctrine of justification but fulfilling a different purpose—became so popular that the chapters of the *Institutes* in which he dealt with them were collected into a volume called *The Golden Book of the True Christian Life*. Calvin also used his theology of justification and union with Christ to configure his account of divine and human agency, the law, and the sacraments.[10]

10. See Billings, *Calvin, Participation, and the Gift*, chaps. 4–5. See also Billings, "John Calvin's Theology of Union with Christ," in Billings and Hesselink, *Calvin's Theology and Its Reception*.

The spread of the doctrine of union with Christ to nonpolemical realms of theology continued in the generations after the Reformation. Heidelberg theologian Caspar Olevian (1536–87), for example, made the double benefit of justification and sanctification in union with Christ central to his covenant theology.[11] Both Puritans in the English-speaking world and members of the Dutch "further Reformation" in the Netherlands utilized a vibrant theology of union with Christ in their works on the Christian life and pastoral theology.[12] Indeed, union with Christ was extremely prominent in the popular piety of many seventeenth- and eighteenth-century Christians in the Reformed tradition. The Holy Fairs are an example of this. These festivals often attracted thousands of participants for around four days of preach-ing, singing, and—at the center—celebrating the Lord's Supper. The theology of the Supper that was preached and practiced was one of union with Christ, a fact that is strongly attested to in the spiritual journals written by lay participants in the festivals.[13]

In contemporary theology, the polemical debates about justification as an aspect of union with Christ have been revived.[14] What has not accompanied this revival of interest, however, has been a recovery of the multifaceted implications of a Reformational account of union with Christ—particularly in areas such as the sacraments, divine and human agency, and the Christian life and ministry. This in itself is a missed opportunity, for the theme of union with Christ had a vitality that spoke to many different aspects of Christian teaching from the sixteenth through the eighteenth century.

Moreover, the need for a renewed theology of union with Christ in Western churches is made acute by at least two major factors. First, the functional or "lived" theologies of salvation in the West have

11. See R. Scott Clark, *Caspar Olevian and the Substance of the Covenant* (Grand Rapids: Reformed Heritage Books, 2008), 137–209.

12. For an excellent analysis of union with Christ in Puritan author John Owen, see Kelly Kapic, *Communion with God: The Divine and Human in the Theology of John Owen* (Grand Rapids: Baker Academic, 2007). On union with Christ in the Dutch further Reformation, see Arie de Reuver, *Sweet Communion: Trajectories of Spirituality from the Middle Ages through the Further Reformation*, trans. James A. De Jong (Grand Rapids: Baker Academic, 2007).

13. See Leigh Eric Schmidt, *Holy Fairs*, 2nd ed. (Grand Rapids: Eerdmans, 2001), 14–15, 158–68.

14. See, for example, Husbands and Treier, *Justification*; N. T. Wright, *Justification*; and John Piper, *The Future of Justification: A Response to N. T. Wright* (Wheaton: Crossway, 2007).

deficiencies in the precise areas where a Reformational theology of union with Christ has strengths. Sociologists have discovered that while many Americans, for example, claim to be "Christian," their theology is often much more deistic than Christian. Salvation is seen in terms of the benefits it provides to the individual and their self-confidence rather than in terms of a restored communion with God and neighbor. Religious traditions are dealt with by "tinkering"—mixing and matching from various Christian and non-Christian sources to fill the purpose of solving one's immediate problems.[15] In contrast to this, a theology of union with Christ centers Christian identity in Jesus Christ himself, and in the claim of the Triune God upon the Christian. Salvation is not self-centered but is a renewal and restoration of the self precisely through orienting the self toward God, toward the church as the body of Christ, and toward the neighbor. Individual believers discover their true identity in communion rather than in a pragmatic, individualistic approach to salvation, and tinkering is replaced by a posture of humble gratitude before God. The God encountered in union with Jesus Christ is at once more majestic and more intimate than the deistic-tending God of the West.

The second reason for the urgent need to recover a theology of union with Christ in the West emerges from the continuing power of fundamentalist-modernist divisions rooted early in the twentieth century. These divisions shape the categories of what divides a "conservative" or "evangelical" church in the West from a "liberal" or "progressive" one. But these very categories—and the church's identity as defined by these categories—reflect a reduction of the gospel. The ecclesial left tends to identify the gospel with a certain type of ethical action. Thus, religion is fundamentally a horizontal affair—horizontal exhortation leading to horizontal action for the sake of love, justice, and so on. The ecclesial right tends to emphasize the importance of the vertical—whether one is "right with God"—but in a way that leaves unclear the precise role of a horizontal life that entails loving the neighbor, as well as the widow and the orphan. Justice is important for many evangelicals, but there is considerable uncertainty about why it is important, as later chapters will explore.

15. See Robert Wuthnow, *After the Baby Boomers: How Twenty- and Thirty-Somethings Are Shaping the Future of American Religion* (Princeton: Princeton University Press, 2007), 13–16, 103–7, 134–35; Christian Smith, *Soul Searching: The Religious and Spiritual Lives of American Teenagers*, with Melinda Lundquist Denton (New York: Oxford University Press, 2005), 118–71.

A theology of union with Christ takes the dualism and polarities that still remain from the fundamentalist-modernist controversy
and unites them into a cohesive, holistic account of the gospel. In a
theology of union with Christ retrieved from the Reformation, justice
is integral for our lives in union with Christ—for through the Spirit
believers receive not only justification but also sanctification, which
animates and enlivens our love of neighbor. Hence, justice cannot be
seen as an optional "extra" for super-Christians. Yet on the other hand,
the gospel can never be reduced to our own acts of justice. For Jesus
Christ, and our union with him, is the good news: in him we receive
both forgiveness and new life by the Spirit. Both gifts are received in
union with Jesus Christ. They can no more be separated than Jesus
Christ himself can be torn into pieces. A theology of union with
Christ can bring together what modernity has polarized and separated.

In order to theologically retrieve a Reformational rendering of the
biblical theme of unión with Christ, this book begins in the opening chapter by exploring the remarkable implications of a common
biblical image for salvation, one that is at the heart of a trinitarian
theology of union with Christ: adoption. Drawing upon the sociological research of Christian Smith, the chapter begins with a portrait
of how the distant God of deism is operative in the theology of
many Christians in the West. In contrast to this, I explore a biblical
theology of adoption as a surprising, if at times unsettling, alternative to this operative deism. In the New Testament, adoption is an
analogy for speaking about the close family relationship of becoming
children of God. It has a trinitarian cast, as believers are united to
Christ by the Spirit, who enables them to cry out to God as "Abba!
Father!" (Rom. 8:14–17). This new, adopted identity becomes for
Christians both a gift and a calling—to walk by the Spirit rather than
by their own power. The way the Reformed tradition adds clarity to
this biblical gift and calling is by emphasizing salvation as received
in the double grace of union with Christ: adoption is first of all a
legal matter of justification through Christ, the one nonadopted
Son of God; justification is received as a gift as believers are united
to Christ. But this newly given, legally valid identity leads to the
discovery of one's new life in the household of God—a new life of
sanctification in which the Spirit calls and empowers Christians to
live into their adopted identity. Although the context for this adopted relationship is communion with God through being united
to Christ, the repeated exhortations from scripture to live into this

new identity indicate to us that Christians are not "adopted" into a low-commitment relationship with a conveniently distant God. To the contrary, the gospel does not so much offer a low-cost "eternal life insurance" as it gives the tremendous privilege of learning to be children of the King, living into our new identity in a kingdom that is coming forth to us from the future.

Chapter 2 explores an implication of a theology of union with Christ that may strike many readers as counterintuitive. The images of union with Christ, abiding in Christ, and participation in Christ present a multifaceted and wide-ranging theology of salvation. No part of human identity goes untouched by union with Christ—one's life is found in Christ, by the Spirit, in service to the Father. But much in modern theology and church life has obscured the negative corollary to union and communion, which scripture also addresses: in ourselves, we are dead, slaves, and can do "nothing" to produce fruit. Thus, although it is missed by many who belong to Reformational traditions as well as by their detractors, a doctrine of the bondage of the will, or what some call "total depravity," corresponds to a doctrine of total communion in which salvation involves a multifaceted communion with God. While neither Calvin nor the early Reformational tradition used the phrase "total depravity," they do claim that no part of human life is unaffected by sin and that sinful humans cannot perform any "saving good" apart from the Spirit's effectual work.[16] This chapter argues that such a strongly stated Reformational doctrine of sin is not a purely negative statement about the human condition. Instead, the early Reformed insistence on the bondage of the will to sin reflects a theology of salvation that has an exalted place for humanity: full humanity is humanity in communion with God. If one really believes that humanity is created for communion with God, then redemption can involve nothing less than the communion enabled by God's Spirit. This chapter retrieves the deeply biblical and christological thought of Augustine and early Reformational theologians to show how it is possible to hold together both sides of the biblical imagery—the imagery of union and communion together with that of slavery to sin. In doing so, it provides a way to affirm a dynamic theology of

---

16. Canons of Dort, third and fourth main points, art. 3, in *Ecumenical Creeds and Reformed Confessions* (Grand Rapids: CRC Publications, 1987), 133. Cf. John Calvin, *Bondage and Liberation of the Will: A Defence of the Orthodox Doctrine of Human Choice against Pighius*, ed. A. N. S. Lane, trans. G. I. Davies (Grand Rapids: Baker, 1996), 68–69.

union with and participation in Christ, while taking very seriously the effects of the fall.

Chapter 3 builds on the previous chapter, adding a second counterintuitive implication to union with Christ: the incomprehensibility of God. As we will note in chapter 2, a theology of union with Christ speaks about oneness, union and participation in Christ, union and communion with God, empowerment and communion by the Holy Spirit. At times, scripture even uses the image of marital sexual union to describe this mystery. On the one hand, it may seem that Western Christian culture—where Christian contemporary music and praise songs are often based on romantic ballads, and young adults are encouraged to wear chastity rings and consider themselves to be "dating Jesus," with "flowers, love notes," and all the trimmings—has a great deal of understanding of this language of union.[17] However, this rendering of communion, intimacy, and union can turn God-the-lover into someone less than God: while a sense of closeness and oneness with God is desired, the God with whom this is desired often doesn't have much "otherness." This is not the Alpha and the Omega, not the mysterious, incomprehensible God who comes to us not only as a lover but always as a stranger as well. This chapter argues that for the language of union with God to function properly, one needs a robust apophatic (negative) theology with a strong sense of the incomprehensibility of God. Ironically, in the hands of Calvin and Bavinck, a thoroughgoing doctrine of divine incomprehensibility does not undermine the language of union and communion; rather, it makes it possible to sustain such language. For those united to Christ in close communion with God, God always remains mysterious, other—God remains God, rather than an idol carved from the technology of romance in Western culture. Calvin and Bavinck show us a path for recovering a key truth that has been obscured in the modern West: a proper construal of God's mystery is vital in affirming the possibility of communion with God.

17. For example, one author writes, "There's nothing weird about thinking of Jesus like your greatest romantic interest, even if you're a guy. He wants that kind of intimacy with you so that he can win your heart with his amazing, perfect love, and make you ready for the big day when you get to live happily ever after with him. So how do you date Jesus? Here are some ways that work for me, but the sky is the limit for creativity—just like any true dating relationship. The key is to make it spontaneous, personal and a major priority. And then you'll find that he begins showing up for dates—sometimes with flowers, love notes, and rainbows!" Julia Ferwerda, "Dating Jesus: The Single Cure for Loneliness," http://www.crosswalk.com/singles/11567469/.

Chapter 4 considers the relation of justice to the gospel in Western Christianity, a relation that has long been a point of confusion and contention. On the one hand, the religious right has tended to frame justice as an optional add-on to the gospel, a form of extra credit for Christians after they are done with the central activities that relate to salvation. On the other hand, the religious left has tended to emphasize justice in a way that makes human acts of justice synonymous with the gospel itself. A theology of union with Christ provides a third way to relate the gospel to justice, thus avoiding the reductionism of both groups. In a theology of union with Christ, to withhold the calling to justice from the new identity we receive in the gospel is to tear Christ apart—to seek to reject the second dimension of union with Christ (sanctification) while holding to the first (justification). But justice is not exhaustive of the gospel either. Instead, justice is defined by its location in Christ, and the law of love fulfilled in Christ becomes the calling that Christians are to pursue in gratitude. When justice is sought through participation in Christ, the primal purpose of the law is fulfilled, which, according to Calvin, is "to unite us to our God."[18] This union with God through the law is enacted in a special way in the Lord's Supper, where believers respond to the presence of Christ with a sacrifice of praise that includes "all the duties of love"—love in the church and loving acts of justice in the world.[19] This chapter brings these biblical themes as developed by Calvin into critical dialogue with early Reformed thought and the Belhar Confession. In doing this, I propose a theology in which Christian identity and practice emerge from the Spirit's work through the Lord's Supper, where believers are brought into communion with Christ and Christ's body and are simultaneously empowered to serve the neighbor in need.

Finally, the book concludes with a chapter that considers how a theology of union with Christ offers a corrective to a popular model for ministry that has valuable strengths but is ultimately misguided: the notion of incarnational ministry. Whether in the circles of youth ministry, urban missions, or foreign missions, references to an "incarnational" approach to ministry are widespread. Yet most forms of incarnational ministry are based on the faulty assumption that the incarnation is a model for ministry, such that Christians should

18. John Calvin, *John Calvin's Sermons on the Ten Commandments*, ed. and trans. Benjamin W. Farley (Grand Rapids: Baker, 1980), 39.
19. *Inst*. 4.18.16.

imitate the act of the eternal Word becoming incarnate. As chapter 5 seeks to show, there is no biblical support for such a notion. Moreover, this notion obscures a central point in Christology—namely, that the incarnation is a unique, saving event rather than a set of activities that Christians are to copy. But rather than simply criticize an incarnational model for ministry, this chapter seeks to provide an alternative in terms of union with Christ. The ministry outcomes sought through "incarnational ministry" can be realized and refined through seeing that the imperative to have "the same mind" as "Christ Jesus" (Phil. 2:5) fits within Paul's matrix of union with Christ. As ones united to Christ, we participate in the Spirit's ongoing work of bearing witness to Christ and creating a new humanity in which the dividing walls between cultures are overcome in Christ. The good news of union with Christ is that Christians do not have the burden of being redeemers; instead, they belong to the Redeemer and bear witness to the living Christ. A theology of union with Christ provides strong grounds for a relational, culture-crossing ministry that is always pointing beyond itself to Jesus Christ—the sole Redeemer, the unique incarnate Word.

Approached in the ways outlined above, this book offers an exposition of a biblical and Reformational theology of union with Christ, as well as a consideration of how this theology radically contrasts with key dimensions of the operative theologies of contemporary Western Christianity. Union with Christ is an illuminating doctrine. It sheds light on our sentimental capitulation to the cultural idols that are less than God, and it shows the way toward a revitalized life in Christ. In terms of theology, it awakens us from our human-centered "dogmatic slumbers," opening our eyes to a God who is both closer to us and more mysterious than we had ever imagined. In our Christian life and ministry, it displaces the heroic role of our own action while calling us to a life of justice and witness that is shaped and enabled by none other than Jesus Christ. This book provides a biblical and theological entryway for rediscovering the mystery of the Christian life—life in Christ.

1

Salvation as Adoption in Christ

*An Antidote to Today's Distant
yet Convenient Deity*

Adopted by the Triune God: A Biblical and Countercultural Account of Salvation

In the course of writing this chapter, my wife and I traveled to Ethiopia to adopt a lovely little girl. We know the country of Ethiopia relatively well, as we both taught in Ethiopia for five months in 2009, and I had spent nine months in Ethiopia earlier in my teaching career. We know that Ethiopia is a wonderful place with beautiful landscapes, welcoming people, and very strong coffee. But it also a country with over four million orphans, according to estimates.[1]

I do believe, as scripture tells us, that we should care for the orphans in the world. "Religion that is pure and undefiled before God, the Father, is this: to care for orphans and widows in their distress" (James 1:27a). Indeed, as chapter 4 in particular explores, Christians should display a special concern for and commitment to those

---

1. A 2006 UNICEF report put the estimate at 4.6 million, and many estimates since that time are even higher. See Indrias Getachew, "Ethiopia: Steady Increase in Street Children Orphaned by AIDS," http://www.unicef.org/infobycountry/ethiopia _30783.html.

in need. But lest pity be our only feeling toward orphans, we should consider that on a different level, all of us are orphans. The God of the Bible has no "natural" or "begotten" children apart from Jesus the Son; all the rest of us need to be adopted. Although there are important differences between the biblical metaphor of adoption and adoption practices today (which we explore below), we should not underestimate the extraordinary power of this biblical analogy: for all of God's people are adopted, both in Israel and in the church (Rom. 9:4; Eph. 1:5). Thus it is good news when Jesus tells us in John's Gospel, "I will not leave you orphaned; I am coming to you" (John 14:18). Instead, through the Spirit, we can be united to Jesus Christ, becoming daughters and sons of God through our union with the one perfect Son of God.

But what exactly is this adoption that we receive? Paul initiates us into this world of adoption in Romans 8. Although by our flesh, or our old self, we are slaves to "the law of sin," the "Spirit of life in Christ Jesus has set you free" (Rom. 8:2). What does this freedom look like? It is freedom to be adopted children of the Triune God. We have been given the Spirit of God, and by the Spirit "Christ is in you." And "all who are led by the Spirit of God are children of God. For you did not receive a spirit of slavery to fall back into fear, but you have received a spirit of adoption. When we cry, 'Abba! Father!' it is that very Spirit bearing witness with our spirit that we are children of God, and if children, then heirs, heirs of God and joint heirs with Christ" (Rom. 8:14–17). In this way, Paul speaks about the drama of adoption that we are caught up into. We are no longer slaves; we are children with an intimate relationship with God. In fact, we don't even pray by ourselves, but the Spirit prays in us words of intimacy— "Abba! Father!"—as those who are in Christ, or "joint heirs with Christ" (8:15, 17).

This image of adoption is key for Paul in speaking about the life of salvation in Christ, as well as the new identity that we enter into in Christ. On the one hand, the Spirit assures Christians that they already belong to God—they can cry out to God as Father, as ones united to Jesus Christ. Yet, as Paul indicates later in the same chapter, this adoption is also a future reality for which "the creation waits with eager longing for the revealing of the children of God" (Rom. 8:19). For "not only the creation, but we ourselves, who have the first fruits of the Spirit, groan inwardly while we wait for adoption, the redemption of our bodies" (Rom. 8:23). We are adopted children of God, able to pray to the Father by the Spirit, yet even this is a foretaste of the consummation of adoption for which the creation groans and waits. But maybe this just sounds like pious God-talk. What, really, *is* so significant about adoption? To get a sense of how radical the message of adoption is, I will adapt a parable from Danish philosopher and theologian Søren Kierkegaard.[2]

Imagine a day laborer living in a great kingdom. The day laborer "never dreamed . . . that the emperor knew he existed, who then would consider himself indescribably favored just to be permitted to see the emperor once, something he would relate to his children and grandchildren as the most important event in his life." But suppose the emperor did something unexpected: "If the emperor sent for him and told him that he wanted him for his son-in-law: what then? Quite humanly, the day laborer would be more or less puzzled, self-conscious, and embarrassed by it; he would (and this is the humanness of it) humanly find it very strange and bizarre . . . that the emperor wanted to make a fool of him, make him the laughingstock of the whole city."[3]

In this parable, the day laborer working in the countryside recognizes the high and exalted place of the emperor. An occasional encounter with the emperor would be delightful—enough so that the laborer could keep his own comfortable life, keep his friends, keep his identity, yet have it embellished by the honor of the emperor. "A little favor—that would make sense to the laborer."[4] But what if the emperor wants to make him his own son? The prospect of adoption in this sense is an offense. It is *too much closeness*—it is the sort of closeness that requires giving up one's own identity. Yes, it is a high and exalted place to be the child of the emperor, the king of the land. But it is too high and exalted—wouldn't he be a laughingstock? Wouldn't he lose all that is precious to him if he were to ascend to be the king's son? In the words of Kierkegaard, the day laborer says, "Such a thing is too high for me, I cannot grasp it; to be perfectly blunt, to me it is a piece of folly."[5] It would be wonderful if the king would send him

---

2. Søren Kierkegaard, *The Sickness unto Death*, trans. Howard V. Hong and Edna H. Hong (Princeton: Princeton University Press, 1980). In the context of *The Sickness unto Death*, Kierkegaard uses this parable to demonstrate that the opposite of sin is faith. Thus, the day laborer must have the courage of faith to accept the emperor's offer.

3. Ibid., 84.
4. Ibid., 109.
5. Ibid., 84.

some money or a letter to cherish as a relic. But the king is asking for so much more. The king is asking to be more than an accessory to his identity. The king wants his full identity, his entire life—wants him to be exalted, the child of the king.

And so it is with God, the King. Yet adoption by the King is *such* a radical notion, we resist it. We would rather have the occasional brush of God's presence, or a relic of his solidarity with us, so that God can be an appendage of *our* identity. But God wants more than that; he wants our lives, our adopted identity. By bringing us into the new reality of the Spirit, we can call out to God—Abba, Father—as adopted children united to Christ. Yet there are few things more countercultural than this process of adoption—losing your life for the sake of Jesus Christ, to find it in communion with the Triune God.

Although Kierkegaard was not directly commenting on Paul's metaphor of adoption, his parable provides a number of points of illumination. First, Kierkegaard doesn't use the term "adoption," but his parable—about an adult who is called to receive a new identity and inheritance—is similar to Paul's metaphor. Paul only used the metaphor of adoption when he was addressing Christians who were living under Roman law and who thus were familiar with Roman adoption practices.[6] In this ancient Roman context, adoption was generally not about babies and childless couples finding a way to have children. Instead, the adoptees were usually adults, and adoption was first of all a legal arrangement to provide an heir who would receive an inheritance and enter into a new household with all its privileges and responsibilities.[7] (Kierkegaard's day laborer feared *both* the privileges and the responsibilities of being a child of the king!) "Adoption," or *huiothesia* (the term Paul uses), is a legal or forensic term in the sense that it refers to the transfer from one family into another. In the ancient world, this legal arrangement gave an adopted son all the rights of a natural son.[8] It was initiated by the head of the family, the *paterfamilias*, and it was customary for this father to affectionately receive the adopted son as a part of his new family.[9]

In light of this ancient background, biblical scholars have made the case for Paul using the term *huiothesia* as a metaphor for salvation

---

6. See Trevor J. Burke, *Adopted into God's Family: Exploring a Pauline Metaphor*, New Studies in Biblical Theology (Downers Grove, IL: IVP Academic, 2006), 60–63.
7. Ibid., 66.
8. Ibid., 69.
9. Ibid., 71.

with certain parallels to this ancient usage.[10] This does not mean that Paul uses the term in exactly the same way that it was used for the Roman family, however.[11] For starters, God has no inherent need to make heirs, but he chooses to adopt sinners into his family as a free, divine act of love. In addition, the metaphor takes on theological content in Paul's hands. For Paul, on the most basic level, adoption is the act of being transferred "from an alien family (cf. Eph. 2:2, lit. 'sons of disobedience') into the family of God."[12]

For Paul, the adoption metaphor is deeply trinitarian, for it is initiated by the Father, mediated by the Spirit, and grounded in the person and work of Jesus Christ. For example, in Galatians 4:4–7 Paul grounds the adoption of sons and daughters in the sonship of Jesus Christ, who is sent by the Father, which is testified to in believers by the Spirit. "God sent his Son . . . so that we might receive adoption as children," Paul says. "And because you are children, God has sent the Spirit of his Son into our hearts, crying, 'Abba! Father!' So you are no longer a slave but a child, and if a child then also an heir, through God." In this way, salvation as adoption is both christocentric—for adoption occurs only in Christ, as a subordinate sharing in his sonship—and trinitarian. The adopted child of God encounters a loving Father through the Spirit's crying, "Abba! Father!" which all occurs in Christ—and so the adopted one is an "heir" of God, united to the Son.

While the metaphor of adoption begins as a legal act, it does not end there: it ends with membership in the household of God (Gal. 6:10; Eph. 2:19), with a calling to act into the reality of this new identity. God's legal act of adopting into the family of God results in a new identity, in an eschatologically conditioned way. Thus, when we are given an identity in Christ, we are called to live into it. For example, the doxological opening of Ephesians 1 says that God "destined us for adoption as his children through Jesus Christ" (v. 5). As the blessings of being in Christ are unfolded in the following verses, Paul returns to the language of adoption and inheritance—that "in Christ we have also obtained an inheritance, having been destined according to the

10. For an overview of the literature on this point, see ibid., 46–71.

11. On areas of disanalogy between its ancient usage in the family and Paul's theological usage, see Ernest Best, *Ephesians*, International Critical Commentary Series (Edinburgh: T&T Clark 1998), 125. Richard Longenecker emphasizes the way in which the immediate theological context for each usage of the term "adoption" is decisive for its meaning. See Longenecker, *Galatians* (Dallas: Word, 2002), 172.

12. See Burke, *Adopted into God's Family*, 27.

purpose of him who accomplishes all things according to his counsel and will, so that we, who were the first to set our hope on Christ, *might live for the praise of his glory*" (1:11–12, emphasis added). This new identity of one belonging to a new family in Christ is sealed by the Spirit in the verses that follow: "In him you also . . . were marked with the seal of the promised Holy Spirit; this is the pledge of our inheritance toward redemption as God's own people, to the praise of his glory" (1:13–14). The adopted identity in Christ, sealed by the Spirit, leads to living "for the praise of his glory" (1:12), but also provides the ground for numerous ethical exhortations in Ephesians: the call to unity (4:13); to prayer (6:18); to speaking and living the truth in Christ (4:15, 21, 25; 6:14); to living in "love" rather than in anger, malice, and bitterness (4:21–5:1).[13] All of these exhortations are to reflect the behavior of those who have been conferred a new adopted identity in Christ and who seek to live into this inheritance received as children of God in Christ.

In contrast to some theologians who have associated adoption only with justification, Paul's overall usage of the adoption metaphor describes both the legal dimension of being transferred into God's family and the transformative dimension of growing in God's family. By associating adoption only with justification, theologians have sometimes tended to emphasize the legal at the expense of the transformative side of adoption. Trevor Burke has criticized certain Reformed scholastic thinkers, in particular, for making adoption a subset or benefit of justification without recognizing its distinct meaning.[14] While Burke makes a good point, I suspect some of the reason for the confusion comes from the following: Theologians have often spoken about the act of *becoming adopted* as a forensic act, which is a valid point (as Burke agrees). But the forensic sense of becoming adopted does not exhaust the meaning of Paul's metaphor, because the result of that act is that one is adopted to be a son or daughter of God, placed in the security of God's family, and given a new identity to live into in an eschatologically conditioned way. Some theologians have thus been too quick to assume that the meaning of "adoption" is exhausted by the act of *becoming* adopted. Significantly for this chapter, however, this is not a mistake that John Calvin makes. Calvin uses the image

13. See Andrew T. Lincoln, *Ephesians*, Word Biblical Commentary (Dallas: Word, 2002), 19.

14. Burke, *Adopted into God's Family*, 23–26.

of adoption as a way to describe the double grace of justification *and* sanctification received in union with Christ. Calvin understood that as an image for salvation, the act of becoming adopted is a legal, forensic action, but it has another dimension as well: as an image for the way Christians are to act as children of the Father who promises "to nourish us throughout the course of our life."[15] Indeed, the Spirit gives new life, displayed in love of God and neighbor, which "shows that the Spirit of adoption has been given to us (cf. Romans 8:15)."[16]

In giving this exposition of Paul's metaphor of adoption for salvation, I am not claiming that it is the only or the most significant soteriological term for Paul's theology of union with Christ. But it is a metaphor that is important yet often neglected. In particular, it highlights the radical character of life in Christ as a change in identity, as being conferred a new identity in Christ as children of God—filled with the Spirit, united to Christ, and given access to the Father in God's household. Like the day laborer in Kierkegaard's parable, it is a biblical metaphor that shows us an astonishing state of affairs: the high King, the Lord of the universe, desires for us to be his adopted children. Thus, while God is holy and transcendent, he is not at a convenient distance. God's gracious, loving call is, in fact, a threat to our autonomy, our deep and pervasive strategies to keep hold of our lives rather than losing them for the sake of Jesus Christ.

God at a Convenient Distance: Today's Cultural Deism as a Contrast to Salvation as Adoption

Recently, a series of studies confirmed just how countercultural this notion of salvation as adoption is. The results of these studies are compiled in two books, *Soul Searching* and *Souls in Transition*.[17] These

15. *Inst.* 4.17.1. In this section, Calvin goes on to explain that the Lord's Supper is a key source of nourishment provided for God's children.

16. *Inst.* 3.14.18. This example from Calvin, in particular, applies Paul's image of adoption to sanctification. For more on Calvin's theology of adoption in terms of the double grace, see J. Todd Billings, *Calvin, Participation, and the Gift: The Activity of Believers in Union with Christ*, Changing Paradigms in Historical and Systematic Theology (Oxford: Oxford University Press, 2007), 105–16.

17. Christian Smith, *Soul Searching: The Religious and Spiritual Lives of American Teenagers*, with Melinda Lundquist Denton (New York: Oxford University Press, 2005); Christian Smith, *Souls in Transition: The Religious and Spiritual Lives of Emerging Adults*, with Patricia Snell (New York: Oxford University Press, 2009).

are the most comprehensive studies of the religious beliefs of American teens and young adults ever conducted. While all sorts of religious groups were surveyed, both statistical analysis and in-depth interviews revealed that a common theology was functional for the vast majority of American teens, regardless of their religious tradition. It is what we might call an "American theology" or a "cultural theology" that can be summed up by the phrase "moralistic therapeutic deism" (MTD) and the following creed:

1. A God exists who created and orders the world and watches over human life on earth.
2. God wants people to be good, nice, and fair to each other, as taught in the Bible and by most world religions.
3. The central goal of life is to be happy and to feel good about oneself.
4. God does not need to be particularly involved in one's life except when God is needed to resolve a problem.
5. Good people go to heaven when they die.[18]

What emerges from this functional creed? Tragically, it is not a biblical notion of salvation as adoption. Rather, to begin with the D of MTD, the God we encounter here is a deistic God. This God created and ordered the world but now stands back at a distance, except when there is a crisis. While some who were surveyed may believe that God gave us his Son and adopted us by his Spirit, these beliefs are not mentioned: they are crowded out, made unimportant in relation to the other convictions expressed in the MTD creed. Why? Because on a deeper level, they think we have no need for a media-tor—our sin has not alienated us from God. Instead of forgiveness and communion with God, the purpose of religion is therapeutic (the T of MTD): religion should help us be happy and feel good about ourselves. How does it do this? By helping us make decisions, because God wants people to be good, nice, and fair (thus the M: moralistic). Note that there is no particular need for a holy God to bestow grace upon sinners since people are basically good already and will go to heaven if they play by the rules. We are not orphans; there is no need for a new identity in Christ. Such is the assumption of MTD.

18. Smith, *Soul Searching*, 162–63.

In a major follow-up study to *Soul Searching*, *Souls in Transition* examined the beliefs of eighteen- to twenty-three-year-olds, labeled "emerging adults." To a certain extent, we still see the characteristics of MTD. Most emerging adults assume that they are the master of their life, their identity, their religion. "They as individuals can determine what is right, worthy, and important. So they themselves can pick and choose from religion to take or leave what they want."[19] No religious tradition per se is needed for this process. At most, one may need to pick and choose the good verses from the Bible, leaving behind "the crazy parts," as one emerging adult expressed to me.

But *Souls in Transition* also reveals a breakdown of MTD, what amounts to a crisis for many emerging adults. In moving from the teenage years to young adulthood, emerging adults begin to sense that they are not free and self-made after all, that they may even be slaves, as the apostle Paul suggested (Rom. 6–7).

> Emerging adults are determined to be free. But they do not know what is worth doing with their freedom. They work very hard to stand on their own two feet. But they do not really know where they ought to go and why, once they are standing. They lack larger visions of what is true and real and good. . . . Many know that there must be something more, and they want it. Many are uncomfortable with their inability to make truth statements and moral claims without killing them with the death of a thousand qualifications. But they do not know what to do about that, given the crisis of truth and values that has destabilized their culture. And so they simply carry on as best they can, as sovereign, autonomous, empowered individuals who lack a reliable basis for any particular conviction or direction by which to guide their lives.[20]

This paragraph describes a crisis of identity. Emerging adults want to believe things, to *be* someone other than just another conformist who capitulates to every social trend. But ironically, emerging adults are often paralyzed from making deep faith commitments because of a social conformity deeper than any particular commitment to God, Jesus Christ, or the Holy Spirit: conformity to the idea that religion depends upon the individual, that it should "remain a personal matter, something an individual may or may not choose to get into because

19. Smith, *Souls in Transition*, 286–87.
20. Ibid., 294.

it is meaningful to him or her."[21] Yet Jesus says, "I am the way, and the truth, and the life" (John 14:6), and he calls his disciples to take up their cross and follow him, to lose their lives for his sake. But this contradicts the deeply held American ideology that strives not only to tolerate all different religious beliefs but also to "keep options open, not to get too committed, to push dealing with religious matters off to some future date."[22] Emerging adults want God to be more than a butler, a convenient yet distant deity. Yet, in conformity to the ideologies that reduce faith to a matter of personal preference and fulfillment, their faith has been sectored off, compartmentalized. Faith has been reduced to a necklace one wears as part of a self-made identity rather than a whole new set of clothes one wears—"put[ting] on the Lord Jesus Christ" (Rom. 13:14)—as a new identity found in him.

Emerging adults, in this way, are simply conforming to broader trends in modern Western culture. Paralyzed in a state of indecision, we are enticed by our culture to settle for gods that are actually less than God (what the Bible refers to as "idols"). Our culture tells us to satisfy our longings with money or hookup sex or even our own heroic efforts to "save the world," when only God can satisfy. By conforming to our culture in these ways, we settle for a God who is a lifeguard saving us from occasional mishaps, appearing only when it is convenient. But that is not the living God—Father, Son, and Spirit—the one in whom we should find our new adopted identity. Because we are paralyzed from losing our lives for the sake of Jesus Christ, we end up with idols instead. We can easily say, "yes, we're children of God, and God is happy with us," but we don't think we need a new identity given by God. In doing this, not only do we deny the adoption Paul speaks about, but we also settle for idols rather than the living God.

Against our common cultural assumption, we as sinners, according to scripture, are not bright-eyed, good-natured children of God. Indeed, the only "natural" child of God, as noted earlier, is Jesus Christ. All the rest of us need to be adopted. As Paul says in Galatians, apart from Christ we are slaves—thus we need *adoption* to be children in God's household. "But when the fullness of time had come, God sent his Son, born of a woman, born under the law, in order to redeem those who were under the law, so that we might

21. Ibid., 286.
22. Ibid., 287.

receive adoption as children. And because you are children, God has sent the Spirit of his Son into our hearts, crying, 'Abba! Father!' So you are no longer a slave but a child, and if a child then also an heir, through God" (Gal. 4:4–6).

We display our sinful rather than adopted identity through the idols we construct in place of the living God. We feel weak, so we project our need for power onto God. We want solidarity against our enemies, so we construct a God who is always on our side. This human tendency to project idols onto God is widely recognized, even among atheistic philosophers such as Ludwig Feuerbach and Karl Marx. But it is also recognized among theologians such as John Calvin, who writes, "They do not therefore apprehend God as he offers himself, but imagine him as they have fashioned him in their own presumption. When this gulf opens, in whatever direction they move their feet, they cannot but plunge headlong into ruin. Indeed, whatever they afterward attempt by way of worship or service of God, they cannot bring as tribute to him, for they are worshiping not God but a figment and a dream of their own heart."[23] Some may think that Calvin, with his critique of idolatry, is being a killjoy by replacing the nearness and familiarity of the idol with a distant deity. But the opposite is the case. One of Calvin's key objections to idolatry is that it makes God too distant, not too close. "For we know that we are accustomed to imagine God absent, except when we have some sensible experience of his presence."[24] Yet God is not absent, even when our idols are absent. Although Calvin believes that we do need physical, sensible signs of God's presence—provided through the sacraments—these are signs whereby God "offers himself" to unite us to Jesus Christ rather than idols that we construct for our own purposes.

In adoption, God comes closer to us than MTD allows. In adoption, our central cultural ideal of being a self-made person is put on the cross. But in adoption, we also enter into the playful, joyous world of *living as children of a gracious Father, as persons united to Christ and empowered by the Spirit*. In the final two sections of this chapter, I want to explore different dimensions of this transformation from slaves who are under the illusion of being autonomous, "self-made persons" to children of God who are united to Jesus Christ.

23. *Inst.* 1.4.1.

24. Comm. on Gen. 8:1, CTS. See Heiko A. Oberman, "The Pursuit of Happiness: Calvin between Humanism and Reformation," in *Humanity and Divinity in Renaissance and Reformation*, ed. John O'Malley (Leiden: Brill, 1993), 278n80.

Learning to Be Children of God: Receiving the Double Grace in Union with Christ

The life of salvation is not the dull task of trying to be "a good Christian," maintaining cultural conformity with those around us so that we receive "eternal life insurance" for the afterlife. No. The new life of salvation is a journey of nonconformity, a process of learning how to become daughters and sons of the Triune God.

Ironically, even though this is a countercultural process, we don't learn to be children of God by trying really hard or by pulling ourselves up by our bootstraps as individuals. Instead, we enter into a reality created by God's own word where we find our lives not in our own efforts or moral discipline but in Jesus Christ. John Calvin, drawing on the writings of Paul and John, with their emphasis on union with Christ and abiding in Christ, has a helpful exposition of this new identity. Calvin says that this reality of salvation as adoption is that by the Spirit we receive a double grace in union with Christ in his death and resurrection. "Christ was given to us by God's generosity, to be grasped and possessed by us in faith. By partaking of him, we principally receive a double grace: namely, that being reconciled to God through Christ's blamelessness, we may have in heaven instead of a Judge a gracious Father; and secondly, that sanctified by Christ's spirit we may cultivate blamelessness and purity of life."[25] As Calvin makes clear, in union with Christ we receive two distinct yet inseparable gifts: justification, in which we are declared righteous before God as ones who are clothed with Jesus Christ, and sanctification, the gift of a new life, a new creation, which manifests itself in Spirit-empowered gratitude.

In Calvin's account, this double grace of union with Christ moves us from our hardened, self-sufficient slavery to a way of being that is centered in Jesus Christ and freed for eager service to God in the world. The first gift of union with Christ is forensic, which means that it is God's change in decision toward us, like a judge in a courtroom. In defining justification in the *Institutes*, Calvin first describes this legal, courtroom context for the term and then writes, "We explain justification simply as the acceptance with which God receives us into his favor as righteous men. And we say that it consists in the remission of sins and the imputation of Christ's righteousness."[26]

25. *Inst.* 3.11.1.
26. *Inst.* 3.11.2.

Christ's righteousness is imputed onto us: righteousness is credited to our case before God because of Jesus Christ. This may seem to be an impersonal notion, but it occurs amidst our union and closeness with Christ. Calvin says, "Christ, having been made ours, makes us sharers with him in the gifts with which he has been endowed. We do not, therefore, contemplate him outside ourselves from afar in order that his righteousness may be imputed to us but because we put on Christ and are engrafted into his body—in short, because he deigns to make us one with him."[27]

Moreover, although adoption should not be the only rubric under which justification is considered,[28] consider how the language of adoption can help to illuminate the role of justification. For any adoption to be valid, in the ancient world as well as our own, the adoptive parents must have *legal rights* to the child. The child cannot just start acting like the child of the new parents. That new relationship is secure only when it has a legal basis. When "forensic" pardon is received in Christ, sinners are acquitted of their guilt and are legally adopted as children. The legal dimension is indispensable—and it is what provides the context for sanctification as a transformative process by the Spirit. Those who are legally pardoned and received into God's family are freed from the "severe requirements" of the

27. *Inst.* 3.11.10.

28. On an exegetical level, this is a fairly obvious point, as the terms "justification" and "adoption" are not identical for Paul. But there is a more subtle issue here as well. One important feature of justification, which advocates of the New Perspective on Paul have pointed out, is the ecclesial level—that justification refers to the (horizontal) process of becoming a member of God's covenant people. That is a true and significant insight. At times, certain authors in the New Perspective on Paul have downplayed the vertical dimension of justification that involves God's forgiveness and acquittal of the sinner. With my emphasis on adoption, some might think that I seek to construe justification in purely ecclesial terms, as entry into the covenant people. But that is not the case. (To make this clear, later in this paragraph I refer to God's forensic act in the following terms: "When 'forensic' pardon is received in Christ, sinners are acquitted of their guilt and are legally adopted as children.") Thus, while inclusion into God's family is an important aspect of justification, Paul's thought requires us to speak of the acquittal of sinners as well. For a brief account of the New Perspective on Paul and its criticisms, specifically in relation to N. T. Wright, see Kevin J. Vanhoozer, "Wrighting the Wrongs of the Reformation? The State of the Union with Christ in St. Paul and Protestant Soteriology," in *Jesus, Paul, and the People of God: A Theological Dialogue with N. T. Wright*, ed. Nicholas Perrin and Richard B. Hays (Downers Grove, IL: InterVarsity, 2011). Vanhoozer seeks to show how the recovery of Paul's metaphor of adoption could be a way to move forward in the discussion between Wright and his recent detractors.

law (of which they fall short) so that they can act like children who "hear themselves called with fatherly gentleness by God," Calvin says, and "will cheerfully and with great eagerness answer and follow his leading."[29] Thus, Paul's notion of "justification by faith" fits with adoption, for being "engrafted into Christ through faith" makes one "a son [or daughter] of God, an heir of heaven, a partaker in righteousness," according to Calvin.[30] We do not become children of God by striving to please God. We become children of God through embracing Jesus Christ as our righteousness, through putting faith in Jesus Christ, who lived, died, and rose again for our sake. We add nothing to this righteousness of Jesus Christ, which is received as a gift as we lose our old self and find ourselves anew "in Christ" as God's adopted children.

In Calvin's day, many Christians saw their salvation as the product of their own works, similar to MTD today, in which the only righteousness we have before God is through our own works. In contrast, Calvin wants to be crystal clear that our salvation is "not through works," though it is also "not without works," which display the love of God and neighbor in our lives. For "in our sharing in Christ, which justifies us, sanctification is just as much included as righteousness," Calvin says.[31] For him, in salvation we receive not only forgiveness (justification) but also new life (sanctification) as a gift. Thus, sanctification is not simply "our response," initiated by our asking "what would Jesus do?" Sanctification, like justification, is a gift that we receive in union with Christ.

Hence, the formal relationship between justification and sanctification is crucial: they are distinct yet inseparable. There is no temporal gap between these two gifts. It is impossible to receive one without the other. Indeed, since both are contained in Christ, "these two which we perceive in him together and conjointly are inseparable."[32] To try to acquire God's pardon without entering into the new life given in Christ would be to tear Christ into two—or "rend Christ asunder," in Calvin's words.[33] Put in terms of adoption, to separate justification from sanctification would be to accept the legal status of being God's child but to refuse to move to God's house, to call God Father,

29. *Inst.* 3.19.5.
30. *Inst.* 3.15.6.
31. *Inst.* 3.16.1.
32. *Inst.* 3.11.6.
33. *Inst.* 3.11.6.

and to *act* as an adopted child. In terms of Kierkegaard's parable, it may sound attractive to be legally adopted by the king but to stay in your own home at a distance from the palace, yet to do so would be denying this new relationship of being the king's son or daughter. We need not only adoption into God's family and forgiveness of sins; we need also to learn how to grow into our new identity as adopted children of the Triune God.

There are many concrete ways that God shapes us into our new adoptive identity—through worship, hearing and reading God's word, receiving the sacraments, prayer and fellowship, and service toward those in need. For the sake of space, I will limit my focus to two areas that Calvin expounds: prayer and the sacrament of the Lord's Supper. For Calvin, both of these help us enter into our new identity as God's children by the Spirit's power. And they both have the shape of the double grace received in union with Christ.

In prayer, Calvin says, the first thing one must do is realize that we are "destitute and devoid of all good things," so one must "go outside" of oneself to look to God. Specifically, we must "recognize that whatever we need and whatever we lack is in God, and in our Lord Jesus Christ, in whom the Father willed all the fullness of his bounty to abide so that we may all draw from it as from an overflowing spring."[34] This focus on Christ, this hunger for him, is at the root of prayer. Why look to Christ? Because "Christ is the pledge and guarantee of our adoption," Calvin says.[35] In a related way, Jesus Christ is the high priest, one who is praying on our behalf in the holy of holies, at the right hand of the Father. We do not know how to pray on our own. Yet because we belong to Jesus Christ, God's Son, we can enter prayer as God's children—praying "in the name of Jesus," adding our petitions to those of Jesus Christ. This life of prayer in union with Christ is possible only through the Spirit. Indeed, Calvin says, we do not simply exercise our own effort to be adopted children in prayer, for the Spirit is "witness to us of the same adoption, through whom with free and full voice we may cry, 'Abba, Father.' Therefore whenever any hesitation shall hinder us, let us remember to ask him to correct our fearfulness, and set before us that Spirit that he may guide us to pray boldly."[36] Left to ourselves, we would fearfully

34. *Inst.* 3.20.1.
35. *Inst.* 3.20.37.
36. *Inst.* 3.20.37.

resist pouring out our hearts to the King of the land. But the Spirit, the agent of adoption, enables us to do so, revealing a Father who is "gently summoning us to unburden our cares into his bosom."[37] Occurring in the context of the double grace of union with Christ, our praying is in light of the indicative—that we *have been* united to Christ (as Paul says in Rom. 6), receiving free, justifying pardon and new life as gifts. Knowing that our righteousness and new life is in Jesus Christ, our consciences are calmed, and we can freely call on God as a gentle Father by the Spirit. And in the process of doing so, we obey God, who asks us to abide in Christ and to act as sons and daughters of the almighty King.

The language of adoption is also central for how Calvin talks about receiving God's word spoken, and also our focus here—God's word made visible through the signs of the bread and cup in the Lord's Supper. From his first sentence on the Lord's Supper in his key work, *The Institutes*, adoption is central for Calvin. "God has received us, once for all, into his family, to hold us not only as servants but as sons."[38] As adopted children, we not only obey or serve God; we are first of all *recipients* of the Father's abundant generosity. "To fulfill the duties of a most excellent Father concerned for his offspring," Calvin says, "he undertakes also to nourish us throughout the course of our life. And not content with this alone, he has willed, by giving his pledge, to assure us of this continuing liberality."[39] Out of extravagant love for the adopted children who have entered the King's house, God provides a "spiritual banquet, wherein Christ attests himself to be the life-giving bread, upon which our souls feed unto true and blessed immortality," for "Christ is the only food of our soul, and therefore our Heavenly Father invites us to Christ."[40]

Why is it crucial to rest in the righteousness of Christ our priest in prayer, and to feed upon Christ in word and in the sacrament of the Lord's Supper? Because to become adopted children, we do not simply copy the Son, asking "what would Jesus do?" We are actually incorporated into the Son's own life—that is what union with Christ is. In union with Christ, we receive forgiveness, which enables adoption and new life as adopted children, by the Spirit's power. You can't become an adopted child of God by trying really hard to be one—by

37. *Inst.* 3.20.5.
38. *Inst.* 4.17.1.
39. *Inst.* 4.17.1.
40. *Inst.* 4.17.1.

exercising spiritual disciplines, by giving to those in need, or by loving your neighbor. All of these actions should be fruits of your union with Christ—the fruit of Christ's work *for* you (justification) and Christ's work *in* you (sanctification). The good news is that in Jesus Christ, we receive forgiveness and new life. We did not manufacture this news. The news is not about our own efforts to imitate Christ or to do what Jesus would do. First and foremost, the good news of the gospel is the gift of actually being united to Jesus Christ—a gift received from God in a way that activates us to live into this new life, coming to us as part of God's new creation.

What Does It Mean to Be "Progressive?" The Convergence of Identity and the Future in Salvation as Adoption

Our identity as adopted children in union with Christ is our true identity, our real identity. Moreover, it is a part of the new creation of God. Yet this new identity has already been received. Within a few verses in Romans 8, Paul points to both sides: "You have received a spirit of adoption. When we cry, 'Abba! Father!' it is that very Spirit bearing witness with our spirit that we are children of God" (8:15–16). As the Spirit assures us, the identity of being children of God has already been received, for "we *are* children of God." Yet it is also a reality that belongs to the future and is experienced now as a foretaste of God's future; the full reality of adoption is not yet: "We know that the whole creation has been groaning in labor pains until now; and not only the creation, but we ourselves, who have the first fruits of the Spirit, groan inwardly while we wait for adoption, the redemption of our bodies" (Rom. 8:22–23). We have received this new identity, but we also "wait for adoption." In fact, we "groan inwardly" while we wait. Those in Christ have received the "first fruits of the Spirit" but are still waiting for a consummation of this identity in Christ.

We have been adopted, but our new identity is coming to us from the future—an identity that is the Spirit's new creation. But what does this mean, really? If we receive the invitation from the king of the land to be adopted children, why should we leave our comfortable homes and take the journey of entering into this new identity? Isn't that risky? Moreover, doesn't that violate who I am?

Beneath the paralysis that keeps many in our culture from giving over their identity to Jesus Christ lies a question about the future: who owns the future? We live in a context where many people and ideas claim to be "progressive." Think about it for a moment: the essential point of claiming to be progressive is that one owns the future, that the future is progressing toward the position I hold. So, for example, Barack Obama claims to be progressive, bringing in the way of the future; but likewise, the conservative Tea Party movement could call itself progressive, claiming that the way of the future is not in big government programs. Musicians, actors, and others in popular culture claim to be progressive, bringing in the new to outdo the old. In politics and popular culture, various positions claim to be progressive, which is another way of saying, "I own the future on this issue."

Yet in view of changing cultures and times, one could begin to have serious doubts about whether we have any sense at all of what it means to be progressive. My generation, Generation X, was told that the future belongs to us. Younger generations are told the same thing. But of course, that's not really true since every generation has a generation following it. Things that seemed progressive to my generation are likely to seem retrograde to the next. At various points in recent history, practices like eugenics and racial segregation were championed as progressive. The fact that they no longer seem progressive to us just shows how much the future is out of our grasp.

However, the question of who owns the future is one that scripture specifically addresses. Revelation 1:8 reads, "'I am the Alpha and the Omega,' says the Lord God, who is and who was and who is to come, the Almighty." Then in the final chapter of Revelation, Jesus Christ himself says, "'I am the Alpha and the Omega, the first and the last, the beginning and the end'" (22:13). This statement means not just that Jesus was at the beginning and the end, but that Jesus Christ "is the origin and goal of all history."[41] Jesus is the Lord of history throughout, even to its end, which is our future.

---

41. Richard Bauckham, *The Theology of the Book of Revelation* (Cambridge: Cambridge University Press, 1993), 27. On the phrase "Alpha and Omega," which God attributes to himself in Revelation 1 and Christ attributes to himself in Revelation 22, Mitchell G. Reddish notes that "all of history is under the control of God, not just its beginning and ending. In later rabbinic writings the first and last letters of the alphabet were used to denote something in its entirety. Abraham was said to have kept the law from *alef* to *tav* (the first and last letters of the Hebrew alphabet), meaning that he obeyed the entire law. In a similar way, to describe God as the Alpha and the Omega is not a restriction of God to only the beginning and the end but is a declaration of the totality of God's power and control. God is 'the Almighty,' and as such all 'salvation and glory and power belong to our God' (Rev. 19:1). Nothing is outside the purview

Thus, although we cannot state with great confidence a public policy that will be truly progressive in ten or fifty years, we can state with great confidence something about the future: it is heading toward Jesus Christ, as Lord of all. In terms of adoption, this means that living into our adoption is living into God's future, God's kingdom—a future that Jesus himself owns, even when it looks ambiguous and uncertain to us. Moreover, as we live into this new identity, we need not worry that we are losing our true identity. For Jesus Christ is the perfect image of God, and the image of God in us is being restored as we grow into our adopted identity.

Calvin says it this way: In the original creation, humans were created good—they were "united" with God.[42] In the fall, humans were alienated from God and other creatures. But we still have a trace of the image of God in us, which he calls a "participation in God."[43] Thus, when the Spirit comes to us in redemption, uniting us to Jesus Christ, we do not lose our true identity; rather, it is restored. Since we were not created to be autonomous, self-made people but were created to be in communion with God, when the Spirit leads us back into communion with God in Christ, we do not lose our true selves. We regain them.[44]

Our new self in Christ, which comes forth from the future, is our true self. We won't find it by introspection but will find it by looking to Jesus Christ, the one we receive in the gospel. When this happens, those in Christ will be "very much more themselves than they were before," according to C. S. Lewis.[45] "To enter heaven is to become more human than you ever succeeded in being on earth," he says.[46] Why? Because to be fully human is not to be autonomous but to be in communion with God, as we will explore further in the next chapter.

Let me end with a clarification about how this new identity is lived out in our pluralistic world. Am I saying that we should receive the

---

of God. The claim that God is the one 'who is and who was and who is to come' is a restatement of the same idea." Reddish, "Alpha and Omega," in *The Anchor Bible Dictionary*, ed. David Noel Freedman (New York: Doubleday, 1996), 1:161.

42. *Inst.* 2.1.5.

43. *Inst.* 1.2.1.

44. Calvin's development of these themes will be explored in more detail in chap. 2 below.

45. C. S. Lewis, *Mere Christianity*, rev. ed. (San Francisco: HarperSanFrancisco, 2001), 161.

46. C.S. Lewis, *The Problem of Pain*, rev. ed. (San Francisco: HarperSanFrancisco, 2001), 127–28.

good news in a way that proclaims Jesus Christ as the savior of the world, the one hope, the one true light, thus the one in whom we find our identity? Yes, I am. We should live into this new life in Christ with boldness, losing our lives for his sake. And we should bear witness to Jesus Christ to those around us.

But isn't that arrogant and presumptuous? On that point, we must remember a key biblical truth: Jesus Christ is the way, the truth, and the life, but that does not mean that *we* are the way, the truth, and the life. Whenever we bear witness to Jesus Christ we are on firm ground. Jesus Christ, as Alpha and Omega, is the owner of the future. No truth will come along in ten or a hundred years that "surpasses" him. That is who Jesus Christ is, according to the New Testament. But this is different than saying "I know all the truth" or "I own all the truth." No, the Christian confession is that I am owned *by* the one who is truth, so I bear witness to him.[47] We are called to bear witness to Jesus Christ in a way that reflects his own life of servant-hood, of love of neighbor, of love of enemy.[48] Yet we must be clear about the source of this new, adopted identity that we have received: Jesus Christ himself. As the one who owns the future, he deserves our childlike trust as we live into our new, adopted identity—an identity that will last longer than our fashions, our political views, even our own good works. For by the Spirit, we can receive forgiveness and new life as we participate in Jesus Christ himself, enabling us to call God "Abba, Father" for eternity.

47. For a development of this distinction, see "The Crucified One Is Lord: Confessing the Uniqueness of Christ in a Pluralistic Society," in *The Church Speaks: Papers of the Commission on Theology, Reformed Church in America, 1985–2000*, ed. James I. Cook (Grand Rapids: Eerdmans, 2002), 129–53. In addition, chap. 3 below provides an adaptation of this theme through the thought of Franciscus Junius, who gives an eschatologically conditioned account of how all true human knowledge of God derives from Jesus Christ. Developing Junius's insight, we could say that, first and foremost, Jesus Christ is the one who truly knows God, and Christians participate in his knowledge in their union with him by the Spirit.

48. I explore these themes further in the following chapters.

2

Total Depravity in Sin, Total Communion in Christ

How the Bondage of the Will Mirrors a
Theology of Salvation as Communion

The Starting Point: Biblical Images of Union with Christ and Corresponding Images of Sin

Union with Christ by the Spirit is a key biblical and theological motif for salvation. In scripture, this theme is broadly canonical and has a covenantal sense, as God's Old Testament promises of cleansing and new life are fulfilled in Jesus Christ and are extended, in this same Christ, not only to Jews but also to Gentiles. The theme is apparent in Jesus's call in the Synoptics to discipleship and to bear fruit, as well as in the imagery of becoming "participants of the divine nature" (2 Pet. 1:4) and in the key image of the church as being "prepared as a bride adorned for her husband" (Rev. 21:2). But the imagery of union with Christ receives its fullest development in two New Testament locations: Paul's letters and John's Gospel. In Paul, union with Christ in his death and resurrection is one of the most comprehensive images used for salvation itself, undergirding his nearly ubiquitous claim that believers can now find their life "in Christ." In John's Gospel, union with Christ is connected with both faith and obedience—abiding in Christ, as a branch abides in a tree. "I am the vine, you are the branches," Jesus says. "Those who abide in me and I in them bear much fruit" (John 15:5a).

But one does not have to delve far into scripture to see the negative corollary to these rich images for salvation, for every notion of salvation has a corresponding notion of sin—the very thing salvation heals. Indeed, to finish the sentence from John 15:5 above, "Those who abide in me and I in them bear much fruit, *because apart from me you can do nothing.*" Lest we second-guess whether "nothing" in John really means nothing, the next verse says, "Whoever does not abide in me is thrown away like a branch and withers; such branches are gathered, thrown into the fire, and burned." How could this be? In John, these are two sides of the same coin: a person bears fruit only through union with and abiding in Christ, which means that one bears no fruit apart from that abiding. The duality regarding this abiding in Christ is also present in John 8:31–38: one either abides in Christ and his word, which leads to freedom (8:31), or one remains in sin and is "a slave to sin" (8:34), for "there is no place in you for my word" (8:37).

Paul uses similar language. One is either a slave to sin or a slave to righteousness—even a "slave of Christ," he says (1 Cor. 7:22). After speaking about union with the death and resurrection of Christ in the early verses of Romans 6, Paul writes, "Do you not know that if you present yourselves to anyone as obedient slaves, you are slaves of the one whom you obey, either of sin, which leads to death, or of obedience, which leads to righteousness? But thanks be to God that you, having once been slaves of sin, have become obedient from the heart to the form of teaching to which you were entrusted, and that you, having been set free from sin, have become slaves of righteousness" (Rom. 6:16–18). When speaking about union with Christ, Paul adds another image to describe the ability of fallen humans to please God on their own: the image of death. Colossians 2:13 says that "when you were dead in trespasses and the uncircumcision of your flesh, God made you alive together with him." Dead in your trespasses, dead in your sin: that's a strong image for the power of sin! But it's inherently connected to what follows: "God made you alive together with him [Christ]" (Col. 2:13). While we could not save ourselves, while we were utterly dead and helpless to attain salvation, God united us to Jesus Christ, the one in whom we have life (Rom. 5:8). The power of God's salvific action in uniting us to Christ is connected to the utter powerlessness of sinners to save themselves.

What are we to do with these biblical images about the power of sin apart from union with Christ—that one can do "nothing," one is a "slave to sin," one is "dead" in their sin? If we want to receive scripture's teaching about union with Christ, we must accept the strong language about sin that accompanies it. We should not say that Christ is the vine and we are the branches but then disregard "apart from me you can do nothing." We should not cling to Paul's language about union with Christ but cut off the language he directly connects to it—that of slavery to sin and of being dead in one's sin apart from God's saving action to unite us to Christ.

If scripture is our ultimate guide about salvation as union with Christ, we cannot help but speak about the slavery or bondage of the will to sin—about such indelicate topics as "total depravity." When we receive the powerful, multifaceted image of union with Christ for salvation, it means that what we are saved from—sin—is powerful and multifaceted as well.

Debunking Misunderstandings about the Bondage of the Will[1]

There is a reason that I began this chapter by examining scripture. The doctrine of the bondage of the will to sin is not an ivory-tower creation of gloomy theologians with a pessimistic outlook on life; it does not result from a deterministic philosophical mind that wants to glorify God and, in the process, demean humanity to a fated existence. No. The doctrine of the bondage of the will to sin emerges from the language of scripture about sin's power: apart from union with Christ, one can do "nothing," one is "dead," one is a "slave." These are strong words. And the Reformed strand of Augustinianism explored in this chapter takes these strong words very seriously.

1. While I use the conventional phrase "bondage of the will" to speak about the Reformed strand of Augustinianism, even this phrase needs qualification. A more precise designation might be the "bondage of choice." Augustine, along with Luther, Calvin, and the Reformed scholastics discussed below, affirms that the will is free in the sense of being voluntary, choosing particular options over others. Yet the "bondage of choice" means that the scope of possible choices for the fallen will has been limited; the will can voluntarily choose many things, but on its own it cannot will any salvific good. For more on the ways that the fallen will is still free in spite of this "bondage," see the section "Developments Related to the 'Freedom' of the Bound Will" below.

But what is often missed is that in John's Gospel, in Paul's letters, and even in a close reading of the Augustinian tradition, these images for sin never appear by themselves. They appear with their corollary: union with Christ, communion with God, the saving work of the Holy Spirit. Looking at both sides of the coin together, we can begin to see how a doctrine of the will's bondage to sin is not misanthropic. Rather, it teaches that full humanity is humanity united to God, in communion with God, something we witness most clearly in the person of Jesus Christ. Communion with God was characteristic of humanity in the original creation, and it is being restored and enhanced in salvation, in the healing of sin and participation in the life of Christ.

Before exploring this claim further, let us first clarify a few areas in which there are common misunderstandings about Reformational teaching on the bondage of the will, generally known by its often caricatured T in the acronym TULIP, signifying total depravity.

First, the bondage of the will to sin does not mean that we see no good in human beings unless they are Christian. It means that humans cannot perform any good *for the sake of salvation* apart from the Spirit, as we will explore further in a later part of this chapter. It is worth noting that the phrase "total depravity" is not used by Reformers such as Calvin. Moreover, as Marguerite Shuster notes, the phrase "total depravity" is misleading when understood intensively: that is, humans are as bad as they could possibly be. Total depravity in this sense would mean "that we could not possibly be more wicked than we are."[2] Although that is sometimes what total depravity is misconstrued to teach, it is simply not Augustinian or Reformed doctrine. Rather, the "total" should be understood extensively: "The doctrine means that depravity extends to the whole of the person, sparing no human faculty or power." This means that "all of our faculties" are "corrupted," so that "there is no 'Archimedean point' of moral integrity on which we can stand to deliver ourselves."[3] Stated differently, the doctrine of total depravity teaches that no part of a human person takes the initiative in the movement toward God. Rather than movement toward God being undertaken autonomously, it is always initiated and enabled by God's Spirit—enabled, in other words, by communion with God.

2. Marguerite Shuster, *The Fall and Sin: What We Have Become as Sinners* (Grand Rapids: Eerdmans, 2004), 160.
3. Ibid., 165.

Second, it is simply not the case that a general optimism about human nature leads to positive results in terms of societal good and love for neighbor, nor that pessimism about human nature leads to negative results. Despite the common Hollywood ploy for the villains to be those who "don't believe in the goodness of people," there are numerous counterexamples. As I explore further in chapter 4 by drawing upon the work of Philippe Theron, apartheid in South Africa was undergirded by naïve optimism about human nature, the assumption that different races could engage in "separate development" in a way that would be beneficial for both groups.[4] Yet the results of that optimism were anything but positive. At the other end of the spectrum, in the contemporary political debates about free market and regulation, it is arguably the more "left-wing," regulatory side that displays greater pessimism about the inherent goodness of human nature. But this pessimism can be seen as constructive, for the purpose of positive societal results. Examples could be multiplied indefinitely.

Third, we should recognize at the outset that there are deeply conflicting strains in contemporary Western culture, strains that make the doctrine of the will's bondage seem strange to some and intelligible to others. On the one hand, sociological studies show that most Americans see themselves as autonomous, self-made individuals. Young adults in particular, as we noted in chapter 1 through our consideration of Christian Smith's research, believe that religion is simply a matter of choosing what seems best and what pleases them personally, not a matter of truth or, even more extreme, a matter in which humans need God in order to know the truth about God. The American tendency is toward a radical libertarian view of freedom, where "freedom" assumes that we autonomously choose between this and that, in a way that is exalted above the influence of advertising, peer pressure, or culture.

On the other hand, many in modern culture are quick to call such "freedom" an illusion. In a seemingly unlikely pairing, many modern social scientists would agree with the Reformed scholastics that if we

---

4. As Theron says, "If proponents and opponents of the theological defense of apartheid had taken human greed, fear, pride, appetite for self-aggrandizement, passion for power, etc. more seriously, they would have heeded the Heidelberg Catechism's warning that we are prone by nature—that means, rather fundamentally!—to hate God and our neighbor." Theron, "One Savior, One Church: Reconciliation as Justification and 'New Creation,'" in *The Unity of the Church*, ed. Eduardus Van der Borght (Leiden: Brill, 2010), 281.

are to speak about freedom at all, we cannot define it as "uncaused" or devoid of any type of necessity. One hears similar sentiments in much contemporary literature and music. In the song "The King of Pain," for example, The Police use images of captivity to speak about how our souls are in bondage and slavery even when we think we're free. In fact, we need to be rescued, the song suggests, like a hat stuck in a treetop or a flag that has no will but that of the wind that blows it. Ironically, the Reformed tradition actually has a more robust view of human freedom—even in its fallen state—than many modern sources.

Nevertheless, in a contemporary Western context, the main popular instinct that the Reformed tradition must reject regarding the human will is that "freedom" means absolute, individualistic autonomy. The idea that we are sovereign individuals who choose in an exalted fashion, above all influences and "causes," may seem like common sense in an individualistic society. But it is also naïve, flying in the face of what both theological and nontheological disciplines tell us about freedom.

Augustine and His Reformed Reception: Looking to the Incarnation for a Doctrine of Grace

One enigma in contemporary scholarship on Augustine is the relative lack of attention to his Christology. Despite the fact that his Christology was developed in the course of his discussion of other topics, Augustine's insights were nonetheless profound.

Augustine's reception in the Reformation was characterized by Reformers such as Calvin seizing upon Augustine's references to the incarnation.[5] These references occurred in Augustine's debate with Pelagius on grace. Such a connection may seem puzzling and thus needs some unpacking, which we will do by following the train of thought through one passage in Augustine.

> In an assumption at once uniquely wonderful and wonderfully unique, God took up our nature, the flesh and rational soul of the human Christ, so that without any preceding merits of his own justice, this human being began to be the Son of God, so that from the beginning

5. In Calvin, see *Bondage and Liberation of the Will: A Defence of the Orthodox Doctrine of Human Choice against Pighius,* ed. A. N. S. Lane, trans. G. I. Davies (Grand Rapids: Baker, 1996), 129–30.

of his own existence he was one person with the Word who is without beginning.[6]

The humanity of Jesus Christ is not preexistent. It comes to existence in the Virgin Mary. But the deity of Jesus Christ is the eternal Word, that which is "without beginning," that which assumes the human flesh and soul of Jesus Christ in time, in Mary. In the course of this, Augustine notes the implication that the humanity of Christ is "without any preceding merits." How could it have "merited" anything? For "from the beginning of his own existence he was one person with the Word." In the next sentence, Augustine expands on this point.

> Nor is anyone so blindly ignorant of this event and of the faith that he would dare to assert that although the Son of Man was born of the Holy Spirit and the Virgin Mary, he *earned* the rank of being Son of God through free choice by living well and doing good works without sinning. The Gospel refutes this by saying "The Word was made flesh" [John 1:14]. Where was this done except in the womb of the Virgin, the place where the human Christ began?[7]

Like later christological thinkers in the East such as Cyril of Alexandria, who defends Christ's deity in the womb by giving Mary the title *theotokos*, meaning God-bearer, Augustine is emphatic that the human Jesus does not earn the honorific title Son of God through good works, nor is he "adopted" by the Father at a later point in his life after he has proven himself. No. Even in the womb, the divine Word had fully assumed the humanity of Christ.

Augustine continues by making his point for grace clear.

> This birth, which joined the human to God and the flesh to the Word in the unity of one person, was undeniably gratuitous. Good works followed; they did not earn this birth.[8]

If Christ was not adopted because of his prior merit or his prior human action—or even his human receptivity—then we must conclude that the Word's joining to the flesh was "undeniably gratuitous," Augustine

---

6. Augustine, *On Rebuke and Grace*, 11:30, in *Theological Anthropology: Sources of Early Christian Thought*, ed. and trans. J. Patout Burns (Philadelphia: Fortress: 1981), 100–101.

7. Ibid., emphasis added.

8. Ibid.

argues. The fruit of this union of God and humanity is "good works," but that should not be confused with the source of the union, which was solely from the grace of God.

Augustine goes on to spell out implications of the incarnation for his debate with Pelagius, arguing that his analysis of the incarnation can lead to insights about the way grace works throughout the Christian life. How could this be? Several levels of explanation are at work. If grace is a matter of divine and human agency working in harmony, what better place to look than the incarnation, where divine and human agency are in *complete* harmony? A related explanation is that, in considering what it means to be fully human, we must look not only to the first Adam but also to the second Adam, who is higher than the first. Since Jesus Christ is the perfect image of God, and Christians are being conformed to the image of Christ in salvation, we should seek a notion of freedom and a doctrine of grace that derives from this second Adam. Certainly, Jesus Christ is unique. He is the only begotten Son of God, while we can be daughters and sons only by gracious adoption. Yet in salvation, Christians participate in Christ and come to share in his new humanity. If Christ's humanity is constituted through God's gratuitous grace, then the *new humanity* that believers share must also be constituted by gratuitous grace. Indeed, if there were anyone who could autonomously merit the favor of God, wouldn't it be Jesus Christ? But even Christ's humanity was assumed by God as an act of pure grace, of unmerited favor—so also for those who are "in Christ."

This profound christological insight for anthropology was not lost on Calvin nor the Reformed and Lutheran scholastics after him. Indeed, in scholasticism this insight was further developed into the anhypostatic-enhypostatic distinction, which claimed that Christ's humanity does not have an "independent existence apart from its union to the Logos."[9] This later became a key insight in Karl Barth's theological anthropology.[10] While this technical distinction was certainly a development—not simply a restatement of patristic terminology—it shares insights displayed by Augustine, as discussed above, as well as by other patristic writers.[11] Within the Reformation and post-Refor-

9. Kelly Kapic, *Communion with God: The Divine and Human in the Theology of John Owen* (Grand Rapids: Baker Academic, 2007), 83.

10. See Kimlyn J. Bender, *Karl Barth's Christological Ecclesiology* (Aldershot, UK: Ashgate, 2005), 63–64.

11. While I am not claiming that Augustine was an explicit source for the patristic development of this technical distinction, his reception on this point in the Reformation

mation period, this notion underwent development as well. While later Reformed thinkers such as John Owen incorporated this insight with great clarity and precision,[12] an earlier form of the insight was already present in Reformers such as Calvin and Vermigli.[13] Calvin in particular used this insight to emphasize the "salvation as communion with Christ" side of the coin (which we saw in Paul and John), even as he exposited his view of the bondage of the will to sin, as we will explore below.

Communion with God, the Bondage of the Will, and the Double Grace of Union with Christ

Contrary to the frequent caricatures of Reformed theology in which God is seen as diametrically opposed to humanity, Calvin and the mainstream Reformed tradition follow this Augustinian line of thought in claiming that true humanity is humanity in communion with God. Therefore, as a consequence of the example from Augustine, emphasizing divine agency does not mean diminishing or demeaning the human. Saying that redemption is 100 percent empowered by God does not mean that humanity is belittled to nothingness. No. Instead, full deity and full humanity belong together in communion. Thus an action performed "by the Spirit" is an activation of our human faculties, not a diminishment of them.

Calvin fits this notion into the basic structure of his thought in his important but neglected work *The Bondage and Liberation of the Will*. In this work, Calvin replies to a Roman Catholic critic, Albert

---

helped to solidify the concept for thinkers like Calvin. For an account of the similarity of Augustine's thought on this point to the later anhypostatic-enhypostatic dogmatic distinction, see Luigi Gioia, *The Theological Epistemology of Augustine's* De Trinitate (Oxford: Oxford University Press, 2008), 72–73. For an account that argues for the concept being used by patristic writers such as John of Damascus, see U. M. Lang, "Anhypostatos-Enhypostatos: Church Fathers, Protestant Orthodoxy, and Karl Barth," *Journal of Theological Studies* 49 (1998): 630–57.

12. See Stephen R. Holmes, "Reformed Varieties of *Communicatio Idiomatum*," in *The Person of Christ*, ed. Stephen R. Holmes and Murray A. Rae (London: T&T Clark, 2005), 78–86.

13. For an account of the concept in Calvin's Christology, see E. David Willis, *Calvin's Catholic Christology* (Leiden: Brill, 1966), 79. For an account of Vermigli on this point, see William Klempa, "Classical Christology," in *A Companion to Peter Martyr Vermigli* (Leiden: Brill, 2009), 333.

Pighius, who claims that Calvin's doctrine of the bondage of the will contradicts the church fathers and demeans the created goodness of human beings. Calvin's defense is to cite certain church fathers, especially Augustine, and to provide further clarifications of his position. In addition, Calvin makes an ad hoc use of Aristotle (for his own distinct theological purpose), employing the distinction between "substance" and "accident." A substance is the essence constituting something (e.g., that we all share human "nature"), and an accident is a characteristic in which members with the same substance can differ without losing the substance (e.g., that one person has brown eyes and another has green eyes—both people retain a human nature or substance despite their accidental difference of eye color). Using these terms, Calvin claims that the substance of human nature is good.[14] As he states in the *Institutes*, the original, created human nature is not only good; it is "united to God." Indeed, Adam is righteous through a "participation in God."[15] However, in the fall, the accidental characteristic of sinning is added,[16] alienating humans from God, from neighbor, and ultimately from themselves. In this fallen state, human beings seek their identity "in themselves" or "in the flesh." They seek to be human apart from God. But of course, that is simply repeating the sin of Adam—following one's own wisdom rather than lovingly trusting in God. While fallen humans share the accidental characteristic of sinning, this characteristic does not completely vanquish the *imago Dei*, which Calvin says is a "participation in God."[17] Again, this characterization of the *imago Dei* makes sense with Calvin's view of humanity: to *be* fully human is to be united to God, and although sin seeks autonomy from God, there is still a trace of this union with or participation in God in all humanity.

In redemption, then, is where Calvin's Aristotelian distinctions do especially important work. When Paul speaks about being "crucified with Christ" and putting to death the flesh, or the old self, is *this* misanthropic? Does this make salvation a *rupture* of identity—leaving behind all that we were and taking only what is new? No, Calvin says. The Christian life, involving the mortification of the flesh, is a *restoration* of who we were created to be.[18] How? Recall the language of

14. Calvin, *Bondage and Liberation*, 46–47.
15. See *Inst.* 2.1.5; 2.2.1.
16. Calvin, *Bondage and Liberation*, 46–48.
17. *Inst.* 2.2.1.
18. Calvin, *Bondage and Liberation*, 210–13.

communion and union with Christ in John and Paul. This communion and union is a *restoration* of the created goodness.[19] In Aristotelian terms, the accidental characteristic of sinning is gradually diminished and overcome in redemption, restoring the good, created "substance" of human nature, which is in communion with God. When we deny ourselves as the first step in the Christian life, according to Calvin, this is *not* denying our *created* selves; it is denying our "old selves," our false selves that seek to be autonomous. There is continuity between creation and redemption, and God's grace *restores* the creation rather than simply replacing it. In the words of Calvin, the purpose of grace "is to restore the nature that has fallen and has been overturned and make it stand upright."[20] This "upright" posture, though, is never autonomous but is always in dependent communion with God, since that is what it means to be human. For, as Calvin points out about the vine and the branches in John 15, humans never bear fruit pleasing to God "in themselves" but only insofar as they abide in the vine.[21]

It is not simply Calvin's view of Adam that underlies this entire framework of true humanity as being in communion with God, but it is also Augustine's incarnational reflections about the second Adam, Jesus Christ, who is higher than the first. In the incarnation we see perfect harmony between divinity and humanity, but, as Augustine noted, Christ's humanity has no autonomous merit or power on its own. It exists because the divine Word of God has assumed the humanity of Christ. Thus, as believers grow in Christ, they grow in communion with God *mediated by the hypostatic union*. Because of this, the idea of a "true humanity" that is *not* in divinely initiated communion with God is a contradiction in terms.

Does the denial of an autonomous space for human action in Christ mean that Christians become completely limp and passive because of God's work? Stated differently, if divine and human agency is not partitive, such that God does part and the human does part, will humans refuse to live an active Christian life? No. While it's true that both justification and sanctification are *received* in union with Christ

---

19. Indeed, because the second Adam, Jesus Christ, is higher than the first, life in Christ not only restores the good creation but lifts humanity higher than the original creation. For more on this specific point in Calvin, see Henri Blocher, "Calvin's Theological Anthropology," in *John Calvin and Evangelical Theology: Legacy and Prospect*, ed. Sung Wook Chung (Louisville: Westminster John Knox, 2009), 83–84.

20. Calvin, *Bondage and Liberation*, 99.

21. Ibid., 231.

(not achieved by the sinner autonomously), this reception is an activating one. In other words, sinners are moved from death to life, from passivity to activity, as they are enabled by the Spirit to participate in Christ. The new life of the Spirit in sanctification is received as a gift. But it activates our capacities. As we see in Jesus Christ, true humanity (in harmony with God) is active humanity—actively obedient to the Father, active in loving God and neighbor. While Christians receive participation in Christ as a gift, the result of this reception is an enlivening of our capacities by the Spirit. As Calvin says in the *Bondage and Liberation of the Will*, God does not "cause" faith or action in us without our assent. Yet "assent is properly called ours, but not in such a way that it should be understood to derive from us."[22] Declaring that God deserves the credit for the fruit of the preaching of the gospel, Calvin warns that "this is not because in doing everything by the power of his own Spirit [God] excludes the ministry of his servants, but so as to secure for himself the entire praise for the action, just as the effectiveness derives from him alone, and whatever labour people do without him is empty and barren."[23] Thus, communion with the Spirit is what makes our faith and action our own. Stated differently, God *does* use our will, our mind, our ministry, and our efforts to preach the gospel and to live faithful Christian lives. But wherever there is fruit, the credit should not be divided between God and us. When we pray and the prayer is answered, we should not congratulate ourselves for praying with wisdom and diligence. No. In all things, we give praise to God, because even sanctification is a *gift*, first and foremost, that we receive from God.

At this point, in seeing not only justification but also sanctification as a gift received in union with Christ, we are at the heart of the issue on an experiential level for Christians. If sanctification is a matter of me drawing deeply upon myself to do good things for God, then my own holiness—and my own effort—becomes an end in itself, and preaching should focus on Christ only to the extent that he is a moral exemplar who goads us to work harder. Why? Because in this way of thinking, since Christ's justifying work is done, it is up to us to achieve our sanctification.

But this is where the gospel as union with Christ is so radical. It says, do not look to yourself, but look to Jesus Christ for your new

22. Ibid., 120.
23. Ibid., 163.

identity. As the Heidelberg Catechism says, our "only comfort in life and in death" is not in looking to ourselves but is "that I am not my own, but belong—body and soul, in life and in death—to my faithful Savior Jesus Christ."[24] When you stop looking to yourself, something peculiar is likely to happen: God and neighbor can come back into focus as objects of love.

I grew up in a common form of American Christianity that basically treated anxiety like a fruit of the Spirit. If you were not worried about your own holiness, something was wrong. In relation to this, Reformed teaching on the double grace and the will's bondage is *very good news*: rather than being "tossed back and forth without any certainty," with "our poor consciences . . . tormented constantly," as the Belgic Confession says, we come to rest in Jesus Christ, knowing that new life is a gift received in union with him.[25] In this way, we are freed to actually love and delight in God and neighbor. Otherwise, our praying, our acts of mercy, our evangelism, all are done to build up our own holiness—which blocks God and neighbor from being our focus. When both our justification and our new life are found in Jesus Christ, then this burdensome, disingenuous Christianity is replaced by Spirit-empowered gratitude.

But how can we receive or even have faith unless we are free to do so on our own? This frequent question assumes that true humanity is humanity autonomous from God rather than united to God. The Reformation doctrine of the bondage of the will to sin asserts that, apart from the Spirit's regeneration, the fallen will is unable to do any good that could contribute to salvation. No part of the fallen human being is untainted by sin such that it could take the first step toward God—that is what total (extensive) depravity is. But this claim is not a new speculation born out of the Reformation. It is simply the consequence of a theology of salvation and communion that John's Gospel and Paul's letters are well aware of: in the words of Christ, "apart from me you can do nothing" (John 15:5).

One faces a similar issue in interpreting Paul's imperatives, which, if taken out of context, may appear to make divine and human agency partitive and competitive: "Do not grieve the Holy Spirit of God, with which you were marked with a seal for the day of redemption" (Eph.

---

24. Heidelberg Catechism, question 1, in *Ecumenical Creeds and Reformed Confessions* (Grand Rapids: CRC Publications, 1987), 13. Footnotes to supporting scripture texts in the CRC translation are not included here.

25. Belgic Confession, art. 24, in *Ecumenical Creeds and Reformed Confessions*, 102.

4:30). Is Paul postulating an autonomous way of speaking about the Christian will, such that Christians "grieve" God unless they obey him from an autonomous space? No. Once again, this is part of Paul's eschatological way of speaking. "Do not grieve the Holy Spirit," like "put on the Lord Jesus Christ" (Rom. 13:14), is an imperative to live into the God-given identity that Christians have already received in Christ. For example, in Ephesians, the neighbor-love imperatives of 4:25 through 5:1 are rooted in the indicative of union in Christ: "for we are members of one another" (4:25). Ephesians does not exhort us to make ourselves members of Christ's body; rather, being a member of Christ's body is the accomplished fact that leads to the exhortation to speak only what is "useful for building up," avoiding the evil talk and bitterness that would "grieve the Holy Spirit" (4:29–30).[26] Similarly, Paul roots the imperative of Romans 13:14 in the indicative of union with Christ, which is prominent in the book of Romans.[27] Only by removing such imperatives from the eschatological "now" but "not yet" that conditions Paul's theology of union with Christ can one use such passages to support the notion that Christian action has a space that is autonomous from the Spirit's work.

Why is it impossible for the fallen human to take the first step toward God? Because it would be a contradiction in terms, both scripturally and logically, when the scriptural framework outlined above is owned. To be human is to be in communion with God. Thus, *it is impossible to act "in oneself" in taking a step toward God*, because acting "in oneself" is part of the very definition of sin—the corollary to salvation as communion.

If we are to move the implications of this position to a post-Reformation era, we can see how it differs from a classic Arminian position. On the one hand, unlike Pelagius, Arminians affirm that fallen humans cannot choose God on their own. Yet, in contrast to the Reformed explanation, the Spirit's prevenient grace lifts the sinner to a state of equilibrium in which the sinner can either choose or reject

---

26. See Andrew T. Lincoln, *Ephesians*, Word Biblical Commentary (Dallas: Word, 2002), 313.

27. Close readers of the biblical text who do not self-identify as Reformed note these basic features along with Reformed readers. For example, James Dunn makes the case that the Romans 13 imperatives are rooted in an eschatologically conditioned understanding of union with Christ, and that "put on the Lord Jesus Christ" refers to an action that is enabled by the Spirit. See Dunn, *Romans 9–16*, Word Biblical Commentary (Dallas: Word, 2002), 790–94.

God's gospel. But this explanation is impossible without assuming that true humanity is autonomous from God rather than in divinely enabled communion with God. Why? Because if one chooses God in that moment of equilibrium, the decisive movement toward God was empowered "by oneself," rather than effected "by the Spirit."

Yet Arminians could object that their view of prevenient grace affirms divine initiative and communion with God the Spirit in the moment of decision. That is true, in a certain sense. But Arminians don't confess that divinely enabled communion goes "all the way down," so to speak. There is divine initiative not just at the conception of Christ in Mary but throughout the incarnation. We do not abide in Christ the Vine at the beginning, only to be replanted after Christ has given us new life. No. We abide in Christ "all the way down." Apart from this abiding, John says, we can do nothing. The Arminian denial of the effectual or causal dimension of the Spirit's work occurs to preserve a certain type of autonomous space for the will. But if sin is acting "in ourselves" and obedience is acting in communion with God, then it is simply impossible to move toward God by acting "in ourselves." Only by the Spirit's effectual work can one move toward communion with God. Or, stated differently, *only by communion with God can we move toward communion with God.* That's what the Reformed teaching of the bondage of the will affirms.

Certainly Augustine and the Reformed tradition give us specific, biblical reasons to believe that the Spirit's work is effectual, such as the Philippians 2:13 statement that "it is God who is at work in you, enabling you both to will and to work for his good pleasure." Scriptural exegesis of this and other passages used to support the Spirit's effectual work will continue to be an important part of the theological discussion of this topic.[28] But what is often missed by both advocates and critics of the Reformed tradition is this: salvation as communion with God implies the will's bondage apart from the Spirit's regeneration, and both justification and sanctification are *gifts* in union with Christ. Just as we saw with the images of union with Christ in Paul and John, a state of total (extensive) communion with God through union with Christ requires the other side of the coin—namely, that

---

28. For an account of key scriptural passages in relation to a range of theological interpretations of the effectual work of the Spirit, see Kevin J. Vanhoozer, *First Theology: God, Scripture, and Hermeneutics* (Downers Grove, IL: InterVarsity, 2002), chap. 4.

there is a total (extensive) scope for human depravity, for humanity "in itself" apart from the Spirit.

Why Is This Position So Surprising Today?

In presenting my account of this neglected dimension of the Reformational doctrine of the bondage of the will, I have observed that historical theologians generally value the argument, while the response of many others has been surprise, even shock. Could this really be Calvin's position, a Reformed position on the bondage of the will?

Allow me to offer two snapshots. First snapshot: At an ecumenical conference, I described how, in Calvin's view, grace *restores* the good human nature that was united to God rather than destroying it. In response, a Roman Catholic scholar insisted that this couldn't be Calvin's position—it is the Catholic position! At the time, I tried to clarify the sense in which Calvin makes this claim by pointing to *The Bondage and Liberation of the Will*, which—although neglected in both scholarly and popular circles—is quite clear. In retrospect, perhaps I should have just granted a sense in which his second claim was true. Yes, it is a catholic position. But Calvin and Reformed theologians in the centuries after Calvin considered themselves to be catholic.[29]

Snapshot two: A student said that she had heard about total depravity in TULIP for many years, but she had no idea that this doctrine actually affirms a rich notion of salvation as communion with God. Her response? "Why didn't anyone ever tell me this? This actually sounds like *good* news!" She wondered where the Reformed tradition had gone wrong in losing this key part of its teaching.

Developments Related to the "Freedom" of the Bound Will: From Luther to the Reformed Scholastics

Indeed, where did the Reformed tradition go wrong, to the point of obscuring the communion aspect of the total depravity/total communion connection? In responding to the reactions of the Roman Catholic

29. For more on the catholic character of the thought of Calvin and early Reformational theology, see J. Todd Billings, "The Catholic Calvin," *Pro Ecclesia* 20, no. 2 (Spring 2011): 120–34.

scholar and the student, it might be tempting to talk about the alleged decline of the Reformed tradition on this point of doctrine into the so-called legalism of Reformed scholasticism. But that is simply not the case.[30] The bondage of the will continued to be taught in Reformed circles after Calvin, and while it underwent development in a number of areas, these developments generally enhanced and built upon the insights discussed in this chapter, rather than undermining them. After Calvin, Reformed theologians became increasingly sophisticated in their patristic scholarship, and while they continued to work with an Augustinian theology of grace, they extended the Reformed project of critically retrieving from other patristic and medieval sources as well.[31] In this they deepened the catholicity of their theology in a distinctively Reformed way. This means that some of the "catholic" dimensions discussed here, such as the emphasis on the *imago Dei* and human agency in communion with God, are extended and clarified after Calvin, not diminished.

One question in particular received considerable development in Reformed scholasticism: since the "bondage of the will" is a soteriological claim—that is, since the human will can make no progress toward salvation apart from the Spirit—in what sense is the "bound" will still free? While Reformed scholastics eventually analyzed this issue with philosophical tools such as modal logic, the basic question intersects with quite existential ones: If a sinner can do nothing but sin apart from the Spirit's regeneration, is that sinner really free enough to be considered responsible? Are virtuous non-Christians not able to do "good" in some sense? If they are, then how can the Reformed claim that sinners can do no "good" apart from the Spirit's renewing work be upheld?

On the deeper theological point about whether the "bound" will is still free, there was a gradual development of thought that is worth our while to recount, for there are key insights from Luther and Calvin that later Reformed thinkers sought to retain, even as they further developed aspects of the teaching.

---

30. In the next section ("Why Is Total Communion So Surprising? The Problem with the TULIP Acronym") I explore one of the actual reasons why the connection between total depravity and total communion is surprising to many today.

31. See J. Todd Billings, "Norms and Methodologies for Theology in the Reformation and Early Modern Period," in *The Oxford Handbook to the Reception of Christian Theology*, ed. Richard Cross and Sarah Coakley (Oxford: Oxford University Press, forthcoming).

Luther's teaching on free will was not a general inquiry into commonsense notions of freedom but rather a soteriologically motivated attack on free will as a teaching that could obscure the Christian gospel itself. In his theses in the Heidelberg Disputation, Luther states his position on free will quite directly. For instance, in thesis 13 he says, "Free will, after the fall, exists in name only, and as long as it does what it is able to do it commits a mortal sin."[32] Luther explains that he is not annihilating the will but that the will "is not free except to do evil."[33] The will is not coerced to do evil, but when the uncoerced will does what is in the capacity of a fallen human to do, the result is sin. In support of this, Luther cites John 8:34b, "everyone who commits sin is a slave to sin," as well as Augustine, who said that "free will without grace has the power to do nothing but sin."[34] Thesis 14 continues: "free will, after the fall, has power to do good only in a passive capacity, but it can always do evil in an active capacity."[35] After the fall, the will, which was once free, can do good only when it is acted upon by a source outside itself (thus Luther's talk of a "passive capacity"). The will is dead and enslaved; it *can* live, but it must be *brought to life*, for it is unable to bring itself to life.[36] In terms of the larger theological framework, the will can do no good apart from the effectual work of the Spirit.

Why does Luther insist upon the importance of this negative account of the fallen will? His target is a theology of glory, a theology that Gerhard O. Forde exposits in a way that shows its prominence not only in the sixteenth century but also today.[37] A theology of glory seeks to divide the agency and honor for salvation between God and human beings—for God would surely make righteousness accessible to those who do their best, right? In the terms of the moralistic therapeutic deism creed, "God wants people to be good, nice, and fair to each other, as taught in the Bible and by most

32. Martin Luther, *Luther's Works*, ed. Jaroslav Jan Pelikan, Hilton C. Oswald, and Helmut T. Lehmann, vol. 31, *Career of the Reformer I* (1957; repr., Philadelphia: Fortress, 1999), 48.

33. Ibid., 31:49.

34. *The Spirit and the Letter* 3.5, in *Patrologiae cursus completus*, ed. J. P. Migne (Paris, 1865), 44:203.

35. Luther, *Luther's Works*, 31:49.

36. See Luther's explanation of thesis 14 in ibid.

37. See Gerhard O. Forde, *On Being a Theologian of the Cross* (Grand Rapids: Eerdmans, 1997).

world religions."[38] So what does God do for people when they are "good, nice, and fair?" "Good people go to heaven when they die," the MTD creed says.[39] In MTD theology God conforms to our own common sense; likewise, humans are able to please God quite well on their own. In his sixteenth-century context, Luther attacked theologians who sought to give assurance by saying *facere quod in se est*, "do what is in you," which Forde notes "might aptly be translated 'just do your best' or 'do what you can,' and God will not deny you grace."[40] In thesis 16, Luther leaves no doubt about what he thinks of this theology: "The person who believes that he can obtain grace by doing what is in him adds sin to sin so that he becomes doubly guilty."[41]

To the theologian of glory, both in the sixteenth century and today, such a thesis seems devastating. The theologian of glory looks at works in a commonsense way and classifies them as good or evil. From this perspective, we have access to God's way of evaluating righteousness and find that, in the end, we're pretty good people, at least when we try our best. But that is theology without a cross—the cross that reveals God's judgment of actions that we thought were "good," showing them to be sinful and thus leaving us exposed as sinners who have no hope apart from a savior outside ourselves. According to Luther, to "do what is in you" results in sin, and the idea that God will reward you for trying your best makes you "doubly guilty." The theologian of glory is always hopeful about what humans can do to save themselves. Today the solution proposed in many churchly circles in response to apathetic, nominal Christianity and the lack of church growth is to "try harder"—to become purpose-filled, get organized, and be a "passionate" Christian. But what if trying harder isn't enough? What if it is insufficient not only to revive a nominal Christian but to save a sinner from God's judgment? If trying harder isn't enough, some will be tempted to despair.

But a certain type of despair can bear good fruit, in Luther's view. Affirming the bondage of the will can be a way to affirm despair in precisely the right thing, that is, despair in the old self, in the attempts

38. Christian Smith, *Soul Searching: The Religious and Spiritual Lives of American Teenagers*, with Melinda Lundquist Denton (New York: Oxford University Press, 2005), 162.

39. Ibid., 163.

40. Forde, *Theologian of the Cross*, 50.

41. Luther, *Luther's Works*, 31:50.

at self-salvation. Luther writes, "Now you ask, 'What then shall we do? Shall we go our way with indifference because we can do nothing but sin?' I would reply, By no means. But, having heard this, fall down and pray for grace and place your hope in Christ in whom is our salvation, life, and resurrection."[42] Salvation is not in ourselves; it is not enabled by doing our best, by "trying to be a good Christian." Instead, as we have explored in this chapter, salvation is "in Christ," in communion with God in Christ by the Spirit. Only in Christ can we find "salvation, life, and resurrection." Thus, one of the purposes of recognizing the will's bondage is to lead to a type of despair that opens one to the communion with God found in Christ. As thesis 18 states, "It is certain that man must utterly despair of his own ability before he is prepared to receive the grace of Christ."[43]

Integrating this insight into the thought of this chapter, then, one might say not only that total depravity is the theology of sin that corresponds to total communion as salvation, but also that recognizing the "no" in the bondage of the will is a key part of our recovery—a crucial dimension of coming to truly acknowledge the significance of salvation in Christ. Not just youth who have MTD as a functional creed but also scores of others inside and outside the church, particularly in the West, have little idea how desperately they need to be rescued by one who is outside themselves: Jesus Christ. Certainly, Christ lives within the people of God, as he has united himself to them by the Spirit. But Christ is never constituted by our own efforts, by our own life "in itself." Rather, Christ is the savior external to ourselves who has given life in union with him. Thus, coming to affirm our own total depravity can be a step on the path toward recognizing that in Jesus Christ "is our salvation, life, and resurrection."

Tracing the Reformed strand of thought on this point, we can see that Calvin shares Luther's soteriological concerns, affirming the bondage of the will in strong terms. As argued above, he coordinates this with an overall soteriology that frames salvation as (total) communion with God, with no positive place for the autonomous will. Yet Calvin also nuanced his position. Although the will is not free to choose good or evil as was the human will before the fall, Calvin insisted that the "bound" will is still responsible. As Luther notes above, the will actually chooses what it desires. Moreover, the will

42. Ibid.
43. Ibid., 31:51.

is not driven or coerced by an external force to sin, but it is "self-determined" in the sense that "of itself it directs itself in the direction in which it is led."[44] It is "bound" to sin "so that it can choose nothing but evil," but "it does so of its own accord and gladly, without being driven by any external impulse."[45] So while fallen sinners necessarily sin in their actions, their actions are indeed the result of their own will and not external force.

Thus, although neither Luther nor Calvin is comfortable speaking with his Roman Catholic interlocutors about a "freedom of the will" after the fall, this is because "freedom of the will" was being used in such a way as to undercut the soteriological point of the bondage of the will. Yet, given that the will is bound to sin, is there a sense in which the bound will is still free? Even among Calvin's evangelical peers, such as Peter Martyr Vermigli, the answer was yes. Indeed, since Calvin affirms the continuing presence of a will that makes choices, one could say that his greatest concern was not to deny the will's "freedom" so much as to recognize that the scope of the will's choice is limited to sinful possibilities. This view is required in order to maintain the "no" of the will's bondage, a "no" that leads one to look for salvation coming from outside oneself—from Jesus Christ.

While not denying these important soteriological points, a more robust notion of human responsibility could be seen developing already in Vermigli, contributing to what became a popular distinction between the necessity of the consequent and the consequence.[46] With Vermigli and the generations after him who worked with this distinction, the assumption was that fallen humans will necessarily sin. But necessity is not always incompatible with contingency. There are, in fact, different kinds of necessity. While that discussion can become quite complicated in its reliance upon modal logic, an example may help illustrate the point. The basic idea is to show how a contingent act can be compatible with necessity.

44. Calvin, *Bondage and Liberation*, 69.

45. Ibid.

46. While Vermigli and the later Reformed tradition sought to maintain Luther's soteriological insight about the bondage of the will, Luther, in a brief treatment, claimed that the distinction between the necessity of the consequent and the consequence was "completely useless." See *Luther's Works*, ed. Jaroslav Jan Pelikan, Hilton C. Oswald, and Helmut T. Lehmann, vol. 33, *Career of the Reformer III* (1957; repr., Philadelphia: Fortress, 1972), 194–95.

The soldiers freely crucified Christ.
Hence, the crucifixion of Christ was a contingent act.
The crucifixion of Christ was decreed (and foreknown and prophesied) by God.
Hence, the crucifixion of Christ was necessary on account of God's decree (and foreknowledge and foresaying).[47]

Thus, in the first two statements we can see how the crucifixion of Christ was, in itself, a contingent act. Indeed, as authors such as Franciscus Junius (1545–1602) emphasized, one should note that the will had other real possibilities in the first statement, for the soldiers contingently chose to crucify Christ. Yet on another level, such an act was necessary—not "in itself" but "by a necessity of consequence on account of the decree of God."[48] In other words, God decrees the final act (the consequence), making it necessary. But the human acts leading to this act are contingent (the consequent), such that the act is chosen among various possibilities.

By the beginning of the seventeenth century, Franciscus Gomarus (1563–1641) provided an explanation for how fallen sinners can choose objects that appear to be good but are not "good," following the soteriological line of reasoning of Luther and Calvin that the fallen will can do no good. How can this be, when fallen sinners choose apparently good objects with their will? Gomarus makes a teleological argument: A truly good action must be directed toward God as its goal, or *telos*. Yet this is not possible except through the Spirit's regenerative work. In considering how the so-called glorious deeds of heathens might be evaluated, Gomarus says that "they lack the pure source (*fonte*), namely faith (*fide*), and their goal (*fine*), namely the honor of God. How can anyone dignify these [works], I ask, to call them good?"[49]

Although not developed in a teleological way, a similar clarification can be found in the Canons of Dort (1619), which state that all

47. Willem J. van Asselt, J. Martin Bac, and Roelf T. te Velde, eds., *Reformed Thought on Freedom: The Concept of Free Choice in Early Modern Reformed Theology* (Grand Rapids: Baker Academic, 2010), 114. This reasoning on crucifixion is a classic example of the necessity of the consequence, given in this case in an exposition of the thought of Junius. The numbering of each premise in the original text has been removed.
48. Ibid.
49. Franciscus Gomarus, "Theological Disputation on Free Choice (1602)," in Van Asselt, Bac, and te Velde, *Reformed Thought on Freedom*, 132–33.

people, because of their fallen will, are "unfit for any saving good."[50] "Good" in this soteriological sense is not possible without the Spirit's renewing work. Nevertheless, the phrase "saving good" (together with Gomarus's teleological account) makes it possible to explain how non-Christians perform all sorts of actions that are "good" in the common usage of the term but not a "saving good."

Moving to later scholastics such as Gisbertus Voetius (1589–1676), Francesco Turrettini (1623–87), and Bernardinus de Moor (1709–80), we see increasingly sophisticated accounts that expand upon the notion of human responsibility and freedom while strongly affirming the soteriological bondage of the will.[51] None of these figures ground human responsibility in an individualistic, libertarian notion of freedom. Instead, like good catholic and Reformed thinkers, they see all human activity as dependent upon God; God's agency actually upholds human agency rather than diminishes it. In the midst of the accounts in Reformed scholasticism, a Reformational doctrine of the bondage of the will was not lost but was further developed and clarified.

Why Is Total Communion So Surprising? The Problem with the TULIP Acronym

For many laypeople today, as well as for a surprising number of pastors and scholars, the TULIP acronym—or its implicit notion that predestination is the center of Reformed theology—provides their basic framework for Reformed doctrine. It is in this context, then, that they understand the bondage of the will. While I have critiqued elsewhere the use of the TULIP acronym by the "new Calvinists,"[52] I suspect that the theology circulating around this widespread acronym is at least part of the reason that the Reformed emphasis on total com-

50. The will in bondage makes "all people . . . unfit for any saving good, inclined to evil, dead in their sins, and slaves to sin." Canons of Dort, third and fourth main points, art. 3, in *Ecumenical Creeds and Reformed Confessions*, 133.

51. See Van Asselt, Bac, and te Velde, *Reformed Thought on Freedom*, 145–229.

52. J. Todd Billings, "Calvin's Comeback? The Irresistible Reformer," *Christian Century*, December 1, 2009, 22–25. It is worth noting that for decades Calvin scholars have argued against the notion that predestination was the "central dogma" from which Calvin's other teaching was derived. Yet this is still a popular conception of Calvin's theology in some circles. See Richard A. Muller, *After Calvin: Studies in the Development of a Theological Tradition* (Oxford: Oxford University Press, 2003), 94–98.

munion has been lost by many.[53] For those who have not been initiated into TULIP circles, here is a basic explanation from my earlier article:

T   stands for Total Depravity: Sinners are totally unable to please God.

U   stands for Unconditional Election: From eternity, God elects some for salvation, an election that does not depend upon a person's behavior or upon foreknowledge of the person's faith or obedience.

L   stands for Limited Atonement: Christ's atoning work on the cross is intended only for the elect.

I   stands for Irresistible Grace: Humans who come to faith do not synergistically act in cooperation with the Holy Spirit; rather, the Spirit overcomes human resistance.

P   stands for Perseverance of the Saints: The elect remain steadfast in their faith and do not fall away.[54]

As Ken Stewart has noted, although this acronym is often used as a key to the theology of Calvin, Calvinism, or the Reformed tradition, it does not date before the twentieth century.[55] Moreover, as noted earlier in this chapter with regard to the term "total depravity," the TULIP acronym is easily and frequently misunderstood. I use the term "total depravity" in this chapter only after qualifying exactly what I mean by it. TULIP as it is commonly understood sounds negative—the T, L, and I in particular strike many as misanthropic and coercive. For some, it confirms their suspicion that Reformed theology is negative and misanthropic, since they assume that TULIP defines Reformed theology.

However, the notion that Reformed theology should be defined by TULIP is a misunderstanding on several levels. First, TULIP is an attempted summary of the seventeenth-century Canons of Dort—and a poor summary at that. (For example, the Canons never speak of

53. Of course, the reasons why a teaching would be a surprise depend on the particular context and background of the ones who are surprised. But TULIP—and the accompanying notion that Reformed theology is centered in predestination—is a broadly shared assumption about the Reformed tradition that tends to downplay the notion of salvation as communion.

54. Billings, "Calvin's Comeback?," 22.

55. See Kenneth J. Stewart, "The Points of Calvinism: Retrospect and Prospect," *Scottish Bulletin of Evangelical Theology* 26, no. 2 (2008): 187–203, esp. 189–90.

the atonement as "limited.") The Canons of Dort emerged from a controversy with the Arminians in the Netherlands and were written as a response to a statement from the Remonstrants. Thus, in many ways the Canons were saying "no" to certain claims (while saying "yes" to Reformed claims).

In its historical context, however, the Synod of Dort was not seeking to write a summary of Reformed doctrine. It never attempted to write a general statement of faith—a statement with a fully stated doctrine of sin, atonement, and salvation. Why? Because in its Dutch context, it already had a general statement of faith: the Belgic Confession. The Canons of Dort were written to provide a clarification of Reformed doctrine on a cluster of issues related to election, sin, and the assurance of salvation. As such, they functioned as a kind of explanatory footnote to the Belgic Confession, which gave a broad summary of Reformed doctrine.

Thus, the Canons were intended to be received not by themselves but as a supplement to the Belgic Confession. Taken together, the Canons of Dort and the Belgic Confession do indeed have a rich theology of communion with God through union with Christ. The Belgic Confession includes a theology of human communion with God before the fall (art. 14), the alienation that takes place through sin (art. 14–15), and the way in which salvation is restoration through justification and sanctification in union with Christ (art. 22–24). Moreover, it develops this theology of communion with God in its account of ecclesiology (esp. art. 28–29) and a powerful sacramental theology rooted in communion with Christ (art. 33–35). Thus, since the Canons function as a supplement to the Belgic, the Canons can both assume and further develop the Belgic's theology of total communion and the bondage of the will. Indeed, while the Canons are most famous for their emphasis on sin, they also teach that salvation is a restoration of communion—a life-giving communion that restores creatures rather than annihilating them:

> Just as by the fall man did not cease to be man, endowed with intellect and will, and just as sin, which has spread through the whole human race, did not abolish the nature of the human race but distorted and spiritually killed it, so also this divine grace of regeneration does not act in people as if they were blocks and stones; nor does it abolish the will and its properties or coerce a reluctant will by force, but spiritually revives, heals, reforms, and—in a manner at once pleasing and powerful—bends it back. As a result, a ready and sincere obedience

of the Spirit now begins to prevail where before the rebellion and resistance of the flesh were completely dominant.[56]

Whatever one thinks about the Canons of Dort, a doctrine of salvation as communion that accompanies a Reformed doctrine of sin can certainly be seen in the documents—when they are received as they were intended, as a supplement to the Belgic Confession. But as long as modern interpreters wear TULIP-colored glasses, assuming that TULIP summarizes the whole of Reformed theology, the result is an imbalanced picture, a theology of total depravity with much less clarity about the gracious communion received in the double grace of union with Christ.

Conclusion

In sum, our chapter has explored how in fidelity to the teaching of scripture, particularly in Paul and in John's Gospel, we need to hold to both sides of union with Christ. "I am the vine, you are the branches," Jesus says. "Those who abide in me and I in them bear much fruit, because apart from me you can do nothing" (John 15:5). If we want to take seriously the biblical images of participating in Christ, being united to Christ, abiding in Christ, and having been adopted in Christ, we must take seriously the accompanying images—that apart from union with Christ, we are dead, in slavery, incapable of producing fruit.

We have explored how Augustine, as well as a strand of the Augustinian tradition (the Reformed), sought to take both sides of the biblical language and imagery seriously. The result is quite surprising for many, forcing us to rethink the idea that we are only human when we are autonomous. In light of Augustine's insight about grace derived from the incarnation, we find that to be fully human is to be in harmony and obedient communion with God. Thus, any partitive attempts to divide salvation between God and human beings are destined to fail. Rather, God's action by the Spirit in the human does not threaten the human's own agency but actually enables it. When humans are empowered by the Spirit to live in Christ—when they act "in Christ" rather than "in themselves"—they are being restored as

56. Canons of Dort, third and fourth main points, art. 16, in *Ecumenical Creeds and Reformed Confessions*, 135–36.

the children of God they were created to be. Thus, claiming that in oneself one can do "nothing" is not a misanthropic teaching about humanity; it is a doctrine of sin that defines true humanity as humanity in total, or full, communion with God—for no autonomous space is found "in Christ." Therefore, human sin is also "total" in its extensive character, for there is no part of "the old self" that can autonomously make a move toward God. Such would be a contradiction in terms, for there is no way to move toward God apart from divinely initiated communion with God.

We have also explored how the bondage of the will has a distinctively soteriological scope, leading to despair in the old self and driving sinners to Christ, as Luther has eloquently argued. With a trajectory beginning with second-generation Reformers such as Calvin and Vermigli, Reformed thinkers sought to hold onto this vital soteriological insight, while also responding to misunderstandings of Reformed teaching that claimed it extinguished the will or, in some cases, lost altogether any notion of freedom. Thus, in a way that carefully upheld the belief that fallen sinners can do no good on their own, later Reformed thinkers developed ways to think through the freedom and responsibility of a will that is in soteriological bondage.

In the end, due to a combination of factors including the multifaceted misunderstandings that the TULIP acronym leads to, both Christians who are Reformed and those who are not tend to think that Reformed teaching on the bondage of the will reflects a negative view of humanity. But rightly understood, total depravity is a way to affirm that redemption involves nothing less than total communion with God in Christ. Ultimately, Reformed teaching does not subscribe to a negative view of humans by affirming the bondage of the will but upholds a high and exalted one: humans were created for communion with God, and redemption involves a restoration of communion with God through the double grace of union with Christ. To see the bondage of the will as purely negative is to remove it from its biblical context, since although "you were *dead in trespasses* and the uncircumcision of your flesh, *God made you alive together with him [Christ]*" (Col. 2:13, emphasis added).

3

Encountering a Mystery in Union with Christ

On Communion with the Incomprehensible God

Communion with God in Calvin in Light of Modern Theology and Spirituality

The stereotypes of Calvin in popular culture are well enough known: Calvin, the alleged tyrant of Geneva, preached an equally tyrannical God—a God high and holy, untouched by the plight of dismal sinners. In this caricatured view of Calvin's theology, God and humanity are functional opposites, and anything that humans receive from God is by means of coercion (i.e., predestination).

Somewhat surprisingly, the assessments of Calvin by contemporary theologians often reflect similar stereotypes. According to several theologians associated with the Radical Orthodoxy movement, because Calvin's theology includes the forensic image of God imputing the righteousness of Christ to sinners in justification, it is based on "divine decree" rather than on the allegedly more appealing medieval vision of creation participating in God. Even if Calvin speaks about participation and communion with God, his language is ontologically ambiguous, we are told, because he does not accept an account of creation as participating in the divine being. Thus, what John Calvin really offers is a theology of a "unilateral gift," one in which the human is completely passive before God, receiving election or divine reprobation by divine decree. In the words of Catherine Pickstock, Calvin fails to speak of "incorporation into the Son" to achieve "reconciliation with the Father," but rather reduces salvation to "simply accepting a transaction carried out by God on our behalf."[1] To these criticisms, one could add a chorus of other voices: Kilian McDonnell, who claims that divinity and humanity become opposites in Calvin, such that a true union in the incarnation is impossible (thus Calvin is said to have a Nestorian Christology);[2] feminist theologians such as Anna Case-Winters, who argues that a binary opposition of God and the world is at play in Calvin's theology, one characterized by divine "domination and control";[3] Eastern Orthodox theologian Joseph Farrell, who argues that Calvin erroneously opposes divine and human agency, failing to realize the proper synthesis of these as Byzantine theology does.[4] It would seem from these critiques that Calvin rarely, if ever, speaks about union with God, union with Christ, and the indwelling of the Spirit—or if he does, he qualifies these statements so heavily as to make them empty of content.

It was the joyful burden of my first book, *Calvin, Participation, and the Gift*, to respond to these divergent criticisms of Calvin. What made this burden "joyful" was that, when one looks at Calvin's writings in their sixteenth-century context and in light of the development of his thought, these criticisms fall flat. Calvin speaks extensively about union with Christ, union with and participation in God, and the indwelling of the Spirit. These references are qualified, yes, but usually with no more qualification than what many contemporary theologians want to claim as well: first and foremost, that union with God is a differentiated union, one that does not annihilate the clear distinction between Creator and creature.

Nevertheless, the themes of union and communion with God are not an afterthought for Calvin but provide the basic imagery and

1. Catherine Pickstock, *After Writing: On the Liturgical Consummation of Philosophy* (Oxford: Blackwell, 1998), 156–57.

2. Kilian McDonnell, *John Calvin, the Church, and the Eucharist* (Princeton: Princeton University Press, 1967), 229–31, 367–71.

3. Anna Case-Winters, *God's Power: Traditional Understandings and Contemporary Challenges* (Louisville: Westminster John Knox, 1990), 64–66.

4. See Joseph P. Farrell, *Free Choice in St. Maximus the Confessor* (South Canaan, PA: St. Tikhon's Seminary Press, 1989), chap. 9, appendix.

structure for key motifs in his soteriology. Calvin did not abandon them in the course of his theological development, but he made increasingly emphatic and extensive additions on this theme in various editions of the *Institutes*, his occasional works, and his commentaries.[5] The images of union with Christ, ingrafting into Christ, partaking of Christ, and adoption were drawn from Paul and Johannine writings in the New Testament and were deeply woven into the fabric of his soteriology. In the broad portrait of his soteriology, Calvin claims that created human nature is good and that Adam was "united to God" and enjoyed "participation in God."[6] Human beings have been alienated from God and from their true, created nature by the fall. But the final end and goal for humanity is a *re-union* of humanity with God in the second Adam, a union even higher than the first. This trinitarian process unites believers to Jesus Christ by the Spirit in order to serve the Father in gratitude. In union with Christ, believers are "participants not only in all his benefits but also in himself." Indeed, "day by day, he grows more and more into one body with us, until he becomes completely one with us."[7] This union is always empowered by the Spirit, for by this Spirit we "come to a participation in God (*in Dei participationem venimus*)."[8] Moreover, through Christ and the Spirit, believers are gathered "into participation in the Father."[9] Since the "perfection of human happiness is to be united to God," this union takes place in redemption.[10] "We are united to God by Christ," Calvin writes. "We can only be joined to Christ if God abides in us."[11] In this way, "men are so united to Christ by faith that Christ unites them to God."[12] Indeed, believers shall "be really and fully united to

5. See J. Todd Billings, *Calvin, Participation, and the Gift: The Activity of Believers in Union with Christ*, Changing Paradigms in Historical and Systematic Theology (Oxford: Oxford University Press, 2007), 68–104.

6. See *Inst.* 2.1.5; 2.2.1.

7. *Inst.* 3.2.24.

8. A literal translation. Beveridge renders the overall passage, "By means of him [the Spirit] we become partakers of the divine nature (*in Dei participationem venimus*), so as in a manner to feel his quickening energy within us. Our justification is his work; from him is power, sanctification, truth, grace, and every good thought, since it is from the Spirit alone that all good gifts proceed." John Calvin, *Institutes of the Christian Religion*, ed. Henry Beveridge and Robert Pitcairn (Edinburgh: Calvin Translation Society, 1845), 1.13.14.

9. *Inst.* 1.8.26

10. *Inst.* 1.15.6.

11. Comm. on 1 John 4:15, CC.

12. Comm. on 1 John 4:15, CTS.

Thee [Almighty God] through Christ our Lord."[13] Yet being united
with God does not make believers "consubstantial with God," as if
they were a fourth member of the Godhead, but rather it takes place
in Christ by "the grace and power of the Spirit."[14] Calvin also speaks
of a coming beatific vision, a "direct vision" of the Godhead, "when
as partakers in heavenly glory we shall see God as he is."[15] This final
end is also "the end of the gospel," which Calvin says is "to render us
eventually conformable to God, and, if we may so speak, to deify us."[16]

Thus, by arguing that Calvin has a well-developed theology of
union with God in Christ, my first book put Calvin's thought in an
unexpected place for his contemporary critics: closer to their own
theologies, which emphasize salvation as restoration, communion,
and union with God.[17] In this place, rather than simply being a weak
foil in contemporary discussions, such as discussions of grace and
gift-giving, Calvin's theology might be seen as carrying contemporary

13. Comm. on Jer. 31:34, CTS.

14. *Inst.* 1.15.5.

15. *Inst.* 2.14.3.

16. Comm. on 2 Pet. 1:4, CTS. Calvin's willingness to speak of deification at this
point is in response to the statement in 2 Peter 1:4 about believers becoming "participants of the divine nature." Passages like this one were key to patristic teaching about
deification. For an analysis of Calvin's commentaries on the biblical passages that
were frequently read by the church fathers in terms of deification, see Carl Mosser,
"The Greatest Possible Blessing: Calvin and Deification," *Scottish Journal of Theology*
55, no. 1 (2002): 36–57. Calvin gives a Western, Augustinian account of the theme of
deification as an exegetical and soteriological motif; as such, he clearly maintains a
Creator-creature distinction and also gives an account that differs significantly from
Eastern Orthodox accounts of *theosis.* See J. Todd Billings, "United to God through
Christ: Calvin on the Question of Deification," *Harvard Theological Review* 98, no.
3 (July 2005): 315–34; Billings, "The Contemporary Reception of Luther and Calvin's
Doctrine of Union with Christ: Mapping a Biblical, Catholic, and Reformational
Motif" (paper presented at Calvin Studies Society and North American Luther Forum,
Luther Seminary, St. Paul, MN, April 8, 2011).

17. While the critics above are mistaken in thinking that Calvin does not have a
theology of salvation as restoration, communion, and union with God, there are still
significant differences between their proposals and Calvin's account. One very important difference, as I note in *Calvin, Participation, and the Gift,* is that Calvin's account
of justification is deeply forensic in orientation. This is particularly clear in Calvin's
additions to the 1559 *Institutes* where he rejects Osiander's proposal for a nonforensic
account of justification. For more on this important feature of Calvin's theology, see
Calvin, Participation, and the Gift, 53–62, 106–16. For more on Calvin's dispute with
Osiander in contemporary scholarship, see Billings, "John Calvin's Soteriology: Key
Issues in Interpretation and Retrieval," *International Journal of Systematic Theology*
11, no. 4 (October 2009): 428–47.

promise. Even as it remains part of a sixteenth-century rather than twenty-first-century theological project, it is nevertheless possible, as John Webster has argued, for a theology of retrieval to speak to present concerns.[18]

But now, particularly for those who accept the main argument of my first book, I face a different kind of challenge for a theologian of retrieval: if Calvin presents insights for contemporary theology, I have thrust his thought forward into a wide-ranging discussion of deification, union with God, and union with Christ. On the one hand, I am happy about the possibility of Calvin no longer being just a foil for some but becoming a possible dialogue partner. On the other hand, there is a danger of assimilating Calvin into the popular categories or trends of contemporary culture that are preoccupied with "union with God," which leaves him among a rather motley crew: panentheists who love to speak of union with God, young evangelicals who sing of union with God while wearing chastity rings and talking about "dating Jesus," and the spiritual-but-not-religious crowd that also speaks of a mystical union with the divine. Have I just added Calvin to the chorus of those who emphasize union with God to the point of dismissing God's otherness, domesticating the Holy One of Israel into a comfortable lover?

18. See John Webster, "Theologies of Retrieval," in *Oxford Handbook of Systematic Theology*, ed. John Webster, Kathryn Tanner, and Iain Torrance (Oxford: Oxford University Press, 2007), 590–92. In the process of giving a historical account of Calvin's thought that is nonetheless a retrieval, I have sought to avoid the pitfalls of other attempts at a theology of retrieval—like the reading of Luther by Finnish theologian Tuomo Mannermaa. Mannermaa has helped to revive interest in the significant theme of union with Christ in Luther's theology. In engaging this theme, Mannermaa sought to retrieve a Luther who is useful for contemporary Lutheran-Orthodox dialogue. Mannermaa claims that a central strand of Luther's theology of justification relates to *theosis* and that this was missed in earlier historical accounts of Luther's theology. This feature in Luther's theology is said to set him apart from colleagues such as Philip Melanchthon and from much in the Lutheran confessional tradition. This disjunctive historiography, which seeks a "novel" interpretation of Luther with relatively little attention to Luther's historical context and theological development, leads Mannermaa to an account of Luther's theology that has serious historical problems. See Carl Trueman, "Is the Finnish Line a New Beginning? A Critical Assessment of the Reading of Luther Offered by the Helsinki Circle," *Westminster Theological Journal* 65 (2003): 231–44; Billings, "Contemporary Reception of Luther." While much of my detailed historical analysis of Calvin's theology of union with Christ occurs in other works (see note 6 in the introduction), the account that I retrieve in this book seeks to read Calvin's theology in light of his theological development and his sixteenth-century context.

For the record, I am not opposed to the image of God as a lover or spouse to his people. This is a biblical image, and it has had an important place in the Reformed tradition, particularly in preaching on the union with Christ that is celebrated at the Lord's Supper. However, on the one hand, at this moment in Western culture, there is a tendency to use the language of "union" and "communion" with God in a way that displaces God's transcendence, identifying God with the world or, more specifically, with ourselves and our own desires. On the other hand, among nominal Christians in particular, a functional deism pervades much of Western Christianity, as sociologists such as Christian Smith have demonstrated among young adults. It seems that either God is transcendent in the sense of being distant or God is close in the sense of being a reflection of ourselves. Or perhaps God is both at the same time in these popular forms of theology.

One key feature that separates Calvin's theology of union with God through Christ from these modern trends is the terse but significant negative theology running through Calvin's doctrine of God. Calvin's negative theology claims, first and foremost, that God is fully known only by God and that, while God may be known partially by creatures, he cannot be comprehended. But interestingly, Calvin's theology of transcendence does not contradict the claims of union highlighted in my first book, or make God into the distant, deistic deity. Rather, this theology of divine incomprehensibility is intimately tied to his notion of union and communion with God. Calvin makes both moves simultaneously by retrieving a category from patristic theology: accommodation.

In retrieving a theology that holds divine mystery together with a knowledge of and communion with God, this chapter moves in a different direction from the assumptions of moralistic therapeutic deism. In MTD there is a belief in God, but the mystery of God is affirmed in a way that assumes there is "no right answer."[19] Regarding different beliefs in God, divine mystery combines with American individualism to ground an easy subjectivism: the "typical bywords" are "'Who am I to judge?' 'If that's what they choose, whatever,' 'Each person decides for himself,' and 'If it works for them, fine.'"[20]

---

19. Christian Smith, *Soul Searching: The Religious and Spiritual Lives of American Teenagers*, with Melinda Lundquist Denton (New York: Oxford University Press, 2005), 145.

20. Ibid., 144.

It is no wonder that such a set of beliefs has little claim upon the lives of its adherents. In MTD, divine mystery means that God is simply an unknown, God is in the realm of opinion rather than knowledge, and there is little sense of how to sort through the various opinions about God.

Drawing upon Calvin and a trajectory of Reformed thought after him opens the possibility of a radically different outlook: yes, God is mysterious; yes, our own theology is not adequate to the great glory and majesty of God; but precisely in this mystery, God has made himself known by stooping over in accommodation to us in our weakness. Emphasizing divine transcendence, then, does not make God distant. Divine transcendence and immanence do not point in opposite directions; they are not principles to be "balanced" by a golden mean. Rather, in the matrix of accommodation, emphasizing transcendence makes God's closeness and intimacy with us possible, because it is none other than the Holy One of Israel who has accommodated himself to us in Jesus Christ.

For better or worse, the Reformed theological tradition generally did not follow Calvin in making accommodation the primary category for holding together divine incomprehensibility with the possibility of communion with God. But it did follow Calvin's general direction, supplementing it by adding other patristic and medieval categories and integrating them into a Reformed theological vision. A particularly impressive example of this is Herman Bavinck (1854–1921), who used different terms from Calvin in his theology of divine incomprehensibility but led them to quite similar ends overall. Indeed, later in the chapter I seek to show how early Reformed thinkers retrieved by Bavinck carried on elements of Calvin's doctrine of accommodation more consistently—and more faithfully, I think—than Calvin himself. This improvement upon Calvin came through the extension of the Reformed project of critically retrieving from patristic and medieval theology in the area of negative theology and communion with God. It is this "catholic" character of a Reformed theology of union and communion with God—which has a significant presence in Calvin's writings and is further extended after Calvin—that I seek to retrieve in this chapter. Why? Because it can help avoid the false modern oppositions of "immanence" to "transcendence," and of "knowledge" to "mystery" in articulating the nature of communion and union with God in Christ.

Accommodation and Knowledge of God: Communion with the Incomprehensible God in Calvin

What is the role of the language of accommodation in Calvin's thought? Certainly, if one looks at his overall corpus, Calvin uses accommodation language for a range of interrelated but also distinct purposes: to explain anthropomorphic language about God, including language of God "repenting"; to explain certain commandments of God in Old Testament laws that may appear to contrast with God's own moral law;[21] to portray God's action through material means in the sacraments; and to speak about the incarnation as an expression of God's revelatory, accommodating love.[22] What do these diverse uses have in common? While there are exceptions, Calvin perennially frames language of accommodation in terms of the relationship between God's transcendence and knowledge of himself, on the one hand, and the limited nature of human knowledge, on the other.

Although Calvin makes a brief use of the notion of accommodation in the 1536 *Institutes*, his first significant use of the notion in relation to knowledge of God occurs in the 1539 *Institutes*. The timing is significant because 1539 is the year Calvin set out his "program" both for his commentaries and for his continued work on the *Institutes*. In the years following, Calvin used the notion of accommodation extensively in his commentaries and in additions to the *Institutes*. But as Arnold Huijgen has argued,[23] this passage from 1539 on the doctrine of God had a considerable influence on how accommodation would be used in later editions:

> The Anthropomorphites, also, who imagined a corporeal God from the fact that Scripture often ascribes to him a mouth, ears, eyes, hands, and feet, are easily refuted. For who even of slight intelligence does not understand that, as nurses commonly do with infants, God is wont in a measure to "lisp" (*balbutire*) in speaking to us? Thus such forms of speaking do not so much express clearly what God is like as

21. See Jon Balserak, *Divinity Compromised: A Study of Divine Accommodation in the Thought of John Calvin* (Dordrecht: Springer, 2006), 67–70.

22. For an overview of the various uses of accommodation in Calvin, see Balserak, *Divinity Compromised*.

23. See Arnold Huijgen, "Divine Accommodation and Divine Transcendence in Calvin's Theology," in *Calvinus Sacrarum Literarum Interpres: Papers of the International Congress on Calvin Research*, ed. Herman J. Selderhuis (Göttingen: Vandenhoeck & Ruprecht, 2008), 119–30, esp. 121–26.

accommodate the knowledge of him to our slight capacity. To do this he must descend far beneath his loftiness.[24]

Lest we think that we can know God on the level of God, Calvin tells us that God speaks to us in revelation as a nurse does with infants. According to the Battles translation, God speaks with a "lisp," but others translate *balbutire* as God's "stammering," "prattling," or even "babbling." As David Wright wrote on this passage, "God's babbling to us conveys not a pristine (*ad liquidum*) picture of what he is like but only that knowledge which is adapted to our slender capacity. Divine accommodation, it seems, both reveals and conceals. Its double-edged force is nicely caught by the verb *balbutire*."[25]

A number of interrelated assumptions are at work in this key passage from Calvin. First, there is a repeated contrast between the way that God is—or God's knowledge of himself—and human apprehensions of God. One can detect a common patristic notion here that only God fully knows God on the level of God; human understanding is something different. Indeed, elsewhere when Calvin spoke about a human apprehension of the divine essence, he advised, "Let us willingly leave to God the knowledge of himself."[26]

Second, because of the asymmetry between God's knowledge of himself and human knowledge of God, all human knowledge of God is partial, incomplete, and accommodated to human weakness. This applies to the comprehension of God's essence in particular. As the Catechism of 1538 says, God's "nature is incomprehensible, and remotely hidden from human understanding"; and in that of 1542: "our understanding is not capable of comprehending his essence."[27]

A third dimension of this image of accommodation must not be missed, however. Why does a nurse speak baby talk to an infant? Why does someone "condescend" from a high and exalted place? Out of love and a desire for communion and fellowship. For Calvin, the partial and incomplete character of human knowledge of God is inextricably tied to God's loving desire for fellowship with creatures. God is not an "object" in the world, meant to be observed by humans. It is God

24. *Inst.* 1.13.1. This section from the 1539 edition is identical in the 1559 edition.
25. David F. Wright, "Calvin's Accommodating God," in *Calvinus sincerioris religionis vindex*, ed. W. H. Neusner and B. G. Armstrong (Kirksville, MO: Sixteenth Century Journal Publishers, 1997), 4–5.
26. *Inst.* 1.8.21.
27. Translation from *Inst.* 1.5.1, n. 3.

who makes himself known. All revelation is accommodation because all revelation is an act of condescending love that seeks fellowship and, to some extent, mutual knowledge of the other. God's knowledge of the creature will always surpass the creature's knowledge of God, but the fact that the creature has any knowledge of God at all is due to God's astonishing, condescending love.

This feature of God's accommodation is displayed in his account of the incarnation as an act of loving, revelatory accommodation. Note the way that Calvin, in his commentary on 1 Peter 1:21, closely ties together God's act of condescension in Christ, communion with God, and limited human capacity:

> There are two reasons why there can be no faith in God, unless Christ put himself as it were in the middle (*quasi medius interveniat*), for we must first ponder the vastness of the divine glory and at the same time the slenderness of our understanding. Far from certain is it that our keenness could climb so high as to apprehend God. Therefore all thinking about God, apart from Christ, is a bottomless abyss which utterly swallows up all our senses. . . . The other reason is that when faith ought to join us to God, we shy away from and dread all approach; unless the Mediator meets us to free us from fear. . . . Hence it is clear that we cannot trust in God (*Deo credere*) save through Christ. In Christ God so to speak makes himself little (*quodammodo parvum facit*), in order to lower himself to our capacity (*ut se ad captum nostrum submittat*); and Christ alone calms our consciences that they may dare intimately (*familiariter*) approach God.[28]

Due to our small human capacity, God "makes himself little" and lowers "to our capacity." Why would God do such a thing? So that humans may have some apprehension of and fellowship with God, enabled by God's accommodation in Christ to "intimately approach God." The vastness and greatness of God, which renders him incomprehensible to human perception, is the condition for God's condescension for the sake of mutual intimacy. Presumably, God could have made himself known in a more exalted way, but then human consciences would not dare to "intimately approach God." Ultimately, such a God would be a different God than the one made known in Jesus Christ—the God who is at once incomprehensible and yet makes close relational

---

28. Translated and quoted in F. L. Battles, "God Was Accommodating Himself to Human Capacity," in *Readings in Calvin's Theology*, ed. Donald K. McKim (Grand Rapids: Baker, 1984), 42.

communion possible. Calvin's negative theology is tightly woven together with a theology in which communion with God is the intended end of creation and redemption. Without divine incomprehensibility, God's loving condescension would not be necessary or meaningful. Not only with scripture as revelation and with the incarnation but also with the law and the sacraments, Calvin used this tightly woven language of accommodation to speak of God's condescension to human capacity for the purpose of enabling divine-human communion. The law given in God's covenant is an accommodation to human weakness in which God "humbles himself" to "enter into a common treaty" with his people.[29] This accommodation is to fulfill the law's purpose, which is "to unite us to our God."[30] On the sacraments, Calvin speaks about Christ instituting baptism and the Lord's Supper "in accommodation to our weakness, to raise us upward toward himself."[31]

Without God's loving accommodations in the law, the sacraments, scripture, and most of all, the incarnation, knowledge even of God's incomprehensibility would not be possible. With the terse, concise language of accommodation, Calvin presents incomprehensibility as a positive feature of his doctrine of God, while also presenting loving communion as the mode for God's revelatory acts.

Before concluding this section on Calvin's notion of accommodation, it is worth taking a step back to consider how Calvin's approach to this notion fits into his theological method relative to the doctrine of God.

Calvin repeatedly returns to the study of scripture and the church fathers to develop his theology of accommodation in relation to the doctrine of God.[32] Calvin's study of scripture led him to see the Bible's creaturely images for God (anthropomorphisms) and the Old Testa-

---

29. John Calvin, *John Calvin's Sermons on the Ten Commandments*, ed. and trans. Benjamin W. Farley (Grand Rapids: Baker, 1980), 45.

30. Ibid., 39.

31. John Calvin, "Last Admonition to Joachim Westphal," in *Tracts and Treatises on the Reformation of the Church*, trans. H. Beveridge (Grand Rapids: Eerdmans, 1958), 2:428.

32. While biblical and patristic sources are particularly significant for Calvin's theology of accommodation in relation to the doctrine of God, Calvin's language of accommodation also reflects his participation in the sixteenth-century humanist rediscovery of ancient rhetoric. See Olivier Millet's excellent work, *Calvin et la dynamique de la parole: Etude de rhétorique réformée* (Geneva: Editions Slatkine, 1992), esp. part 3.

ment law as examples of God's accommodation, as noted above. Calvin also developed his theology of divine mystery in his exposition of the Psalms. Herman Selderhuis points out how Calvin holds together a paradox in his Psalms commentary. On the one hand, God is high and exalted and "cannot be measured by our standards." On the other hand, God is so high and great that he can "stoop to any location." For "precisely from his exalted position God casts his eyes upon the humble and lowly." Rather than God's "inconceivable glory" making God distant from human need, it is precisely this glory that is displayed as he comes near to humans in need.[33] In the Psalms commentary, as elsewhere in Calvin's writings, "accommodation" became a way to speak simultaneously about God's transcendence and God's remarkable love and care for human beings.[34]

Calvin's engagement with the church fathers also helped him develop his theology of divine accommodation. John Chrysostom— and the sixteenth-century appropriation of his work—appears to have held unique significance for Calvin. According to Huijgen, the image of a nurse babbling to a child, which Calvin uses to depict accommodation, can be traced to Erasmus's preface to Chrysostom's "Homilies against the Anomoeans."[35] Chrysostom's sermons themselves use the language of accommodation, with a heavy emphasis on the incomprehensibility of God in response to the "anthropomorphites." (In fact, the emphasis on divine incomprehensibility in these sermons is so strong that the Catholic University of America Press translation has titled them *On the Incomprehensible Nature of God.*) In addition to Chrysostom, Augustine was also a significant source for Calvin's doctrine of accommodation, according to Battles[36]—an observation that is not surprising given Calvin's use of Augustine in many aspects of his thought. In his use of Chrysostom, Augustine, and others, Calvin exercised a concern similar to that of a variety of patristic writers in the way that he relates accommodation to the doctrine of God: God is not a creature; in fact, God is incomprehensible, utterly transcending human knowledge of God. What patristic scholars call "apophatic" thought with regard to the

33. H. J. Selderhuis, *Calvin's Theology of the Psalms* (Grand Rapids: Baker Academic, 2007), 53.

34. See ibid., 47–51.

35. Huijgen, "Divine Accommodation," 123.

36. See Battles, "God Was Accommodating Himself," in McKim, *Readings in Calvin's Theology*, 26, 28–30, 33.

negative theology of the church fathers was certainly not foreign
to Calvin.

In brief, Calvin was attempting to retrieve the essentially catholic concern for the incomprehensibility of God, as well as to avoid
projecting the creaturely onto God through literal interpretations of
anthropomorphisms. This catholic sensibility, on Calvin's part, contrasts not only with that of the anthropomorphites he writes against
but also with common views of divine mystery and communion in
modern thought. According to Calvin, it is God who is accommodating in revelation, not the human effort to ascend to God. Precisely in
this emphasis on divine initiative in revelation, Calvin preserves both
the mystery and the divine origin of revelation. Although there is a
close relation between the knowledge of God and the knowledge of
self in Calvin's theology, this should not be confused by describing his
method in terms of "correlation" (in the words of Edward Dowey).[37]
Such language obscures the more fundamental assumption behind
Calvin's language about revelation as accommodation: namely, that
God's knowledge of God is higher than, and superior to, human
knowledge of God. Given this asymmetry, God must condescend
and accommodate to human capacity in order to be known on our
lower, creaturely level.

Between Deism and Pantheism: Communion with the Incomprehensible God in Bavinck

When Herman Bavinck, professor of systematic theology at the Free
University in Amsterdam, published his four-volume *Gereformeerde
Dogmatiek* (*Reformed Dogmatics*) from 1895 to 1901, he was not
seeking to directly imitate Calvin's approach to accommodation.
Yet Bavinck inhabited a confessional Reformed tradition that shared
much with Calvin's approach to this issue. Although I will explore an
important difference between Calvin and Bavinck on this issue, I want
to begin by highlighting two areas of substantial commonality: First,
like Calvin, Bavinck gives a thorough and robust negative theology—in
a way that closely links divine incomprehensibility to the possibility
of human communion with the divine. Second, like Calvin, Bavinck

37. Edward A. Dowey Jr., *Knowledge of God in Calvin's Theology*, 3rd ed. (Grand
Rapids: Eerdmans, 1994), 18.

displays catholic instincts in this aspect of his doctrine of God, continuing and extending Calvin's earlier efforts to deepen the patristic and medieval echoes in a Reformed doctrine of God. As Bavinck does this, he frames his approach as a way to avoid two popular trends of his day: deism on the one hand and pantheism on the other.

Many theologians in Bavinck's day, as in our own, considered the negative theology of patristic and medieval thought to be subbiblical, Platonic meanderings. Nevertheless, Bavinck vigorously defended this language, presenting the incomprehensibility of God as one of the key presuppositions of his entire doctrine of God. Bavinck's volume on the doctrine of God begins with a chapter on divine incomprehensibility, opening with the stunning words that "mystery is the lifeblood of dogmatics." The mysterious nature of God does not make dogmatics impossible, but rather, as dogmatics "faces the incomprehensible one," the dogmatician is moved to "adoration and worship."[38] Why? Because the "knowledge of God-in-Christ . . . is life itself." Although "between [God] and us there seems to be no such kinship or communion as would enable us to name him truthfully," God nevertheless reveals himself in order to enable human fellowship with him.[39]

While the incomprehensibility of God is a key presupposition for properly interpreting scripture for Bavinck, it is also a teaching to which scripture testifies. For "the revelation of God in the Old Testament . . . does not exhaustively coincide with his being."[40] The Old Testament gives "true and reliable" knowledge of God by the "signs and pledges" of God's presence (e.g., "the stone at Bethel," "the cloud in the tabernacle, the ark of the covenant"), but these signs "do not encompass or confine him"—for God dwells in darkness, and "one cannot see God and live (Exod. 33:20; Lev. 16:2)."[41] In the New Testament, "God dwells in inaccessible light," for "no one has seen him or can see him (John 1:18; 6:46; 1 Tim. 6:16)," and "no one knows him except the Son and the Spirit (Matt. 11:27; 1 Cor. 2:11)."[42]

Thus, in his articulation of negative theology, Bavinck insists that "God infinitely surpasses our understanding, imagination, and

38. Herman Bavinck, *Reformed Dogmatics*, vol. 2, *God and Creation*, ed. John Bolt, trans. John Vriend (Grand Rapids: Baker Academic, 2004), 29.
39. Ibid., 30.
40. Ibid., 33.
41. Ibid.
42. Ibid., 34.

language."[43] Together with earlier Reformed theologians, he affirms that God cannot be defined in human terms and that God has no name.[44] Thus, "neither in creation nor in re-creation does God reveal himself exhaustively."[45] Does this negative emphasis threaten communion with God? No. For Bavinck, it is the condition for the possibility of communion with God. "[God] cannot fully impart himself to creatures. For that to be possible they themselves would have to be divine."[46] In other words, the partial character of human knowledge of God is necessary if God is to have communion with humans as creatures and avoid destroying their otherness by absorbing them into the divine. Thus Bavinck affirms that while God "cannot be comprehended," God "can be apprehended."[47] In this apprehension is the true object of human love and desire—a love that finds fulfillment only in the infinite God. "God is the sole object of all our love," Bavinck says, "precisely because he is the infinite and incomprehensible one."[48] God's incomprehensibility uniquely qualifies him to be an intimate lover of his people.

At points, Bavinck uses a vocabulary similar to Calvin's in speaking about the condescension of God in revelation that makes human knowledge of God possible. Particularly in his section on biblical anthropomorphisms, Bavinck makes it clear that not just some but all biblical language about God is accommodated to human capacity and is in this sense anthropomorphic. God graciously gives us names to describe him, but "not a single one of them describes God's being as such."[49] Instead, in order to facilitate human knowledge of God (which is below God's knowledge of himself), God "speaks to us of himself" in "human language," and "for the same reason he manifests himself in human forms" in scripture. "From this it follows that Scripture does not just contain a few scattered anthropomorphisms but is anthropomorphic through and through."[50] At times, Bavinck uses language similar to Calvin's to describe this process: "In order to convey the knowledge of him to his creatures, God has to come down

43. Ibid., 40–41.
44. Ibid., 40.
45. Ibid., 36.
46. Ibid., 36.
47. Ibid., 47.
48. Ibid., 48.
49. Ibid., 99.
50. Ibid.

to the level of his creatures and accommodate himself to their powers of comprehension."[51] In addition, Bavinck describes this process in terms of analogy: all human knowledge of God is "analogical" such that, although God is "unknowable in himself," he is "able to make something of himself known in the being he created."[52] By analogy, Bavinck says, humans can gain a knowledge of God, but this knowledge "is only a finite image, a faint likeness and creaturely impression of the perfect knowledge God has of himself."[53]

A key way that Bavinck pulls together the language of accommodation and analogy is through the notion of archetype and ectype: "God's self-consciousness is archetypal; our knowledge of God, drawn from his Word, is ectypal."[54] In other words, just as Calvin's language assumes two different levels of knowledge of God—God's knowledge and an inferior, derivative level of human knowledge of God—Bavinck is claiming that human knowledge of God is "inadequate, finite, and limited," and yet sufficient for the purpose of facilitating human fellowship with God. God puts "his splendid names in our mouth," even though these names do not provide an "essential, quidditative, adequate knowledge of God."[55] Using the example of the incarnation, Bavinck speaks about how "the fullness of the deity dwelt in Christ bodily." Yet God's glory was also "concealed" by the incarnation.[56] Truly, "those who saw [Christ] saw the Father," yet this "seeing" was not the way that God sees God, but an ectypal knowledge, a derivative knowledge accommodated to human capacity.

Who are Bavinck's dialogue partners in formulating his doctrine of incomprehensibility and communion with God? Like Calvin, in addition to scripture, Bavinck looks to the church fathers. But Bavinck draws upon the patristic writings more extensively and generously than Calvin on this point, and he extends his appropriation to medieval theologians as well. For example, when Bavinck outlines his position on anthropomorphisms, he draws repeatedly

51. Ibid., 110. Bavinck also positively quotes Matthias Flacius (1520–75), who used language quite similar to Calvin's language of accommodation, saying that "with a view toward our feeble minds, it pleased the Holy Spirit, the author of Scripture, to stammer in our fashion." S. Glassius, *Philologiae sacrae* (Jena: Steinmann, 1668) 116, quoted in ibid., 105.

52. Bavinck, *Reformed Dogmatics*, 2:48.

53. Ibid., 110.

54. Ibid., 107.

55. Ibid.

56. Ibid.

upon Augustine. On divine incomprehensibility, he cites Irenaeus and Basil. Calvin also drew positively upon these patristic writers, though for him Chrysostom was a central source for his notion of accommodation in particular. But in addition to these, Bavinck draws constructively upon Origen and repeatedly quotes Pseudo-Dionysius, Thomas Aquinas, and John of Damascus positively on divine incomprehensibility and anthropomorphisms. While Bavinck does not always agree with these figures, he does engage them seriously, often agreeing with their formulations. In particular, from Pseudo-Dionysius, a church father who was quite consistently viewed negatively by Calvin,[57] Bavinck draws upon the insight from Pseudo-Dionysius that God "is both 'nameless and yet has the names of everything that is.'"[58]

In addition to displaying a catholic sensibility by drawing upon patristic and medieval theologians, Bavinck also utilizes a doctrine that received considerable Reformed development after Calvin: God's covenant with Adam (or the covenant of works). In his discussion of this covenant, Bavinck claims that because God is "elevated above humanity in his sovereign exaltedness and majesty," no "fellowship" between God and human beings is possible apart from God's initiating, condescending covenantal action. He says, "For then God has to come down from his lofty position, condescend to his creatures, impart, reveal, and give himself away to human beings. . . . But this set of conditions is nothing other than the description of a covenant."[59] Rather than pantheistically "pull God into what is creaturely" or "deistically elevate him endlessly above it," we should recognize that "God is infinitely great *and* condescendingly good; he is Sovereign but also Father; he is Creator but also Prototype. In a word, he is the God of the covenant."[60] Because the doctrine of God's covenant with Adam speaks about God's relation to humanity before the fall, it makes this point about the necessity of God's condescension with particular clarity for Bavinck. "True religion . . . cannot be anything other than a covenant: it has its origin in

---

57. See Johannes Van Oort, "John Calvin and the Church Fathers," in *The Reception of the Church Fathers in the West*, ed. Irena Backus (Leiden: Brill, 1997), 2:694.

58. Bavinck, *Reformed Dogmatics*, 2:102. For example, after the section describing this position in Pseudo-Dionysius, Bavinck states his own position that "on the one hand, God is without a name; on the other hand, he possesses many names." Ibid., 104.

59. Ibid., 569.

60. Ibid., 570, emphasis added.

the condescending goodness and grace of God. It has that character before as well as after the fall."[61]

Bavinck presents a retrieval of catholic and Reformed thought as an alternative to the pantheism and deism of his own day. He does so by framing divine transcendence in a way that affirms divine mystery, but always in relationship to creatures. God accommodates and condescends to the level of human beings to make loving fellowship possible.

At this point, we are at the brink of an issue on which there appears to be some divergence between Bavinck and Calvin: does *all* human knowledge of God require God's condescending, accommodating initiative? Bavinck gives a clearly affirmative answer to this question, while at a certain point in Calvin's thought there is much more ambiguity.

A Contrast between Calvin and Bavinck: The Beatific Vision, the Incarnation, and Accommodation

It is a common assumption in the literature on accommodation in Calvin that all human knowledge of God is "accommodated" knowledge. But the question arises, is this accommodation because of human finitude or human sin, or both? At first, there would seem to be a simple answer: Calvin uses the language of accommodation to describe the way God relates to Adam and Eve in the garden, so accommodation must be a result of not just sin but also finitude. But the question is a subtle one. David Wright makes a common claim about Calvin's theology when he says that "all knowledge of God is accommodated knowledge" but then goes on to claim that "we must make do with the prattling of God until hereafter he speaks to us face to face."[62] Wright does not note the possible tension between these two statements. If accommodation is indeed a permanent feature of human knowledge of God, then it follows that we must make do with the prattling of God for eternity. But Wright contrasts this accommodated prattling with the final face-to-face vision of God, suggesting that this beatific vision is not accommodated knowledge—in which case we must qualify the claims of Wright, Dowey, Van der Kooi,

---

61. Ibid.
62. Wright, "Calvin's Accommodating God," in Neusner and Armstrong, *Calvinus sincerioris religionis vindex*, 19.

and others that all knowledge of God in Calvin's theology is accommodated.[63] Van der Kooi, for example, makes a common move
in recent scholarship when he quotes Calvin on the necessity of
accommodation in the garden and infers that accommodation is
not simply the result of sin but that some form of accommodating
mediation is "always necessary" for human knowledge of God.[64] But
what about knowledge of God in the final blessed state?

Although Calvin does not speculate about the details, he does
seem to suggest that human knowledge of God that differs qualita-
tively from the accommodated knowledge described above may be
possible. The issue comes in the way Calvin interprets 1 Corinthians
15:24—"Christ will deliver the Kingdom to his God and Father"—
both in his section in the *Institutes* on the two natures of the Mediator and in his 1 Corinthians commentary. Calvin wrote that the final
vision of God will be a "direct vision of the Godhead, . . . when as
partakers in heavenly glory we shall see God as he is."[65] Following
church fathers such as Hilary with his interpretation, Calvin thinks
that Christ will have "discharged the office of Mediator" and thus
"will cease to be the ambassador of his Father." In light of this,
even the title "Lord" is a temporary title for Christ, for "to him was
lordship committed by the Father, until such time as we should see
his divine majesty face-to-face. Then he returns the lordship to his
Father so that—far from diminishing his own majesty—it may shine
all the more brightly. Then, also, God shall cease to be the Head of
Christ, for Christ's own deity will shine of itself, although as yet it
is covered by a veil."[66] In his 1 Corinthians commentary, Calvin adds
that "when the veil has been removed, we will see God plainly, reign-
ing in his majesty, and no more will Christ's humanity be intermediate (*media*), which [now] restrains us from the vision of God lying
beyond."[67] Another translation renders these final phrases such that

63. For example, Dowey: "To conclude, this concept of *accommodation with
respect to all knowledge of God*, whether meant in principle for man as creature or as
sinner, is the horizon of Calvin's theology." *Knowledge of God*, 17, emphasis added.
64. See Cornelis van der Kooi, *As in a Mirror: John Calvin and Karl Barth on
Knowing God*, trans. Donald Mader (Leiden: Brill, 2005), 42–43.
65. *Inst.* 2.14.3.
66. *Inst.* 2.14.3.
67. Translated and quoted in Richard A. Muller, "Christ in the Eschaton: Calvin
and Moltmann on the Duration of the *Munus Regium*," *Harvard Theological Review*
74, no. 1 (1981): 47.

"Christ's humanity will no longer stand in the middle, keeping us from the final view of God."[68]

Perhaps not surprisingly, the history of interpretation of these passages is a checkered one. Jürgen Moltmann, in *The Crucified God*, uses this passage to argue that the incarnation becomes "superfluous" for Calvin at the eschaton.[69] A. A. van Ruler uses this passage as justification to speak about the end of Christ's work of incarnate mediation, which was contingent upon the presence of sin in the world and would be "laid aside" at the eschaton.[70] Heinrich Quistorp, in his work on Calvin's eschatology, uses the passage to speak about how Christ's humanity "recedes into the background" following the final judgment.[71]

These passages from Calvin raise a number of issues. One issue is whether Christ's reign over us is temporary or lasts forever. Richard Muller and Robert Doyle, in separate ways, seek to demonstrate from other passages in Calvin that Christ's rule is eternal.[72] In their view, a careful reading of Calvin, against Moltmann and Van Ruler, does not see the reign of Christ as limited in scope.

In addition, Muller argues that when Calvin speaks of the "veil" to be removed in order to see God plainly, it is not Christ's humanity but our own human infirmity that keeps us from a final view of God. Thus, Christ's humanity is no longer "in the middle" because the elect are so deeply united to Christ that they enjoy the final vision of God from a place of complete union with Christ's humanity. Nevertheless, according to Muller, Christ's humanity no longer being "in the middle" does have implications for revelation. Ontologically, Christ's humanity still mediates communion with God, but epistemologically, "Christ's humanity no longer acts as an intermediate bearer of revelation between us and the vision of God."[73] Yet it does

68. Translated and quoted in Robert C. Doyle, *Eschatology and the Shape of Christian Belief* (Carlisle: Paternoster, 1999), 14.

69. Jurgen Moltmann, *The Crucified God: The Cross of Christ as the Foundation and Criticism of Christian Theology* (New York: Harper & Row, 1974), 257–59.

70. A. A. van Ruler, *Gestaltwerdung Christi in der Welt* (Neukirchen: Buchhandlung des Erziehungsvereins, 1956), 35, quoted in ibid., 260.

71. Heinrich Quistorp, *Calvin's Doctrine of the Last Things*, trans. Harold Knight (Richmond: John Knox, 1955), 167–71.

72. See Muller, "Christ in the Eschaton," 31–59; Robert C. Doyle, "The Context of Moral Decision Making in the Writings of John Calvin" (PhD diss., University of Aberdeen, 1981), 317–22.

73. Muller, "Christ in the Eschaton," 48.

have a "mediate" role as bearer of revelation in that the humanity of believers becomes directly situated before God, enabling a direct vision of God because of its union with Christ's humanity.

Remarkably, despite recent interest in Calvin's notion of accommodation, the implications of this point in Calvin's theology for accommodation have been largely missed. One of the few references occurs in Balserak's book on accommodation in Calvin, which claims, significantly, that knowledge of God in the beatific vision is an "unaccommodated revelation to his people in glory."[74] (Balserak does not explore the implications of this unaccommodated human knowledge of God for Calvin's overall doctrine of accommodation.) Muller's interpretation is more cautious. In his view, Christ's humanity does not recede or become useless in the final vision of God. Yet his is not exactly an "accommodation" in the sense that "all knowledge of God" is frequently considered accommodated in Calvin. There is, at the very least, tension here with other parts of Calvin's thought. What happened to Calvin's claims, examined earlier, that Christ must be in the "middle" in order for humans to "apprehend God," and that "all thinking about God, apart from Christ, is a bottomless abyss which utterly swallows up all our senses?"[75] Moreover, in commenting on John 1:18, Calvin writes that "God is openly beheld in the face of Christ."[76] Yet his interpretation of the final vision of God suggests that the incarnate Christ's "standing in the middle" is only a temporary phenomenon. Absent from Calvin's account of this final vision of God is the normal vocabulary of accommodation, of God's condescension in Christ to limited human capacity in order to make knowledge of God possible.

Calvin's interpretation of 1 Corinthians 15:24 need not threaten his commitment to maintaining the Creator-creature distinction in the eschaton. If one cross-references this passage with Calvin's interpretation of 2 Peter 1:4 (with its reference to "participation in the divine nature"), he says that "we shall be partakers of divine and blessed immortality and glory, so as to be as it were one with God as far as our capacities will allow."[77] Clearly, Calvin rejects assimilation of the creature into the Creator. In addition, in this commentary passage

74. Balserak, *Divinity Compromised*, 66.

75. Comm. on 1 Pet. 1:21; translated and quoted in Battles, "God Was Accommodating Himself," in McKim, *Readings in Calvin's Theology*, 42.

76. Comm. on John 1:18, CTS.

77. Comm. on 2 Pet. 1:4, CTS.

on the final knowledge of God, its finite character is demonstrated by the limitation in human capacity.

Yet in these brief and provocative passages, Calvin leaves an important aspect of his doctrine of divine mystery ambiguous: the sense in which this final "direct vision" of God is still accommodated, whether it is still the "prattling" of God that humans receive at the beatific vision—and ultimately whether all human knowledge of God requires the divine condescension in the incarnation of Jesus Christ.

While I do not consider this point of ambiguity in Calvin's theology to be a virtue in his thought, the fact that it has so often been missed by his interpreters points to a feature of his thought relevant for this discussion: namely, far from thinking of God and humanity as polar opposites, Calvin seems to think that the union with God that occurs in redemption could be so proper to redeemed humans that not even the mediation (or "middle-ness") of the incarnation is necessary as an accommodating revelation in order for the eyes of humans to gaze upon God.

Yet when later Reformed thinkers "speculate" in areas in which Calvin does not, the result can be a greater preservation of divine mystery and a more consistent christocentrism. For example, consider John Owen, who makes significant use of the archetypal/ectypal theology distinction[78] and offers quite developed reflections about the beatific vision. His work can help us pinpoint the problem with Calvin's texts here. For Owen, the blessed always behold God's glory through the face of Jesus Christ. Drawing on 2 Corinthians 3:18 and 4:6, Owen, and a strand of the Reformed tradition after him, gives a Christ-centered account of the beatific vision in which Jesus Christ is—precisely—in the middle. Even in the eschaton, we apprehend the Triune God through the face of Christ. This approach retains the christocentrism typical of other parts of Reformed theology, in addition to giving a higher view of bodies and creation, thus avoiding the implication that the incarnation was a crassly pragmatic means to facilitate a vision of God uncluttered by Christ's humanity. Moreover, if one follows the principle of Owen that "no man ought to look for anything in heaven but what one way or other he hath some experience of in this life,"

---

78. See Sebastian Rehnman, *Divine Discourse: The Theological Methodology of John Owen* (Grand Rapids: Baker Academic, 2002), 57–71.

then continuing to gaze on the incarnate Christ at the eschaton is absolutely vital.[79] As suggested in the final section on Bavinck above ("Between Deism and Pantheism"), Bavinck's theology avoids Calvin's ambiguity on this point about accommodation. Bavinck's doctrine of the covenant with Adam makes it clear that all knowledge of God is enabled by God's covenantal condescension. On the final vision of God, Bavinck likewise says that "every vision of God, then, always requires an act of divine condescension, . . . a revelation by which God on his part comes down to us and makes himself knowable."[80] Moreover, for Bavinck, the Son is the mediator of all human knowledge of God—even at the eschaton. For "the Son is not only the mediator of reconciliation (*mediator reconciliationis*) on account of sin, but even apart from sin he is the mediator of union (*mediator unionis*) between God and his creation."[81] Jesus Christ will always be the mediator, enabling knowledge that is accommodated and derivative (ectypal), yet true human knowledge of God.

Bavinck's use of the traditional distinction between archetypal and ectypal theology solidifies and clarifies the claim that all human knowledge of God is derivative and accommodated. Reformers such as Luther and Calvin did not explicitly use this medieval distinction. But the distinction became widespread in Reformed and Lutheran dogmatic theology in the seventeenth and eighteenth centuries,[82] and it was used by Puritan thinkers such as Owen. While the distinction was rarely used in the nineteenth and early twentieth centuries, Bavinck

79. John Owen, "Meditations and Discourses on the Glory of Christ," in William H. Gould, ed., *The Works of John Owen* (London: Johnstone and Hunter, 1850), 1:288. For an excellent account of Owen on the beatific vision, see Suzanne McDonald, "Beholding the Glory of God in the Face of Jesus Christ: John Owen and the 'Reforming' of the Beatific Vision," in Mark Jones and Kelly Kapic, eds., *The Ashgate Research Companion to John Owen* (Aldershot, UK: Ashgate, forthcoming). In this section, I am indebted to the insights of Dr. McDonald in correspondence, though the views are my own.

80. Bavinck, *Reformed Dogmatics*, 2:190.

81. Herman Bavinck, *Reformed Dogmatics*, vol. 4, *Holy Spirit, Church, and New Creation*, ed. John Bolt, trans. John Vriend (Grand Rapids: Baker Academic, 2008), 685.

82. See Willem J. van Asselt, "The Fundamental Meaning of Theology: Archetypal and Ectypal Theology in Seventeenth-Century Reformed Thought," *Westminster Theological Journal* 64 (2003): 322–24. While Reformed and Lutheran theologians followed Junius's account (discussed below) on most points, Van Asselt (331–32) points out a difference in the "theology of union" among Lutheran theologians, based on a different account of the communication of idioms.

retrieved it from the earlier Reformed thinkers, helping to revive its place in Reformed theology.[83] This distinction, retrieved by Bavinck as a way to preserve divine mystery and emphasize the *relational* character of our knowledge of God, deserves further elaboration.

A Distinction to Preserve Divine Mystery: Archetypal and Ectypal Theology

While there are medieval antecedents,[84] the clear distinction between archetypal and ectypal theology used in Reformed orthodoxy was derived from Franciscus Junius (1545–1602).[85] Junius's account of God's "accommodated" knowledge to humanity is remarkably christocentric. While it may seem inherently speculative to make this sort of (scholastic) distinction, Junius does so in a way that allows Reformed teaching to be even more consistent than Calvin with Calvin's own notion that "all thinking about God, apart from Christ, is a bottomless abyss." Indeed, rather than representing a move toward later Enlightenment rationalism, it was arguably a way to preserve divine mystery that was later abandoned by thinkers who moved theology in a more rationalistic direction.[86]

In Junius's account, because God is fundamentally distinct from creation and God is the one who fully knows God, there are two types of knowledge of God: archetypal knowledge, which is God's perfect knowledge of himself, and ectypal knowledge, which is knowledge that is derived from archetypal knowledge but that is accommodated to creaturely understanding. Ectypal theology is knowledge of God communicated by God to creatures "through the communication of Grace for his own glory."[87] Thus, with various patristic voices, Junius

83. See R. Scott Clark, *Recovering the Reformed Confession* (Phillipsburg, NJ: P&R, 2008), 147–48.

84. A likely antecedent is the Scotist distinction between *theologia in se* (God's self-knowledge) and *theologia nostra* (our [finite] knowledge of God). See Richard Muller, *Post-Reformation Reformed Dogmatics*, vol. 1, *Prolegomena to Theology*, 2nd ed. (Grand Rapids: Baker Academic, 2003), 227–28.

85. Franciscus Junius was a third-generation Reformed theologian who studied theology in Geneva in Calvin's final years (1562–65).

86. See the argument of Van Asselt, "Fundamental Meaning of Theology," 319–35, esp. 333–35. On the more recent history of the use of the distinction, see Clark, *Recovering the Reformed Confession*, 145–50.

87. Franciscus Junius, *De vera theologia*, trans. Muller, *Post-Reformation Reformed Dogmatics*, 1:235.

holds together the ideas that God is the one who knows God and that God is fundamentally distinct from creation.

Moreover, for Junius, any and all true knowledge of God is received in Christ. Junius describes how this is the case in terms of three forms of human (ectypal) knowledge of God: knowledge of union that Christ alone has in the hypostatic union; knowledge of "vision," which is the beatific vision; and finally, knowledge of God through revelation in this life, while we see through a glass darkly. This third form of knowledge is our current "pilgrim" theology, which awaits eschatological fulfillment in a theology of vision. In the words of Junius,

> The first theology [of union in Christ] is the highest and most perfect (*plenissima*) form of ectypal theology on which we all draw: John 1:16. It is in Christ according to his human nature. The second [theology of vision] is perfect (*plena*) through which the blessed spirits obtain a glorious vision of God in heaven and through which we shall see him as he is (1 John 3:2). Finally, the theology of revelation is not perfect in itself (*non plena re ipsa*), but more (*potius*) through the revelation of faith. It is informed by the principles of the same truth in such a way that, in respect of ourselves, it can appropriately be called perfect: although it is imperfect when compared with the theology of vision for which we hope, as the apostle teaches the Corinthians, 1 Corinthians 13:12. This, indeed, is our theology.[88]

Note that "the theology of revelation is not perfect in itself," but in relation to our limited human capacity, "it can appropriately be called perfect." It is an anticipation of the knowledge of God at the final eschatological vision of God. But for Junius even the beatific vision is, without doubt, mediated by Jesus Christ. Indeed, it is mediated in two ways. First, it is mediated because both "pilgrim" theology and "vision" theology are derived from Christ's knowledge of God, for his knowledge of God is the "prototypical and essential wisdom of God."[89] Our "pilgrimage" in Christ is not toward a beatific vision where we see God "face-to-face" apart from Christ or with Christ no longer "in the middle." No. The entire pilgrimage, and its destination in a theology of "vision," is all part of the believer's union with and participation in Christ.

88. Junius, *De vera theologia*, trans. Van Asselt, "Fundamental Meaning of Theology," 330.

89. Junius, *De vera theologia*, trans. Muller, *Post-Reformation Reformed Dogmatics*, 1:258.

Moreover, while Junius insists on a distinction between God's knowledge of himself (archetypal) and human knowledge of God (ectypal), the ectypal knowledge of God in Jesus's humanity has God's archetypal knowledge as its source. As the Second Person of the Trinity, the Son knows God in an archetypal way—as God knows himself. But those who are in Christ participate in the perfect human knowledge of God in Christ, which is ectypal.[90] In other words, while even in Christ we do not know God exhaustively, as God knows himself, the knowledge of God through Christ truly discloses who God is—in a relational, grace-filled way that is appropriate to creatures.

In Junius's words, "the archetypal theology is the womb or origin (*matrix*) of all others: this ectypal theology in Christ, the mother (*mater*) of all the rest: that the source of all (*fons omnium*), this as it were the common shelter (*castellum*) or means of conception (*conceptaculum*)."[91] Both pilgrim and vision theology occur only in Christ, for "both forms of theology, therefore, Christ has sanctified in his Person: when he used the humble theology in the humility of the flesh, and the exalted theology in his exaltation through which he now is exalted above every name, in such a way that the principle of both forms of theology appears to be in him."[92]

To summarize: Junius's exposition of the distinction between ectypal and archetypal theology provides a way to uphold the mystery of God while seeing not only how all true knowledge of God derives from God's loving and grace-filled self-communication but also very specifically how it derives from that self-communication in Christ. In the words of Junius, "our theology is most of all a communicated theology through which we all draw on the revelation which God chose to give us in Jesus Christ."[93]

Framing the mystery of God in this way does have the consequence that our present pilgrim knowledge of God is "mixed with weakness

90. Thus, in the mystery of the incarnation, God's perfect knowledge of God and a perfect human knowledge of God are united in one concrete Person, but united in a Chalcedonian way that maintains a distinction ("without confusion, without change") while not positing a separation ("without division, without separation"). Christ's perfect human knowledge of God is still accommodated and ectypal—so it is "perfect" in relation to the limitations of human capacity.

91. Junius, *De vera theologia*, trans. Muller, *Post-Reformation Reformed Dogmatics*, 1:258.

92. Junius, *De vera theologia*, trans. Van Asselt, "Fundamental Meaning of Theology," 331.

93. Ibid., 330.

and imperfection" in comparison with Christ's knowledge of God, or even our knowledge of God when we will see face-to-face rather than through a glass dimly (1 Cor. 13:12). Yet our pilgrim theology can bring true knowledge of God (even "perfect," in Junius's terminology) in its communicated form through God's accommodation to our weakness and finitude. Divine mystery should not lead us to despair of knowing anything about God (as is common in MTD), nor should it lead us to anticipate an eschatological point in which we shift our gaze away from Jesus Christ. Rather, as we continue on the great pilgrimage of growing in Christ by the Spirit's power, we come to know God through knowing God in Christ, both now and in the final blessed vision of God.

In relation to our earlier discussion of Calvin on accommodation and the beatific vision, Calvin is often admired by modern theologians for his antispeculative sensibility; but this is a point on which his sensibility may show its profound limitation. Particularly in distinguishing categorically between archetypal and ectypal knowledge of God in the course of theological prolegomena, the Reformed scholastics had to extend their catholic instincts beyond those of Calvin. As Richard Muller notes concerning this distinction and systematic reflection on the beatific vision for the post-Reformation Reformed tradition, "the orthodox derived it from their reading of the medieval scholastic systems" rather than appropriating it from the Reformers.[94] While Calvin has a profound account of the centrality of Christ in knowing God and God's mystery in relation to human knowledge of God, his efforts to maintain catholicity in his doctrine of the knowledge of God may threaten to unwind at this point because he was unwilling to "speculate," which kept him from drawing with enough depth upon parts of his catholic heritage.

Encountering a Mystery in Calvin and Bavinck: Uniting Negative Theology to Union and Communion with God

While certain tensions in Calvin's doctrines of accommodation and the incarnation are further developed in later Reformed teaching, as displayed by Junius and Bavinck, the fact remains that Calvin shares with Bavinck—and the Reformed scholasticism that Bavinck retrieves—a

---

94. Muller, *Post-Reformation Reformed Dogmatics*, 1:260; cf. 1:227–29.

more deeply catholic doctrine of knowledge of God than one finds in the trends of much modern theology. Specifically, Calvin and Bavinck are insightful in the ways they hold together negative theology with the possibility of uniting communion with God. In the hands of Calvin and Bavinck, the emphasis on divine transcendence does not make God distant or in any way sacrifice divine immanence. Rather, divine transcendence and immanence go hand in hand as one inseparable thought. That the incomprehensible God stoops over to accommodate in revelation is an act of astonishing love, fellowship, and intimacy.

As we consider what it might mean to retrieve this theme from Calvin and Bavinck for the church's teaching today, it may be helpful to consider briefly how it contrasts with two modern alternatives, one associated with the ecclesial left and the other associated with the ecclesial right.

For the ecclesial left, Calvin's approach in accommodation contrasts with the notion of God as "absolute mystery" found in modern theologians such as Gordon Kaufman and Sallie McFague. According to Kaufman, God is absolute mystery, which means that God cannot be known on the level of God. On this point, Calvin and Bavinck would heartily concur.[95] But according to Kaufman, God does not make himself known in revelation; rather, all religious images are human projections upon God. Given that status, one should have a human standard for evaluating these images—what Kaufman calls "humanization." As Christians, Kaufman says, our conceptions of God should not be guided by "biblical or traditional images" of God but by a universally accessible ethic of humanization. "The only God we should worship today—the only God we can afford to worship—is the God who will further our humanization, the God who will help to make possible the creation of a universal and humane community."[96]

In a similar way, for McFague God is not self-disclosed by an act of divine revelation.[97] It is in the face of this absence of God's self-

95. Indeed, Bavinck is emphatic on the matter, asserting that for humans "there is no knowledge of God as he is in himself." For God "infinitely transcends our picture of him, our ideas of him, our language of him." *Reformed Dogmatics*, 2:47.

96. Gordon Kaufman, *God, Mystery, Diversity: Christian Theology in a Pluralistic World* (Minneapolis: Fortress, 1996), 29.

97. This brief account draws upon Sallie McFague, *Metaphorical Theology: Models of God in Religious Language* (Philadelphia: Fortress, 1982) and *Models of God: Theology for an Ecological, Nuclear Age* (Philadelphia: Fortress, 1987). For a brief but illuminating overview of McFague's theological project and its connections with Kaufman's theological method, see Sarah Coakley's account in *Modern Christian*

disclosure that we can recognize that "all talk of God" is "indirect"; thus we can develop life-giving metaphors for God.[98] This follows an instinct similar to Kaufman's where the primary goal of God-talk is human flourishing. Religious symbol-systems are inevitable. Therefore, rather than probing what is "given" in divine revelation, one can be liberated by the radical mystery of God to reconstruct religious language about God. The key questions for developing metaphors for God include: Is this language helpful, fruitful, and life-giving to religious believers? Does this language open up relationships of mutuality and responsibility rather than hierarchy and abuse?

In the approaches of Kaufman and McFague, mystery is ultimately set against knowledgeable communion, and the language of analogy and accommodation is conceived of anthropologically rather than theologically. Both are willing to speak about communion with God and divine mystery. But divine mystery is used as grounds for saying that divine self-disclosure is impossible, and we are left in the lonely, isolated world of a liberal Protestantism in which we compete with each other for appealing images of the divine without God's input on the matter. Rather than being brought into a knowledgeable fellowship with a mysterious God, God remains unknown—thus communion with God becomes vacuous and thin. They cannot follow Bavinck's notion that while God "cannot be comprehended," he "can be apprehended"[99]—that God discloses a relational knowledge of himself in revelation. Both Kaufman and McFague are willing to speak about analogies for God but not God-given analogies, divine accommodations that reflect God's extraordinary love. Rather, analogies are human creations, reducible to their function in the human symbol-system of religious discourse. For Calvin and Bavinck, scripture speaks analogically by means of divine accommodation precisely because God both makes himself known to humanity and yet remains veiled in mystery. For both Calvin and Bavinck, mystery and communion are held together, grounded in God's initiative and loving condescension to humanity.

Calvin's and Bavinck's approaches also differ, though in a more subtle way, from operative assumptions in the approaches of evangelicals who speak about "contextualization." The notion of contextualization

Thought, vol. 2, *The Twentieth Century* (Upper Saddle River, NJ: Prentice Hall, 2000), 428–33.

98. McFague, *Models of God*, 34; cf. Coakley, *Modern Christian Thought*, 2:430.
99. Bavinck, *Reformed Dogmatics*, 2:47.

is one that rightly recognizes there is no culture-free version of the Christian faith. All biblical interpretation and all theology emerge from a particular historical-cultural context. What is commonly inferred from this observation, however, is that theological method should be a matter of synthesizing two different spheres: biblical revelation, or "the gospel," should be combined with "culture." Thus, the "gospel" is made "relevant" to the intended audience, whether that audience is the emerging generation of Western youth or a non-Western Christian who needs to encounter Christianity in something other than Western guise. Trends in evangelical publishing reflect this tendency: bright pink Bibles for preteen girls, with notes about beauty and relationships, and macho-looking Bibles for boys, with notes on sports, achievement, and health. The Bible is assumed to be something other than relevant until it speaks to the felt needs of the audience—needs that the audience has because of their sociocultural identity, rather than their identity in Christ per se.

These trends reflect a theology of accommodation that focuses heavily on making the gospel "relevant" to today's culture. But they often miss the point that accommodation is not so much a human act as a divine act. The gospel is understood and lived differently in various cultures. But this is not simply through a human act of "synthesizing the gospel with culture." Rather, as I have argued in some detail in *The Word of God for the People of God*, it is due to the Spirit's work of "indigenization," that is, the Spirit making God's word understandable in various cultural contexts.[100] First and foremost, according to Calvin and Bavinck, the agent of accommodation is the Spirit, not us. Certainly, the Spirit works through instruments—so Calvin will speak, for example, about accommodations in the writings of Moses and Paul—but that is in the context of the unidirectional focus of accommodation generally: from God to creatures. If this insight were to be absorbed within the circles of contemporary evangelicalism, it would be recognized that contextualization is not something that, strictly speaking, *we* should do. Rather than analyze the needs of teenage boys and make their needs the central focus of a study Bible, an attempt should be made to be humbly responsive to God's own condescension in scripture, an accommodation for which Jesus Christ (rather than our own needs) forms the substance and starting

---

100. See J. Todd Billings, *The Word of God for the People of God: An Entryway to the Theological Interpretation of Scripture* (Grand Rapids: Eerdmans, 2010), 105–48.

point. How do the analogies given by God in scripture disrupt and call into question our own cultural portrait of God? How should the fact that God has accommodated himself to us in Jesus Christ reorient our self-perceived needs and desires? These are the sorts of questions that should preoccupy those proclaiming the gospel today. For if we are to have genuine communion with God, we must meet God in the way that God accommodates himself to us in scripture and most fully in Jesus Christ rather than seeking to climb the ladder of self-devised analogies toward the mysterious God. A key insight of Calvin's and Bavinck's notion of accommodation is that it is God who fully knows God—and precisely because of this, God's accommodation must be valued, even though it does not give a face-to-face knowledge of the divine.

Closing Thoughts

I recall a moment in my office when a student declared to me, "I don't like the negative attributes of God"—those that state that God is incomprehensible and not limited in the way creatures are. "The negative attributes just make God seem distant. I just like the positive attributes of God." After our meeting, I was reading Psalm 139, a psalm about intimacy with God. "You have searched me, LORD, and you know me. . . . Before a word is on my tongue you, LORD, know it completely. . . . Such knowledge is too wonderful for me, too lofty for me to attain. Where can I go from your Spirit? Where can I flee from your presence? If I go up to the heavens, you are there; if I make my bed in the depths, you are there" (vv. 1, 4, 6–8 NIV). It struck me that it is precisely the fact that God is *not* like us and that his knowledge is "too lofty" for us "to attain" that makes intimacy with God possible in psalms like this one. Stated in doctrinal terms, God is not limited by time or by space. God's knowledge is inherently higher than our own; it is unattainable by us. Yet as Calvin and Bavinck show us, precisely because of this—together with God's condescending love made known in Christ—worshipful communion with God is possible. As the psalmist says, "How precious to me are your thoughts, God! How vast is the sum of them! Were I to count them, they would outnumber the grains of the sand" (139:17–18 NIV). Intimate communion with God is possible, but it is communion with a God who is inherently other and inherently mysterious to human beings. And while Christians can look forward to "face-to-face" fellowship with God, that knowledgeable fellowship will be just as dependent upon God's condescending love made known in Christ as fellowship with God is now. So let the adopted children of God adore his mystery by focusing their hearts and minds on Jesus Christ, who will always be "in the middle." Precisely in this focus on Jesus Christ, Christians are brought by the Spirit into a mysterious fellowship with the holy and transcendent God who loves his people extravagantly in Christ.

4

The Gospel and Justice

Union with Christ, the Law of Love,
and the Lord's Supper

Justice and the Gospel in North American Congregations

What would it mean for North American congregations to act with justice and to witness to justice as the church in a sinful world? The relationship between the gospel and justice is a profoundly important issue for churches around the world. Yet in North America, the issue has particular contextual challenges as it is often posed in the political realm. While in certain ways the disestablishment of the church is a firm principle in the United States, in other ways, religion plays a very significant role in civic life. Americans witnessed this in the 2008 presidential campaign when Jim Wallis and the "religious left" helped to mobilize a movement in support of Barack Obama's campaign—quoting scripture with just as much frequency as the groups known as the "religious right," who helped get George W. Bush elected four years earlier.

This political example points to the complexities of what it would mean for North American Christians to live into their calling to be people who practice justice. Christians on both sides of the presidential election debate were speaking of "justice." At times, both could be found claiming to speak for the oppressed, the wronged, the marginalized. On one side: who is more marginalized than the poor, those in need of health care? On the other side: who is more marginalized than the unborn baby, those without a voice or any rights under the law? Both sides can speak of justice for the wronged and vulnerable, and of the need for the church to witness to God's just desire for creation. But underlying what looks like agreement, much more fundamental differences are at play. In the words of Alasdair MacIntyre, the real questions are, "whose justice" and "which rationality"?[1]

Even more significant, however, is the relationship between justice and the gospel in the preaching and teaching of American churches. Sociological studies show ironies along this line. Mainline or liberal Christians, who traditionally pride themselves on their concern for social justice, tend to display less commitment to the poor, for example, than self-identified evangelical Christians.[2] The members of denominations claiming to be the "friends of the poor" tend to give less to the poor than members of other churches animated by more "traditional" theological concerns.[3] To put the situation starkly, the churches that talk the most about social and economic justice—those that fit the typical mainline mold—are often less effective than their evangelical counterparts at cultivating concrete commitment to justice issues like poverty in the lives of their members.

In terms of mainline congregations, with dramatically declining membership, an acute question is, *why* should one participate in a worshiping community? Will Willimon puts it this way: "mainline Protestantism is in trouble because we provided people with the theological rationale not to go to church."[4] If the gospel message is that we

1. Alasdair MacIntyre, *Whose Justice? Which Rationality?* (South Bend, IN: University of Notre Dame Press, 1989).

2. Sociologists frequently note that evangelicals give more charitably than their mainline Protestant counterparts, but it is significant to note in particular that evangelicals give more to the "poor and needy" than do their mainline counterparts. See Christian Smith, *American Evangelicals: Embattled and Thriving* (Chicago: University of Chicago Press, 1998), 39, 41. For a recent summary of sociological studies that make similar claims related to evangelical approaches to poverty, see Corwin E. Smidt, Lyman A. Kellstedt, and James L. Guth, eds., *The Oxford Handbook of Religion and American Politics* (Oxford: Oxford University Press, 2009), 197–99.

3. For a study concluding that theological "conservatives" are "more generous" in their charitable giving to the poor than are their liberal counterparts, see Mark D. Regnerus, Christian Smith, and David Sikkink, "Who Gives to the Poor? The Influence of Religious Tradition and Political Location on the Personal Generosity of Americans toward the Poor," *Journal for the Scientific Study of Religion* 37, no. 3 (September 1998): 481–93.

4. Will Willimon, "It's about God," *A Peculiar Prophet* (blog), October 29, 2007, http://willimon.blogspot.com/2007/10/its-about-god.html.

should try hard to be just and kind because that is what God wants us to do, then there is no obvious need for gathering as a community, worshiping Jesus Christ, or seeking empowerment from God's Spirit. If the gospel is nothing more than an exhortation for justice, then one's time is better spent at a Greenpeace meeting or a political lobby meeting than in corporate worship on Sunday morning.

On the other hand, in evangelical churches the relationship between the gospel and justice is often an enigma. The call to justice is frequently seen as an add-on to the gospel, a form of spiritual extra credit for evangelicals. Positively, in recent decades there has been significant renewal among evangelicals that has mobilized them for a wide range of justice ministries, such as work with AIDS victims, sex workers, and the homeless. Yet the theological rationale for such work is often muddy. In particular, there is a lack of clarity on the question of how justice work relates to the free gift of the gospel of Jesus Christ. As *Christianity Today* senior managing editor Mark Galli has noted, among evangelicals it is "rare" that appeals for social action are grounded "in the gospel of grace, in the Cross and Resurrection, in the miraculous gift of forgiveness, and in the immense gratitude that naturally flows from that gift."[5] Instead, according to Galli, evangelicals tend to use moralism, guilt, and shame as motivation for social justice.[6]

In light of these contextual observations, I sense that the challenge for Christians in a North American context is to see how justice fits into a God-focused, Christ-centered gospel, a gospel that is not about our own heroic action but instead is about how we find our place in the drama of salvation, the story of the Triune God made known in Jesus Christ. If justice is integral to the gospel, we need to see *how* it is integral and how it relates to the worship and communal life of the church.

The Eucharistic Gospel and Justice in South Africa: Critically Retrieving the Belhar Confession

In an earlier book, I argued that "scriptural interpretation from diverse contexts can be received as mutual enrichment, gifts of the Spirit

---

5. Mark Galli, "In the Beginning, Grace," *Christianity Today*, October 2009, 26.
6. Ibid., 27.

for the whole church."[7] Seeking a contextually responsive theology should not make us hesitant to look at other contexts but should fuel our interest in and engagement with the scriptural interpretation arising from other contexts. Thus, in assessing how justice relates to the gospel and Christian worship, it may be helpful to look at a different context, one in which justice, the gospel, and the Lord's Supper in particular became tightly bound together, both for good and for ill: the Reformed church in South Africa.

South African Reformed history is instructive both for its failures and for its insight in responding to this history through the Belhar Confession. This confession, accepted in 1986 by the Dutch Reformed Mission Church, spoke to the issues of the church's unity, of reconciliation, and of justice, in direct opposition to both apartheid and the separation of Reformed churches on the basis of race. Lest we think that this cultural particularity makes the Belhar less relevant to the North American context, we should consider the ways the American church has historically legitimated ecclesial separation based on race and class. As Martin Luther King Jr. noted in 1962, "It is still true that the church is the most segregated major institution in America. As a minister of the gospel, I am ashamed to have to affirm that eleven o'clock on Sunday morning, when we sing 'In Christ There Is No East Nor West,' is the most segregated hour in America."[8] Sadly, Sunday mornings in North America today are still frequently segregated; Americans are not in a position to claim that they have nothing to learn from the struggles of South Africa.

In interpreting the South African failure and the Belhar's response, I will use the notion of a "eucharistic gospel"—referring not to a different kind of gospel but rather to the special way in which the Eucharist illuminates the gospel. This eucharistic gospel functions as a hermeneutical locus because issues surrounding the Eucharist and the gospel were central to the story of the segregation, apartheid, and other injustices faced by drafters of the Belhar.

A watershed point in this history occurred in 1857 when the General Assembly of the Dutch Reformed Church (DRC) received from some white members a request for permission to celebrate the Lord's Supper

---

7. J. Todd Billings, *The Word of God for the People of God: An Entryway to the Theological Interpretation of Scripture* (Grand Rapids: Eerdmans, 2010), 108.

8. Martin Luther King Jr., "An Address before the National Press Club," in *A Testament of Hope: The Essential Speeches and Writings of Martin Luther King, Jr.*, ed. James M. Washington (San Francisco: HarperCollins, 1990), 101.

separately from black members of the church. This request was clearly against the Reformed polity of the DRC, which emerged from the Synod of Dort. (Indeed, an earlier request for separate communion had been rejected by the Dutch Reformed Church, for the Lord's Supper was to be administered "without distinction of colour.")[9] Moreover, the 1857 Synod found no biblical grounds for the separation of communion based on race. However, the assembly, wanting to avoid being conservative, doctrinaire, and rigid, gave a pastoral accommodation that "due to the weakness of some," communion and worship could be organized for separate celebrations based on race.[10] (The "weaker" ones referred to were the white members who made the request for separate communion.) Yet this pastoral accommodation "gradually became common practice and still later the norm for the order and structure of the church."[11] Eventually, the trajectory of this 1857 decision led to two different results: First, it led to the establishment of a separate racially based denomination (yet still under the ownership of the DRC) for colored or mixed-race members (1881, Dutch Reformed Mission Church) and later for black members (1951, Dutch Reformed Church in Africa). Second, what began as a "pastoral accommodation" for violating eucharistic polity was eventually developed into an elaborate theology that sought to ground the separation of the races in creation. With its separatist theology of creation, the DRC became an avid advocate of apartheid as a government policy beginning in 1924, claiming that "competition between black and white on economic levels . . . leads to poverty, friction, misunderstanding, suspicion and bitterness."[12] The DRC, and the new ideology emerging from its broken theology of the Lord's Supper and justice, became a major source for the political ideology that led to the system of apartheid.[13]

Decades later, the story of the Eucharist continued to intertwine with this history. At the 1982 meeting of the World Alliance of

9. See Dirk J. Smit, "South Africa," in *Essays in Public Theology: Collected Essays 1* (Stellenbosch, South Africa: SUN Press, 1997), 17.

10. Ibid., 17, 33.

11. Ibid., 33.

12. "Ecumenical Address from the Rev. Dr. Pitikoe," in Reformed Church in America, *Acts and Proceedings of the 196th Regular Session of the General Synod* (New York: Reformed Church Press, 1982), 169.

13. For a fuller genealogy of apartheid theology, see Smit, "South Africa," in *Essays in Public Theology*, 11–27.

Reformed Churches (WARC), "eight representatives of the so-called 'daughter churches' in the DRC-family refused to participate in the official Eucharist, claiming it would be false to do so in an ecumenical context, while they were excluded from the Eucharist in the DRC in South Africa."[14] At this meeting, WARC condemned apartheid and its theological justification as a heresy and suspended the WARC membership of two denominations not taking a stand against apartheid. In this year, the drafting of the Belhar Confession began in the Dutch Reformed Mission Church. In addition, in 1983 a Dutch Reformed Church pastor began a ministry of reconciliation that quite directly sought to counter the failure of 1857. The ministry was known as "koinonia,"[15] and its approach was simple: people from different races who lived in different parts of the city coming together to share meals. A meal would be hosted at the various houses of the participants, so that white and colored participants would eat at the homes of blacks, and so on. In a quite profound way, this sharing of bread and of lives became a force in the anti-apartheid movement, helping to break down the cultural stereotypes and barriers that divided. Although not a formal celebration of the Eucharist, koinonia was a revolutionary activity precisely because of the church's failure to ensure that the Eucharist remained a multiracial, multiclass meal.

Much more could be said about this dramatic history, but for our purposes, I would like to point out three significant ways that these developments in the Dutch Reformed Church departed from the eucharistic gospel.

(1) It was a violation of the scope of the Eucharist as a feast of unity in Christ for peoples from all tribes and nations. The 1857 pastoral accommodation to allow exclusion at the Supper on the basis of race moved against scripture's testimony to the eucharistic gospel. Paul's instructions for the Lord's Supper are very clear: "My brothers and sisters, when you gather to eat, you should all eat together" (1 Cor. 11:33 NIV). "Private suppers" that reflect "divisions among you" are prohibited (1 Cor. 11:18, 21 NIV). Indeed, eating the supper with division is a contradiction, an offense, for in this context Paul writes that "all who eat and drink without discerning the body, eat and drink

---

14. Dirk J. Smit, "On Learning to Speak? A South African Reformed Perspective on Dialogue," in *Essays in Public Theology*, 230.

15. For an account of the koinonia movement from its founding director, see Nico Smith, "Christian Witness and the Plurality of Cultures: The Story of Koinonia South Africa," *International Review of Mission* 83, no. 328 (January 1994): 67–69.

judgment against themselves" (1 Cor. 11:29). While "discerning the body" can refer to discerning the risen Christ at the Supper, it also has implications for the celebrating community: if celebrated in divisive separation from some parts of the body, then Christ's body as the church has not been properly discerned, and it is a meal of judgment.[16] As Paul says in the next chapter, "For just as the body is one and has many members, and all the members of the body, though many, are one body, so it is with Christ. For in the one Spirit we were all baptized into one body—Jews or Greeks, slaves or free—and we were all made to drink of one Spirit" (1 Cor. 12:12–13). When the body of Christ as the church is properly discerned, participants see how this diverse community has been made into one body in Christ, drinking of one Spirit. The gospel reality of this "oneness" that the Lord's Supper celebrates is obscured and contradicted by divisive separation.

(2) It entailed prioritizing church growth and pragmatism over the word of the gospel at the Supper. Lest we think that the movement emerging from 1857 is utterly foreign to contemporary concerns, in many ways it can be understood as an instance where the church was being flexible, evangelical, and "missional" rather than rigidly Reformational. John de Gruchy notes that Reformed churches were not segregated until the "revivals in the mid-nineteenth century": "It was under the dominance of such evangelicalism, rather than the strict Calvinism of Dort, that the Dutch Reformed Church agreed at its Synod of 1857 that congregations could be divided along racial lines." He adds, "Despite the fact that this development went against earlier synodical decisions that segregation in the church was contrary to the Word of God, it was rationalized on grounds of missiology and practical necessity. Missiologically it was argued that people were

---

16. Most modern commentators see either a direct or indirect reference to the unity of the church as the body of Christ in the phrase "discerning the body" in 1 Corinthians 11:19. Commentators such as Blomberg, Hays, Senft, and Stanley interpret "the body" as the body of the congregation. Other commentators claim that "the body" refers first to the body and blood of Christ and secondarily to the body of the congregation, such that "the social is founded upon the salvific," in the words of Anthony Thiselton (summarizing C. Wolff, but also stating his own view). For a brief survey of these views, see Anthony C. Thiselton, *The First Epistle to the Corinthians*, New International Greek Testament Commentary (Grand Rapids: Eerdmans, 2000), 855–58. Gordon Fee makes a significant point that this eating unto judgment moves "in two directions, horizontal and vertical." Neither dimension should be lost. Fee, *The First Epistle to the Corinthians*, New International Commentary on the New Testament (Grand Rapids: Eerdmans, 1987), 532–33.

best evangelized and best worshipped God in their own language and cultural setting, a position reinforced by German Lutheran missiology and somewhat akin to the church-growth philosophy of our own time."[17] The gospel message of one new humanity in Christ, celebrated at the Supper, does not always look attractive to those who are pragmatic or missionally minded in a way that focuses narrowly on adding numbers to the church and maintaining a certain comfort level for those who are already part of the church. Having a pious heart or an ambitious program for mission is no assurance that one is faithfully responding to the good news of the gospel, which overcomes walls of cultural hostility in Christ.

(3) It was optimistic about human nature rather than hoping specifically in the Spirit's work in Christ. While some may think that apartheid suffered from a negative, pessimistic view of humanity, Philippe Theron has convincingly argued that the opposite is the case.

> Far from being pessimistic, apartheid, or separate development as the proponents of this policy preferred to call it, was an impossible political pipedream built on unfounded optimism that it would safeguard racial and cultural identities in an equitable way, establish economic stability, and secure neighborly peace. It was the panacea that served as a social solution for church and society. The alien *(paroikia)* character of the church as a divine institute, signaling the coming of God's eschatological kingdom, was not acknowledged. The fundamental difference between reconciliation as a theological concept, on the one hand, and reconciliation as a social and political settlement, on the other, was not conceded.[18]

The Spirit's work of reconciliation in the gospel is not the same as reconciliation that can be manipulated or manufactured by society in general. The Eucharist is an eschatological feast celebrated in the present. By the Spirit, the church tastes God's coming kingdom in which many separated peoples "have been brought near by the blood of Christ. For he is our peace; in his flesh he has made both groups into one and has broken down the dividing wall, that is, the hostility between us" (Eph. 2:13–14). The union and reconciliation that takes

---

17. John de Gruchy, *Liberating Reformed Theology: A South African Contribution to an Ecumenical Debate* (Grand Rapids: Eerdmans, 1991), 23–24.

18. Philippe Theron, "One Savior, One Church: Reconciliation as Justification and 'New Creation,'" in *The Unity of the Church*, ed. Eduardus Van der Borght (Leiden: Brill, 2010), 271–72.

place in the one Christ is not a general social policy. It is a Spirit-formed concrete reality that calls peoples who were separated by enmity to live in their true, reconciled identity in Christ.

In light of the ways in which the DRC's failures had to do with a lack of fidelity to the Lord's Supper as a meal of union with Christ, the Belhar Confession responds to these failures by highlighting the implications of this central biblical theme. With its focus on church unity, the second article of Belhar emphatically and repeatedly grounds this unity in Jesus Christ and the working of the one Spirit. Indeed, "this unity must become visible so that the world may believe that separation, enmity and hatred between people and groups is sin which Christ has already conquered, and accordingly that anything which threatens this unity may have no place in the church and must be resisted."[19] As such, unity is both "a gift and an obligation": it is a Spirit-given identity of unity in oneness with Christ that the church is called to live into. Not surprisingly, article 2 makes this point with a eucharistic accent: just as believers "eat of one bread and drink of one cup," so they are to pursue and manifest the unity that is in Christ.

This same emphasis can be seen in article 3, on reconciliation: just as "God has entrusted the church with the message of reconciliation in and through Jesus Christ," so the church is called to witness to this "new heaven and new earth" in Christ, living in a new obedience that is incompatible with "irreconciliation and hatred" and "forced separation of people on the grounds of race and color" because these "obstruct" the "ministry and experience of reconciliation in Christ." In this way, the Belhar sets forth union with Christ as the ground to call for unity and reconciliation in Christ.

Article 4 continues by speaking about the church's call to justice. The interpretation of this article is somewhat more ambiguous, however, particularly because the language of union with Christ is not as explicitly present. Instead, the language is framed in terms of God being a God of justice and the church needing to "stand where the Lord stands" by acting with justice.[20] One line in particu-

---

19. For a complete text of the Belhar Confession, see the appendix at the end of this chapter.

20. Dirkie Smit, one of the authors of the Belhar Confession, tries to deal with the paucity of references to Christ in article 4—only one reference at the end of the article—by pointing to the opening line's claim that "God has revealed himself as the one who wishes to bring about justice." Smit says, "In the confession that God 'revealed' himself in this way lies an unspoken reference to Christ and the Scriptures

lar is troubling to some and championed by others: "that God, in
a world full of injustice and enmity, is in a special way the God of
the destitute, the poor and the wronged." This line is much debated
and deserves some consideration with regard to what it is and is
not claiming.

First, many do not recognize that the opening parenthetical phrase
is qualifying rather than intensifying. Here is the basic sense: God loves
all of creation and all people; yet, precisely because there is injustice
and enmity in the world, God is the God of the poor due to their
special need. Thus the parenthetical phrase, "in a world of injustice
and enmity," qualifies the sense that God is "in a special way" the
God of some who are wronged.[21]

Furthermore, the Belhar's text suggests that radically reworking
ecclesiological categories such that "the destitute, the poor and the
wronged" becomes the constitutive definition of God's people is not
the goal or intention. For as article 2 says, "true faith in Jesus Christ
is the only condition for membership of this church."

Yet, on the other hand, problems persist with article 4 that make
it less useful to the church than articles 2 and 3. Since this is a point
that my constructive proposal seeks to ameliorate, it is worth briefly
noting four problems.

First, it is simply not clear what it means to speak in terms of
divine ownership when speaking about justice—namely, that God
is "in a special way the God of" a certain group of people. If it is
because of the particular needs of the poor and the wronged, then
it seems that it would be equally true to say that "in a special way
God is the God of" the tax collectors and those being misled by the
idol of wealth. But then again, it seems that every person would have
"special" needs in this way. Unfortunately, by using the language of

---

and consequently a denial that the statement appealed to natural theology, group
projections, and an ideological or arbitrarily constructed image of God." D. J. Smit,
"In a Special Way the God of the Destitute, the Poor, and the Wronged," in *A Moment
of Truth: The Confession of the Dutch Reformed Mission Church 1982*, ed. G. D.
Cloete and D. J. Smit (Grand Rapids: Eerdmans, 1984), 57. While the Belhar's reference to revelation in article 4 is certainly to be valued, it is not the case that a passing
reference to revelation entails a denial of all forms of natural theology or that it points
clearly to Jesus Christ as the source of revelation. Indeed, particularly in the church's
confession about justice, it seems dangerous at best to assume that Jesus Christ is
implicit or "unspoken"—that is precisely what needs to be explicit.

21. This qualifying rather than intensifying interpretation fits well with Smit's
comments ("In a Special Way," 58).

God's ownership—the God "of" a certain class of people—discussion of article 4 often slips into identity politics rather than a thoughtful concern for justice.

A second problem is that, while biblical language about the poor and the wronged has a dialectical flexibility at times moving toward a metaphorical sense,[22] article 4 tends to speak in a way that suggests a more fixed, modern, sociological sense. While the drafters of the confession sought to avoid this pitfall,[23] both advocates and detractors of the Belhar have often interpreted article 4 in modern sociological terms. Why? In addition to the significant line, "in a special way the God of the destitute, the poor and the wronged," article 4 continues by saying, "the church must witness against all the powerful and privileged who selfishly seek their own interests and thus control and harm others." Taken together, since God is the God "of the destitute, the poor and the wronged," the language of ownership naturally implies that God is "for" the poor and "against" the powerful, thus portraying them as two competing classes of people. But this tends to put people in the fixed categories of "rich" or "poor," "wronged" or "perpetrators." As such, it does not recognize the plasticity of biblical language about the poor. Moreover, as Miroslav Volf has argued, perpetrators are almost always victims themselves, and victims are almost always perpetrators, in different ways.[24] Volf has also noted that when one's overall framing of injustice is in terms of "oppressor" versus "oppressed," one has adopted a schema that seems "ill-suited to bring about reconciliation and sustain peace between people and people groups."[25] For biblical and theological reasons, we should continue to speak at times about the wronged and the perpetrators,[26] but the categories need to stay flexible and dialectical.

22. See J. David Peins, "Poor, Poverty (Old Testament)," in *The Anchor Bible Dictionary*, ed. David Noel Freedman (New York: Doubleday, 1996), 5:401–14, esp. 413; and Thomas D. Hanks, "Poor, Poverty (New Testament)," in ibid., 5:414–23, esp. 415.

23. Smit explains that the commission that formulated the Belhar Confession avoided certain expressions "in order not to create the impression of a class struggle in which God would as it were choose sides for a certain group and against another group" ("In a Special Way," 58). The question, of course, is whether the commission succeeded in doing this. For many readers, the "impression" that the commission sought to avoid is seen as quite directly suggested by article 4.

24. Miroslav Volf, *Exclusion and Embrace* (Nashville: Abingdon, 1996), 101–4.

25. Ibid.

26. See ibid., 104.

A third problem with article 4 is that many of the biblical references supporting the statements in this article occur in a distinctly covenantal context in which the prophets and psalmists are crying out for Yahweh to be faithful to his covenantal promise to Israel. The article eludes any consideration of this covenantal context, along with the profoundly covenantal notion of union with Christ. Without a covenantal context, these statements can be easily misread in flat sociological ways suggestive of God's preference for one socioeconomic group over another.

Finally, on a congregational level, the language of God being the God of the poor easily results in a new set of colonial-type attitudes. As a staff member at a Boston homeless shelter for five years, I saw this frequently in the way Christians treated the homeless poor. As one shelter guest told me with biting irony, "I was in church this morning and they prayed for the homeless. I decided that I should pray for the housed." While Christians should pray for those in need, the rhetoric of special ownership—of God being the God of the poor—can be a way for middle-class congregations to lift themselves up by giving a handout to the poor as "other." In contrast, in the eucharistic vision of the gospel that I explore below—which can be connected to the overall teaching of Belhar, especially articles 2 and 3—the goal is not a handout or a theological "blank check" to members of a particular social class but a neighbor-love that seeks culmination in mutual fellowship at the banquet table of the Lord.

Let me be clear that there is much in the Belhar Confession that is very helpful for the church, which is why I am taking the space to engage it in this chapter. But like many theological documents, some claims are more helpfully formulated than others. My concern is not to "soften" the statements about justice in article 4, but to formulate biblical imperatives toward justice in relation to a theology of union with Christ—just as articles 2 and 3 do. In order to keep with the biblical exhortations to justice expressed in article 4 and to reflect the eucharistic gospel, in this chapter I explain how the gospel leads us into communion with three bodies: first, the body and blood of Jesus Christ, to whom believers are united by the Spirit; second, emerging from the first, the body of fellow believers united to Christ; and third, also emerging from union with Christ, the body of the neighbor, particularly the neighbor in need—what I will call the "wounded body." In speaking about the article 4 categories of the wronged, the poor, and the destitute, I would claim that we should have special regard for those with "wounded bodies" precisely because we love all neighbors. Thus, rather than making the language of justice and special regard dependent on God "owning" a particular group of people (apart from the biblical-covenantal context of God's ownership), I seek to ground the language of justice in union with Christ. We encounter these three bodies at the Table, which is a means of grace by which God reshapes us for communion with Christ's body and the wounded bodies in the world.

Relating Justice to Union with Christ

We begin with some initial observations about the doctrinal place of justice in the Reformed tradition. According to Calvin, the "sum of the gospel" is the double grace of justification and sanctification, gifts that are inseparable yet distinct, received by the Spirit in union with Christ.[27] With this view of the gospel—which is further developed in the later Reformed tradition—love of neighbor and, consequently, justice are folded in as an essential feature of the Spirit's work of regeneration. A life of justice is not an optional part of the Christian life because, although we are not justified "through works," Calvin says, "we are justified not without works . . . since in our sharing in Christ, which justifies us, sanctification is just as much included as righteousness."[28] Indeed, as noted in chapter 1, to separate the new life brought by the Spirit from the forgiveness of sins received in salvation would, in Calvin's view, tear Christ into pieces. For "we must always bear in mind the counsel of the apostle, that free remission of sins cannot be separated from the Spirit of regeneration. This would be, as it were, to rend Christ asunder."[29]

At this point, we need to avoid a common misunderstanding that would turn "sanctification" into a new type of works righteousness. The gospel is nothing less than the double grace of union with Christ; it is not just the forgiveness of sins but also new life. Yet this new life does not make our own *works* the ground or content of the gospel. Our works, even our works of justice in the way of Jesus Christ, are not, in themselves, the good news. The good news is received as a

---

27. *Inst.* 3.3.1.
28. *Inst.* 3.16.1.
29. Comm. on Rom. 8:9, CC.

gift—that in being united to the death and resurrection of Jesus Christ, we receive free pardon and new life by the Spirit. After contrasting the law with justification at the end of Romans 5, Paul poses the question, "Should we continue in sin in order that grace may abound?" (Rom. 6:1). In response, Paul does not turn sanctification into the law, but points back to what is received in union with Christ: "Do you not know that all of us who have been baptized into Christ Jesus were baptized into his death?" (Rom. 6:3). It is only after this indicative of the gospel—of justification *and* sanctification received in union with Christ—that Paul moves to the imperative that correlates with God's law. Third-generation Reformer Franciscus Junius expresses the relationship well by speaking about different degrees, or dimensions, of divine grace in regeneration. The "twofold righteousness" of justification and sanctification are both received as gifts in "communion with Christ": it is not that justification is gift and sanctification is achievement.[30] However, a distinct yet inseparable dimension of this union with Christ is "the action emanating from the new creation,"[31] the Spirit-empowered activation of our lives for love of God and neighbor. Jesus Christ defines the content of this new life, and it is received as a gift—a gift that the Spirit uses to bear fruit in our lives. Yet this fruit, in the form of a life of justice, is never the grounds for our salvation. Thus for the Reformed tradition, our life of justice is *inseparable* from our incorporation into Christ's life, a consequence of receiving the double grace in Christ. The new life received in Christ by the Spirit bears fruit in acts of justice in our lives, yet the new life is a gift. In ourselves, we are not the source of this good—our actions of justice are not the good news of the gospel. Rather, our actions that display love of God and neighbor reflect the gift of new life received in Christ through the Spirit.

Thus, the gospel is not simply forgiveness of our sins or a "get into heaven free" card. Irreducibly, it is participation in Christ's righteousness through receiving forgiveness *and* new life by the Spirit. This new life in union with Christ displays itself in a life of justice, a life formed by the God-focused, Christ-centered gospel. Concretely speaking, celebrating the Lord's Supper is a key way for congregations

30. Franciscus Junius, *De libero hominis arbitrio, ante et post lapsum*, translated in Willem J. van Asselt, J. Martin Bac, and Roelf T. te Velde, eds., *Reformed Thought on Freedom: The Concept of Free Choice in Early Modern Reformed Theology* (Grand Rapids: Baker Academic, 2010), 106.

31. Ibid.

to apprehend and receive the double grace of the gospel and to grow in a life in union with Christ. Calvin taught that the sacraments bring "the clearest promises" from God.[32] Specifically, baptism and the Lord's Supper, in combination with the preached word, are a divine instrument by which the gospel of the twofold grace is held forth to us.[33] While baptism is a sign of the double grace just as the Lord's Supper is,[34] we will continue our focus on the eucharistic gospel in this chapter, exploring the Lord's Supper and its relation to the law of love that expresses justice. To this we now turn.

The Lord's Supper and the Law of Love

A View from the Garden

When believers take the law of God—summarized in the love of God and neighbor—as instruction for the Christian life (the third use), how does this relate to God's purpose in the law? Calvin certainly affirms two negative functions for the law: to reveal our own sinfulness (and need for a savior), and to restrain public acts of wickedness in the civil law. But what about this more "positive" sense of the law, which gives love of neighbor a prominent place in the Christian life, in the Christian's participation in Christ?

For Calvin, the creational purpose of the law, which was present in the garden, correlates with the purpose of the law as instruction for Christians: union with God. As Calvin states, the law contains commands "whose purpose is to unite us to our God. And that

---

32. "But the sacraments bring the clearest promises; and they have this characteristic over and above the word because they represent them for us as painted in a picture from life." *Inst.* 4.14.6.

33. See J. Todd Billings, *Calvin, Participation, and the Gift: The Activity of Believers in Union with Christ*, Changing Paradigms in Historical and Systematic Theology (Oxford: Oxford University Press, 2007), 106–8, 116–41.

34. Thus John Calvin's baptismal liturgy of 1542 speaks of the "double grace and benefit from God in our baptism," which means that "God wills to be a merciful Father to us, not imputing to us all our faults," and that "God will assist us by his Holy Spirit so that we will have the power to battle against the devil, sin, and the desires of the flesh, until we have victory in this, and live in the liberty of his kingdom." Trans. J. D. C. Fisher, *Christian Initiation: The Reformation Period* (Chicago: Liturgy Training Publications, 2007), 114. I am grateful to John Witvliet for bringing to light the significance of baptism as a sign of the double grace in his response to a lecture based on this chapter.

[union with God] constitutes our happiness and glory."[35] Indeed, "the principle end and use of the Law" is "to invite men to God; and, indeed, their true happiness lies in being united to God."[36] This union with God is not a disembodied, ethereal experience. Rather it involves our bodies, our senses, our minds, our actions. For Calvin, "Adam was denied the tree of knowledge of good and evil to test his obedience and prove that he was willingly under God's command."[37] God desired voluntary obedience from Adam so that he "might know he had a Director and Lord of his life, on whose will he ought to depend, and in whose commands he ought to acquiesce." In other words, God's desire for Adam was that he "might acknowledge that he lives not by his own power, but by the kindness of God alone."[38]

It is significant to recognize that this voluntary, active obedience that Calvin connects to union with God interfaces with Calvin's use of a polarity that he finds in both Johannine and Pauline books: the polarity between acting "in oneself" or "in the flesh" and acting "in Christ" or "in the Spirit." Calvin argues that Adam was "united to God" before the fall, that he was righteous through "participation in God."[39] These are not inherent, autonomous qualities of Adam. Rather, they are what we might call "ec-static" qualities that involve an orientation toward God, a trust in God rather than in oneself or other creatures. Paradoxically, the primal, human nature is good precisely because it is united to God in a subordinate relationship of active trust. The delineation of the nature of this union, this active trust, is the law. It is a creational gift from God because the law itself points to the *telos* of human beings in being united in active trust to their Creator and other creatures—a union and fellowship with other creatures that is characterized by justice.

Thus, the fundamental polarity of the law is not just between good and evil but between communion and alienation, union and autonomy. To act in communion with God—to obey the law—is to be truly and fully human. To disobey the law is to trust in oneself, in the flesh. Indeed, the polarity between acting "in oneself" versus

35. John Calvin, *John Calvin's Sermons on the Ten Commandments*, trans. Benjamin Wirt Farley (Grand Rapids: Baker, 1980), 39.
36. Comm. on Isa. 45:19, CTS.
37. *Inst.* 2.1.4.
38. Comm. on Gen. 2:9, CTS.
39. See *Inst.* 2.1.5; 2.2.1.

"in Christ" or "in God" is not only a general orienting polarity for Calvin's view of the law but also provides much of the structure for his practical advice on neighbor-love and justice. Since the *imago Dei* is a "participation in God," Calvin encourages us to contemplate our neighbor in light of this image. For Calvin, "we ought to embrace the whole human race without exception." This should be done "since all [persons] should be contemplated in God, not in themselves."[40]

Viewed in themselves, one's neighbors may not appear worthy of love.[41] But just as Christians are called to live not in themselves but in Christ, the law of God calls Christians to consider their neighbors not "in themselves" but in relation to God. For Calvin, this sets a very high standard for neighbor-love. Just as God's law in the garden evokes a voluntary, grateful response, our love of neighbor should be motivated by a genuine and "sincere feeling of love."[42] Obeying the law of neighbor-love means that one's delight and trust in God overflows to a genuine love and regard for one's neighbor, regardless of whether they are "worthy or unworthy, friend or enemy."[43]

Not only does Calvin emphasize that neighbor-love should be universal, even toward enemies who have harmed us; he also suggests ways that this universal love necessitates a special regard for what I am calling "the wounded bodies." Calvin was no stranger to wounded bodies. Many refugees fled to Geneva, and Calvin displayed great concern for those in need by reorganizing the deaconate to provide food for the hungry, health care for the sick, and related social services.[44] Calvin, reading scripture canonically, saw lines of continuity from Moses the prophet, through the prophetic books, through to Jesus "the prophet" who fulfills the law—for "the justice of God" is "unchangeable," and Christ himself fulfills "in reality . . . what had hitherto appeared only in figures."[45] For Calvin, Christ is the embodiment of justice, the

---

40. *Inst.* 2.8.55.

41. "If we rightly direct our love, we must first turn our eyes not to man, the sight of whom would more often engender hate than love, but to God, who bids us extend to all men the love we bear to him, that this may be an unchanging principle: whatever the character of the man, we must yet love him because we love God." *Inst.* 2.8.55.

42. *Inst.* 3.7.7.

43. *Inst.* 2.8.55.

44. See Jeannine E. Olson, *Calvin and Social Welfare* (Cranbury, NJ: Associated University Presses, 1989).

45. Comm. on Luke 4:17 (*Harmony of the Gospels*, vol. 1), CTS.

embodiment of the law of love, which has particular implications for the rich, who are called by Christ to "bestow on the poor, according to their own ability, what their [the poor's] necessity required."[46] With Calvin's position here, those with special needs do require special concern in actions of love toward them.

With my focus in this view from the garden, I am not trying to downplay the importance of the first two functions of the law—as a mirror to our sin and for civil restraint. Rather, I am seeking to show how God's law, which calls us to justice in its third use, is the fulfillment and restoration of God's created purposes, a fulfillment that configures the love of neighbor, and the neighbor's wounded body, as part of a restoration of communion with God. Moreover, obedience to the law is not done as an anxious work for our salvation or as a bold, heroic human action; obedience to the law takes place in the context of Spirit-empowered freedom and gratitude to God, who has been revealed as a gracious Father through the adoption that believers receive in Christ. These gospel themes appear in a concentrated form in the Lord's Supper.

A View from the Table

Let us begin our reflections on the Table by staying in the garden for a moment longer and considering the Table in the garden. In his Genesis commentary, Calvin suggests that pre-fallen human beings had a need for a material sign of God's love in order to know and live in fellowship with God. In his comments on Genesis 2 and 3, Calvin interprets the tree of life as God's accommodation for the sake of uniting Adam to himself, an external sign of God's promise, for by these signs God "stretches out his hand to us, because, without assistance, we cannot ascend to him. He intended, therefore, that man, as often as he tasted the fruit of that tree, should remember whence he received his life, in order that he might acknowledge that he lives not by his own power, but by the kindness of God alone." Before the fall, we see that humanity needed not only God's spoken word but signs of God's promise to "seal his grace to man," signs that could be seen, smelled, touched, and tasted.[47] Calvin claims that the tree of life was a physical sign of the "eternal Word of God";

---

46. Comm. on Luke 3:18 (*Harmony of the Gospels*, vol. 1), CTS.
47. See Comm. on Gen. 2:9, 3:22, CTS.

thus, even Adam and Eve were directed to find their life in the Son of God rather than in themselves.[48]

As we move from this foreshadowing of the sacrament in the garden to the sacrament of the Supper after the fall, we see that the sacrament fulfills, in a fundamental sense, a similar creational purpose: human beings need physical signs of God's kindness and communion, and the Supper is a gift that provides those signs while still providing fellowship with the Second Person of the Trinity. But in this communion, there is also a healing of the fall's consequences: alienation from God and neighbor. Specifically, for Calvin, this first "vertical" communion with Christ is always connected to horizontal communion with others. "For it is necessary for us to be incorporated, as it were, into Christ in order to be united to each other."[49] This unity is not ethereal or hypothetical. It involves empathic compassion and active love. Just as "no part of our body is touched by any feeling of pain which is not spread among all the rest, so we ought not to allow a brother to be affected by any evil, without being touched with compassion for him." For "we cannot love Christ without loving him in the brethren."[50]

Calvin's eucharistic theology not only holds together vertical and horizontal communion; it also reflects both aspects of the double grace received in union with Christ: both God's free pardon in Christ (justification) and the Spirit's empowerment to live a life of love (sanctification). This is the sense in which the Supper is a "sacrifice of thanksgiving." Unlike the once-for-all sacrifice of atonement, "this kind of sacrifice has nothing to do with appeasing God's wrath, with obtaining forgiveness of sins, or with meriting righteousness." Instead, it is a grateful offering of love to God, since it "is concerned solely with magnifying and exalting God." But significantly, this love is directed to others—even those outside the gathered community of faith. For in the sacrifice of praise "are included all the duties of love."[51]

Thus the Lord's Supper, as an icon of the gospel,[52] not only offers communion with Christ and with Christ's body but also directs the lives of the communicants to the "in God" dimension of the

48. Comm. on Gen. 2:9, CTS. See Randall C. Zachman, *Image and Word in the Theology of John Calvin* (Notre Dame, IN: University of Notre Dame Press, 2007), 168.

49. Comm. on 1 Cor. 10:16, CC.

50. Comm. on 1 Cor. 10:16, CC.

51. *Inst.* 4.18.16.

52. See *Inst.* 4.14.6.

neighbor. This dimension of the gospel is not dispensable, for just as there is no justification without sanctification, the church cannot be without a "sacrifice of thanksgiving."[53] The movement of redemption "in Christ" is inevitably and inseparably a movement toward love of neighbor and toward a concern for justice. And the practice recommended by Calvin of connecting the celebration of the Supper with alms for the poor highlights the extent to which this "love of neighbor" at the Supper has a special regard for the wounded body.[54]

In this account, justice has a clearly delineated doctrinal setting. Justice is set in the christocentric context of life being found through participation in Christ; it is covenantal and communal, part of a celebration of the covenantal sign in the mutual love of community. It is trinitarian, oriented around the imagery of adoption, wherein grateful children receive the gift of the Son sent by the Father through the power of the Spirit. Finally, it safeguards against a works-oriented righteousness through its account of the double grace: Christ accomplished the once-for-all sacrifice for the forgiveness of sins; our "sacrifice of praise" is not to earn favor with God, but because we gratefully love God, we love all that we see that is "in God"—namely, the believing community in Christ and other human beings who "participate in God" by the *imago Dei*. The law and the Lord's Supper work in tandem. The law shows the concrete, embodied way that humans properly "participate" in God, and the Supper is a material sign through which sinners come to participate in Christ by the Spirit and in a life of loving neighbors.

Justice in the Eucharistic Gospel

Living a Justice Defined by Jesus Christ

My reflections above offer a Reformed way to situate a theology and practice of justice. By tying justice to the Lord's Supper, union with Christ, and the double grace, I offer a proposal in the spirit of the Belhar Confession, supplementing article 4 in its exhortation to the church to act with justice. Like article 4 of the Belhar, my

53. "But this is so necessary for the church that it cannot be absent from it." *Inst.* 4.18.16.
54. *Inst.* 4.17.44.

reflections do not prescribe a specific political "road map" for justice. But in response to the question of whose justice, I seek to point clearly to Jesus Christ. Just as articles 2 and 3 point to Jesus Christ as the source and ground for the church's unity and reconciliation, so also I believe we can improve the more general language of article 4 on justice by grounding it specifically in Jesus Christ. Union with Christ should be the source of the church's God-given identity as a people who are unified, reconciled, *and* acting with justice. Jesus Christ, as the gift the church receives in the eucharistic gospel, is the embodiment and definition of justice. In fact, the justice in our lives is not something that we possess but is something that (strictly speaking) Jesus Christ possesses; we display it to the extent that we become possessed by him. Ultimately, while justice is incredibly important to the message of the gospel itself, it is the "justice" that is defined in and through Jesus Christ that is normative for Christians. Seen in light of union with Christ, justice is a derivative, even parasitic, concept. Its positive content should be derived from the expansive yet particular location of Jesus Christ himself. Christ is the spacious one who is "the Alpha and the Omega" (Rev. 21), for "all things have been created through him and for him. He himself is before all things, and in him all things hold together" (Col. 1:16–17). Yet this wide and spacious one—the one who is the truth—is also scandalously particular in the justice he defines. His is a justice of loving God and neighbor, a justice of loving the enemy—a justice of loving all who are "in God" whether they deserve our love or greet us with hatred and injury.

If we accept the claim that justice must ultimately be christologically defined as it is pursued in union with Christ, the liberal Protestant program of reducing the gospel to our acts of justice will not do. Neither will it do to fall into an evangelical reduction of justice to an optional add-on for Christians who want extra credit after properly performing "essential" Christian duties that relate to the life of the soul. Instead, as word and sacrament have the same "office" of holding forth Jesus Christ by the Spirit's power,[55] our pursuit of justice must go hand-in-hand with seeking the renewal of the church's worship, Bible study, and witness.

---

55. Calvin writes, "Let it be regarded as a settled principle that the sacraments have the same office as the Word of God: to offer and set forth Christ to us, and in him the treasures of heavenly grace." *Inst.* 4.14.17.

The Place of the Wounded Body

One of the ways I have extended a theology of union with Christ to include justice is through speaking about three bodies with which those united to Christ are brought into communion. These bodies need to be distinguished but not sharply dichotomized. First and foremost, we have union with Jesus Christ in the Supper, a celebration that points to the union at the heart of the Christian life. This union with Christ's risen body incorporates believers into communion with a second body: Christ's body on earth, brothers and sisters in Christ around the world to whom believers are united in the Spirit's love. Yet believers are called to love a third body as well: that of the neighbor, who is "in God," and the wounded neighbor in particular. The Lord's Supper, like the Christian gospel, is not just a "spiritual" or vertical affair; it necessarily implicates the body of believers and the suffering, wounded bodies of other neighbors as well.

A similar point is made dramatically by William Cavanaugh in writing about a Roman Catholic community under the oppressive Pinochet regime in Chile in the 1970s and 1980s. "In the early days of the military regime, Chile was driven indoors. Behind some doors, champagne corks popped; behind others, there was only an anxious silence. In the streets the military patrols sped by on their hungry search for enemies. Those labeled as enemies faced a terrible dilemma. They could stay at home and await capture, or they could attempt to flee, a choice which would take them out into the streets ruled by the regime." Cavanaugh goes on to write about political dissenters who showed up at the doorstep of priests in Santiago. "They were received, but they were not allowed to stay," he says. Later that evening as the preparations for the Mass were being made, a seminarian spoke up. "He said Christ had been turned away at the door of the residence," Cavanaugh recounts. "Communion in the body of Christ had already been denied in the denial of the two seeking asylum."[56]

Just as it is a contradiction in the South African context to celebrate communion with Christ while exclusively separating Christ's body of believers, so also it is a contradiction in Chile—or the United States or any other context—to celebrate communion with Christ while ignoring the wounded bodies in our midst. The three levels of love

56. William T. Cavanaugh, *Torture and Eucharist: Theology, Politics, and the Body of Christ* (Oxford: Blackwell, 1998), 205.

and communion need to be distinguished because they are not the same, but to separate these three levels by excluding sanctification (and its fruit in a life of justice) from the gospel would be to "rend Christ asunder," as Calvin says.

Part of maintaining the distinction between these types of communion means that one should keep in mind Philippe Theron's point, noted above, about the danger of conflating communion and reconciliation in Christ with reconciliation in society[57]—a confusion that South African apartheid aggravated. Yet these three types of communion are also united, and each level has implications for the others. While the church should not identify the Lord's Supper with a public meal of those in society, the Supper as a means of grace can still have a formative power in developing a public vision. While the koinonia groups in South Africa were not celebrations of the Lord's Supper, they were practices that emerged in the public life of a church seeking to be faithful to the eucharistic gospel. A church shaped by the gospel will find ways to share meals that are in keeping with Jesus's words: "When you give a banquet, invite the poor, the crippled, the lame, and the blind. And you will be blessed, because they cannot repay you, for you will be repaid at the resurrection of the righteous" (Luke 14:13–14). Such a banquet is not the Lord's Supper, but it is nevertheless a sign of God's people who seek to share the table fellowship that they enjoy with those in their midst who have wounded bodies.

In a similar way, in a world of poverty and injustice, the church should seek not simply to give "handouts" to meet the bare necessities of those in need; it should seek to display the hospitality that pursues relationships of mutual love, wherever possible.[58] While there is still a legitimate distinction between communion in the body of Christ and the love of neighbor in society, we cannot act as if one is optional. Moreover, the eucharistic table manners of the church community should help to shape its vision of love for the neighbor in need. Preaching and celebrating the eucharistic gospel should form persons who reflect justice as an aspect of their life in Christ.

Thus, given the close relationship between the gospel, justice, and the Lord's Supper, our concern for the gospel and the church's life

57. See Theron, "One Savior, One Church," 271–72.

58. For further development of this theme, see J. Todd Billings, "The Lord's Supper and the Church's Public Witness: Bringing Together Heaven and Earth, Living between Gift and Promise," *Theology Today* 67, no. 1 (April 2010): 7–14.

of justice should also lead us to renew our eucharistic and liturgical practice. If the Lord's Supper is an icon of the gospel and part of our feeding and empowerment for living in the double grace of Christ, then the celebration needs to be frequent, and the Lord's Supper needs to be a focal point for both preaching and teaching in the church. Calvin was indeed insightful when he suggested that God's word must not only be heard, but smelled, touched, and tasted.[59] Moreover, liturgical renewal of the Lord's Supper needs to take place because of the central focus on the life-giving gospel—not to make the Supper fulfill some other purpose. The Supper does not need to shift its central focus from Jesus Christ onto the community gathered, or even onto the wounded body. It should not be *reduced* to being simply about "how we're all included" or our commitment to help those in need. Yet, in giving a full and frequent celebration of the Supper with its focus on Jesus Christ, these other two bodies should not be eclipsed, since a necessary and derivative consequence of communion with Jesus Christ is communion with his churchly body and loving action toward the neighbor in need. When the gospel of union with Christ is attended to as both forgiveness of sins and renewal in a life of love of God and neighbor (Calvin's "double grace"), renewed activity for a life of justice will be a by-product, by the Spirit's power. For in the covenantal, trinitarian, and Christ-centered state of being in union with Christ, we discover how to commune with our brothers and sisters in Christ *and* our neighbor in need.

Appendix: The Belhar Confession (September 1986)[60]

1. **We believe** in the triune God, Father, Son and Holy Spirit, who gathers, protects and cares for the church through Word and Spirit. This, God has done since the beginning of the world and will do to the end.

59. See the discussion above about Calvin's interpretation of the tree of life.
60. This is a translation of the original Afrikaans text of the confession as it was adopted by the synod of the Dutch Reformed Mission Church in South Africa in 1986. In 1994 the Dutch Reformed Mission Church and the Dutch Reformed Church in Africa united to form the Uniting Reformed Church in Southern Africa (URCSA). This inclusive-language text was prepared by the Office of Theology and Worship, Presbyterian Church (USA), and is used with permission.

2. **We believe** in one holy, universal Christian church, the communion of saints called from the entire human family.

We believe

- that Christ's work of reconciliation is made manifest in the church as the community of believers who have been reconciled with God and with one another (Eph. 2:11–22);
- that unity is, therefore, both a gift and an obligation for the church of Jesus Christ; that through the working of God's Spirit it is a binding force, yet simultaneously a reality which must be earnestly pursued and sought: one which the people of God must continually be built up to attain (Eph. 4:1–16);
- that this unity must become visible so that the world may believe that separation, enmity and hatred between people and groups is sin which Christ has already conquered, and accordingly that anything which threatens this unity may have no place in the church and must be resisted (John 17:20–23);
- that this unity of the people of God must be manifested and be active in a variety of ways: in that we love one another; that we experience, practice and pursue community with one another; that we are obligated to give ourselves willingly and joyfully to be of benefit and blessing to one another; that we share one faith, have one calling, are of one soul and one mind; have one God and Father, are filled with one Spirit, are baptized with one baptism, eat of one bread and drink of one cup, confess one name, are obedient to one Lord, work for one cause, and share one hope; together come to know the height and the breadth and the depth of the love of Christ; together are built up to the stature of Christ, to the new humanity; together know and bear one another's burdens, thereby fulfilling the law of Christ that we need one another and upbuild one another, admonishing and comforting one another; that we suffer with one another for the sake of righteousness; pray together; together serve God in this world; and together fight against all which may threaten or hinder this unity (Phil. 2:1–5; 1 Cor. 12:4–31; John 13:1–17; 1 Cor. 1:10–13; Eph. 4:1–6; Eph. 3:14–20; 1 Cor. 10:16–17; 1 Cor. 11:17–34; Gal. 6:2; 2 Cor. 1:3–4);

- that this unity can be established only in freedom and not under constraint; that the variety of spiritual gifts, opportunities, backgrounds, convictions, as well as the various languages and cultures, are by virtue of the reconciliation in Christ, opportunities for mutual service and enrichment within the one visible people of God (Rom. 12:3–8; 1 Cor. 12:1–11; Eph. 4:7–13; Gal. 3:27–28; James 2:1–13);
- that true faith in Jesus Christ is the only condition for membership of this church.

Therefore, we reject any doctrine

- which absolutizes either natural diversity or the sinful separation of people in such a way that this absolutization hinders or breaks the visible and active unity of the church, or even leads to the establishment of a separate church formation;
- which professes that this spiritual unity is truly being maintained in the bond of peace while believers of the same confession are in effect alienated from one another for the sake of diversity and in despair of reconciliation;
- which denies that a refusal earnestly to pursue this visible unity as a priceless gift is sin;
- which explicitly or implicitly maintains that descent or any other human or social factor should be a consideration in determining membership of the church.

3. We believe

- that God has entrusted the church with the message of reconciliation in and through Jesus Christ, that the church is called to be the salt of the earth and the light of the world, that the church is called blessed because it is a peacemaker, that the church is witness both by word and by deed to the new heaven and the new earth in which righteousness dwells (2 Cor. 5:17–21; Matt. 5:9; Matt. 5:13–16; 2 Pet. 3:13; Rev. 21–22);
- that God's lifegiving Word and Spirit has conquered the powers of sin and death, and therefore also of irreconciliation and hatred, bitterness and enmity, that God's lifegiving Word and Spirit will enable the church to live in a new obedience which

can open new possibilities of life for society and the world (Eph. 4:17–6:23; Rom. 6; Col. 1:9–14; Col. 2:13–19; Col. 3:1–4:6);

- that the credibility of this message is seriously affected and its beneficial work obstructed when it is proclaimed in a land which professes to be Christian, but in which the enforced separation of people on a racial basis promotes and perpetuates alienation, hatred and enmity;

- that any teaching which attempts to legitimate such forced separation by appeal to the gospel, and is not prepared to venture on the road of obedience and reconciliation, but rather, out of prejudice, fear, selfishness and unbelief, denies in advance the reconciling power of the gospel, must be considered ideology and false doctrine.

Therefore, we reject any doctrine

- which, in such a situation, sanctions in the name of the gospel or of the will of God the forced separation of people on the grounds of race and color and thereby in advance obstructs and weakens the ministry and experience of reconciliation in Christ.

4. We believe

- that God has revealed himself as the one who wishes to bring about justice and true peace among people;
- that God, in a world full of injustice and enmity, is in a special way the God of the destitute, the poor and the wronged;
- that God calls the church to follow him in this, for God brings justice to the oppressed and gives bread to the hungry;
- that God frees the prisoner and restores sight to the blind;
- that God supports the downtrodden, protects the stranger, helps orphans and widows and blocks the path of the ungodly;
- that for God pure and undefiled religion is to visit the orphans and the widows in their suffering;
- that God wishes to teach the church to do what is good and to seek the right (Deut. 32:4; Luke 2:14; John 14:27; Eph. 2:14; Isa. 1:16–17; James 1:27; 5:1–6; Luke 1:46–55; 6:20–26; 7:22; 16:19–31; Ps. 146; Luke 4:16–19; Rom. 6:13–18; Amos 5);

- that the church must therefore stand by people in any form of suffering and need, which implies, among other things, that the church must witness against and strive against any form of injustice, so that justice may roll down like waters, and righteousness like an ever-flowing stream;
- that the church as the possession of God must stand where the Lord stands, namely against injustice and with the wronged; that in following Christ the church must witness against all the powerful and privileged who selfishly seek their own interests and thus control and harm others.

Therefore, we reject any ideology

- which would legitimate forms of injustice and any doctrine which is unwilling to resist such an ideology in the name of the gospel.

5. **We believe** that, in obedience to Jesus Christ, its only head, the church is called to confess and to do all these things, even though the authorities and human laws might forbid them and punishment and suffering be the consequence (Eph. 4:15–16; Acts 5:29–33; 1 Pet. 2:18–25; 3:15–18).

Jesus is Lord.

To the one and only God, Father, Son and Holy Spirit, be the honor and the glory for ever and ever.

5

Ministry in Union with Christ

*A Constructive Critique
of Incarnational Ministry*

I begin with a brief autobiographical snapshot. As a student in a Christian college classroom, I am told that, just as God became flesh in a particular culture two thousand years ago, it is my job in relating to another culture to become "incarnate" in that culture. I receive training in cultural anthropology to help make this "incarnation" possible. Eight months later in Uganda, while learning the local language and culture, I wonder: is it really possible for me to become incarnate in another culture? I have no doubt that I am called to be a learner of this new culture and a servant through the witness of my life. But is the eternal Word's act of becoming incarnate really an appropriate model for ministry? Will the Ugandans necessarily "see Jesus" as a result of my efforts at cultural identification? Or am I assuming in this model that my own presence rather than that of Christ is redemptive?

My questions multiplied as I later continued my theological education. When I mentioned the notion that Christians are to "become incarnate" as the Word became incarnate, biblical scholars and systematic theologians told me that the New Testament and orthodox Christian theology taught no such thing. Going back to my professors of missiology and ministry, the response I heard was quite practical: if not the incarnation, what is the alternative model for culture-crossing ministries? This chapter shows how a theology of union with Christ can bridge this broken conversation between biblical studies, theology, and ministry, opening up new possibilities for a dynamic theology of ministry.

Here is my thesis: While certain aspects of "incarnational ministry" are commendable, this chapter critiques its basic assumption: that the incarnation is a model for ministry such that Christians should imitate the act of the eternal Word becoming incarnate. To the contrary, at the center of the Christian gospel is a claim that the incarnation of the Word in the person of Jesus Christ is a unique and unrepeatable event. As such, the incarnation is not an "ongoing process" to be repeated or a "model" to be copied in Christian ministry. Instead, the incarnation should set our focus directly upon Jesus Christ, the servant, to whom Christians have been united. Moreover, the ministry outcomes sought by "incarnational ministry" can be realized and refined through seeing that the imperative to have "the same mind" as "Christ Jesus" (Phil. 2:5) fits within Paul's matrix of union with Christ. As ones united to Christ, we participate in the Spirit's ongoing work of bearing witness to Christ and creating a new humanity in which the dividing walls between cultures are overcome in Christ. Thus, today's church should replace its talk of "incarnational ministry" with the more biblically faithful and theologically dynamic language of ministry as participation in Christ.

While we need to move on from the relatively recent practice of speaking of "incarnational ministry," I am not seeking to devalue the many significant ministries that have been associated with this motto. In youth ministry circles, talk of incarnational ministry has often been used to transition from a program-driven ministry to one that takes relationships of discipleship very seriously. In urban ministry, leaders such as John Perkins have used incarnational ministry as a justification for relocation into needy urban neighborhoods, thus countering the tendency of suburban flight from poor neighborhoods. In missiology textbooks, an incarnational ministry approach is used to justify an "inculturation" model of ministry, where the goal is to overcome the cultural isolation of missionaries in affluent compounds and point instead to a way of valuing the receiving culture. In missional church circles, the notion of incarnational ministry is often used to speak about how the church is sent into the world in ministry rather than simply being inward-focused and engaging in navel-gazing. Indeed, these are all excellent instincts for faithful ministry.

In addition, I should admit that key points in my own life of ministry were shaped or influenced by an incarnational ministry paradigm. The time I spent doing development work in Uganda and working in urban ministry in the United States was especially formative. The incarnational ministry model challenged me to take my own identification with the culture very seriously—including how I lived, the language I spoke, and the relationships I formed. There is something extremely appealing about this relatively new way of conceiving of ministry—as imitating the act of incarnation, in which God came close to us in Christ.

Nevertheless, the power of the parallel between the incarnation and ministry has also led to practical and theological problems. On a practical level, the problems have been recorded in missiological journals for years. Missionaries can find it impossible, practically speaking, to become "one" with the people they are ministering to. Indeed, the goal itself can easily seem to be an illusion. One cross-cultural missionary shares an example: "I recently talked to a couple who were trying to identify with the people and assume an insider role. They lived on the level of the villagers, even though this brought discomfort, stress, and health problems. They tried to convince the villagers that they were not rich; they just wanted to be one with them. However, their [incarnational] model crashed when their newborn became ill and they rushed him home to the States for treatment. No villagers would have had that option."[1] For some, the harder they try to identify with those they minister to, the more they realize they cannot become one with them as the Word became one with humanity. And they begin to question whether their identification with the culture should be an end in itself—as if their own presence (rather than the presence of Christ) was redemptive. Indeed, as we will explore further below, the tendency of practitioners of incarnational ministry to see their own presence as inherently redemptive is one of the fatal flaws that penetrates many forms of incarnational ministry. This kind of thinking can easily slip into individualistic attempts to "make Christ incarnate" in the world as opposed to participating in a worshiping community that is empowered for

---

1. Harriet Hill, "Incarnational Ministry: A Critical Examination," *Evangelical Missions Quarterly* (April 1990): 198.

service in the world through its encounter with the living Christ in word and sacrament.

Yet in the wide-ranging literature on the subject, I agree with many claims made as part of incarnational ministry. Many of them are biblically rooted and theologically and pastorally insightful. But here is the catch: although "incarnational ministry" is used as a convenient shorthand for these approaches, I don't think that imitating the eternal Word's act of becoming incarnate is a necessary assumption for these insights. For the sake of convenience, in the first section below ("A Typology of Incarnational Ministry"), I develop a broad typology[2] of senses for "incarnational ministry." After this survey, in the next section I address the key question: what should be imitated in Philippians 2:1–11? In the third section ("A Theology of Ministry in Union with Christ the Servant"), I explore the ministry insights that emerge from Christians being united to Christ the servant, the incarnate one who reveals God's love, even though the act of becoming incarnate is not to be imitated. This section will reframe, refine, and enhance certain insights from the incarnational ministry discussion. In the chapter's final section ("Participation Ministry as a Constructive Alternative to Incarnational Ministry"), I expound a constructive proposal for how ministry in union with Christ, or "participation ministry," addresses the shortcomings of incarnational ministry and offers a compelling alternative theology of ministry.

A Typology of Incarnational Ministry

Youth Ministry

In youth ministry circles, "incarnational ministry" has become shorthand for affirming that faith needs to become embodied and "incarnate" in acts of love and service. As Kenda Creasy Dean has summarized, it has come to mean that "just as God came alongside us in the person of Jesus Christ, we best represent Christ with young

2. As David J. Hesselgrave notes, incarnational ministry is "seldom carefully spelled out or defined." Thus I seek to highlight some different strands of thought in this typology. Since the language of incarnational ministry has become so widespread in ministry circles, "*its very fuzziness makes careful examination all the more important.*" Hesselgrave, *Paradigms in Conflict: Ten Key Questions in Christian Missions Today* (Grand Rapids: Kregel, 2005), 144–45, emphasis in original.

people by coming alongside them as envoys of his unconditional love."[3] Yet even this simple understanding of incarnational ministry is subject to abuse. As Dean warns in *Starting Right: Thinking Theologically about Youth Ministry*, "the term *incarnational ministry* has been abused by youth ministers who interpret it to mean that they are the incarnate ones. These leaders say to youth, in effect, 'Follow me because I follow Jesus.'"[4] Dean sees how this approach is individualistic in focusing on the youth leader, as well as how it fails to point to Jesus Christ. What should youth leaders think instead? "True incarnational ministry, however, is never about 'following me.' It is always about following Jesus Christ, the true Incarnation of God. We do better to say that we point to the true Christ, as witnesses (as Karl Barth suggested)."[5]

This is a point at which I agree with Dean's evaluation, though I'm sympathetic to the youth ministers who think that the point of incarnational ministry is that they become "incarnate" in youth culture. Indeed, a later essay in the same volume recommends precisely that task as the meaning of "incarnational ministry."[6] Yet, if true incarnational ministry is about bearing witness to the true Christ, why should we call this act of witness "incarnational ministry," as Dean does? Karl Barth, whom Dean refers to, certainly never used this term. As we will explore below, Barth's emphatic language of "witness" means that our own action is not to be confused with the action of the living Christ. For Barth, the church is indeed a sent community, a missionary community, but it exists to point beyond itself to Jesus Christ.

Others in youth ministry circles say that "the substance of incarnational ministry is the valuing of contact between adults and young people in the everyday and ordinary things of life. Friendship and relationship will not only be the means of ministry; they will be the ministry itself."[7] While this is a valuable point—namely, the move from

3. Kenda Creasy Dean, *Almost Christian: What the Faith of Our Teenagers Is Telling the American Church* (New York: Oxford University Press), 93.

4. Kenda Creasy Dean, "Fessing Up: Owning Our Theological Commitments," in *Starting Right: Thinking Theologically about Youth Ministry*, ed. Kenda Creasy Dean, Chap Clark, and Dave Rahn (Grand Rapids: Zondervan/Youth Specialties, 2001), 234.

5. Ibid.

6. See Steve Gerali, "Seeing Clearly: Community Context," in Dean, Clark, and Rahn, *Starting Right*, 285–95, esp. 295.

7. Pete Ward, *God at the Mall: Youth Ministry That Meets Kids Where They're At* (Peabody, MA: Hendrickson, 1999), 38.

a program-driven view of ministry to a relational alternative—it's not clear why this move should be grounded in imitating the unique act of the incarnation. Perhaps it is a way to counter the gnosticism about bodies and everyday life; but the New Testament and the historic church have countered various forms of gnosticism before without needing to make the incarnation a model for ministry.

In sum, when an incarnational ministry model is appealed to in youth ministry circles, it is often used either to advocate norms that do not emerge from the analogy of imitating the incarnation or, when the analogy of imitating the incarnation is in fact used, the results are often problematic: practices that are youth leader–centered rather than Christ-centered. While I can heartily affirm that youth ministry should entail embodied, relational ministry that bears witness to Christ, I need to deny that youth ministry should imitate God's act of becoming incarnate.

Missional Church

One finds a similar state of affairs in missional church circles when it comes to talk about "incarnational ministry." Valid biblical and theological points are made with regard to ministry. Yet most of the points do not actually follow from the use of the incarnation as a model for ministry, as is often claimed. Nevertheless, in a problematic way, some points do rely on the idea that the incarnation is an act to be imitated and repeated in our ministries.

Alan Hirsch in *The Forgotten Ways* provides an example of a popular appropriation of incarnational ministry language within a missional framework. After speaking of God's work through the incarnate Christ, Hirsch claims that "the Incarnation not only qualifies God's acts in the world, but must also qualify ours. If God's central way of reaching his world was to incarnate himself in Jesus, then our way of reaching the world should be likewise *incarnational*."[8] In light of this, Hirsch reads Paul's missionary strategy of becoming "all things to all people" (1 Cor. 9:22) as "incarnational," even though Paul makes no reference to the incarnation as an activity to be imitated in the passage.

As Hirsch unfolds four implications of incarnational ministry—presence, proximity, powerlessness, and proclamation—strangely

8. Alan Hirsch, *The Forgotten Ways: Reactivating the Missional Church* (Grand Rapids: Brazos, 2006), 133, emphasis in original.

enough, only one of the four directly relates to the incarnation. In his discussion of presence, Hirsh says, "The fact that God was in the Nazarene neighborhood for thirty years and no one noticed should be profoundly disturbing to our normal ways of engaging mission." Why? Because it means that while there is a time for "'in-your-face' approaches to mission, . . . there is also a time to simply become part of the very fabric of a community and to engage in the humanity of it all."[9] Hirsch's language is peculiar in some ways—for example, speaking of "God" rather than the "God-man" in Nazareth, such that Christ's humanity becomes instrumental mainly as part of a missionary strategy that we should copy. Yet his main point is a simple one that one needs nothing more than 1 Corinthians 9 to affirm: identifying with a recipient culture is an important missionary strategy.

Hirsch's other three points on incarnational ministry simply relate to the earthly life of Christ: proximity, which has to do with the fact that "Jesus mixed with people of every level of society"; powerlessness, which is Hirsch's word for "servanthood and humility in our relationships with each other and the world"; and proclamation, which is "always [being] willing to share the gospel story."[10] In reflecting on these latter three points, there is no necessary connection between these and the notion of imitating God's act of becoming incarnate. All three are aspects of the ministry of Jesus Christ, the God-human, not the preincarnate Christ; they are imperatives of the New Testament for Christian witness that, as we will explore further in later sections, can be properly rooted in the Christian's union with Christ the servant.

Thus, while Hirsch gives specific practical imperatives for incarnational ministry that do have biblical support, these do not require (or even suggest) Hirsch's overarching claim that we should imitate God's act of becoming incarnate, so that "our way of reaching the world should be likewise *incarnational*."[11] Indeed, as we will see below, the New Testament contains no such teaching.

But there is also a more subtle point at stake in common missional church discussions of the incarnation. As Hirsch hints at, the incarnation is "revelation," thus "the basic motive of incarnational ministry is also *revelatory*—that they may come to know God through Jesus."[12]

9. Ibid.
10. Ibid., 134.
11. Ibid., 133, emphasis in original.
12. Ibid., 132–33.

Darrell Guder gives insight into this sense in his rationale for using the language of "incarnational." "The plot of God's salvation history cannot be reduced merely to propositions about God. Rather, the story reveals both what God intends and how God wants his saving purposes accomplished. One way of talking about this essential coherence and congruence of the message and its communication is to describe God's action as incarnational. By making an adjective out of the noun *incarnation*, we are attempting, theologically, to express this essential congruence of message and its communication of what and how."[13] To summarize Guder's overall point, while certain streams of modernity have tended to reduce the gospel to propositions to be communicated, Guder points out that the Christian message proclaims that God's Word is first and foremost a person: Jesus Christ. God has chosen to communicate his message by means of a person and by means of a community, the church.

Guder's point is a good one, but it is an insight that is *a consequence* of the incarnation, not one that arises from making the incarnation a *model* for ministry. In fact, such insights can be lost when one makes the incarnation a model for ministry. Here is another way to state the insight: In the work of Lesslie Newbigin, whose thought is foundational for the missional church movement, "there can never be a culture-free gospel." Yet, while the gospel will always be "embodied in culturally conditioned forms, [it] calls into question all cultures."[14] Indeed, as the gospel encounters culture, "it will involve contradiction [of the culture], and call for conversion." This involves a conversion that "is the proper end toward which the communication of the gospel looks" and "can only be a work of God, a kind of miracle."[15] Indeed, this "conversion" is the Spirit's work, not simply a human work. In my own work on revelation, I draw upon Newbigin, along with Andrew Walls and Lamin Sanneh, in speaking about how the Spirit both "indigenizes" the gospel and calls all cultures to transformation through it.[16] The cultural concreteness with which the gospel is translated into various cultural environments could be said to be

13. Darrell Guder, *The Incarnation and the Church's Witness* (Harrisburg, PA: Trinity Press International, 1999), 4.

14. Lesslie Newbigin, *Foolishness to the Greeks: The Gospel and Western Culture* (Grand Rapids: Eerdmans, 1986), 4.

15. Ibid., 6.

16. See J. Todd Billings, *The Word of God for the People of God: An Entryway to the Theological Interpretation of Scripture* (Grand Rapids: Eerdmans, 2010), 105–48.

incarnational in the sense that it mirrors and dimly reflects the action of God through the incarnation of Christ.

Yet in this process of the gospel encountering culture, the incarnation is simply not a model for ministry that we should follow. Consider what happens when we take the incarnation as a model: I, as a Westerner, think that the gospel needs to be "incarnated" into Ugandan culture when I live as a Christian witness. Thus, if the incarnation is a model, I start with my own Western, culturally formed view of the gospel and seek to "incarnate" it or translate my view of the gospel into Ugandan culture. In the process of this analogy, my Western view of the gospel is elevated to be parallel to the divine Word, which is then "contextualized" for a Ugandan culture. This approach takes what Newbigin calls a "miracle" and turns it into a human act, under human control. Authors such as Guder are very careful to avoid such a view of the "translation" of the gospel.[17] With Barth, Guder finds it problematic to think of the church as a "continuing incarnation"; he agrees that we are not equivalent to Jesus Christ but rather that we are "subordinate" to Christ, bearing witness to Christ.[18] Though his book *The Incarnation and the Church's Witness* includes a defense of the adjectival use of the word "incarnational" for the church's mission, he also lists numerous cases in which using the word "incarnational" can be harmful and misleading.[19] While Guder presents rich insights in his missional theology of the church, in the end he would be better off avoiding the term "incarnational" in reference to the church's action. Why? Because what Guder is speaking about is a revelational *consequence* of the incarnation for the church's life, rather than the action of the church itself being "incarnational," in either imitating or continuing the unique incarnation of Jesus Christ.

Finally, we should make sure that one more important insight from the missional church is retained, even though it is sometimes framed as a feature of incarnational ministry: namely, that the church is sent as a community into the world in mission.[20] The key scriptural source

17. Darrell Guder, *The Continuing Conversion of the Church* (Grand Rapids: Eerdmans, 2000), chap. 5.

18. Guder, *The Incarnation and the Church's Witness*, 15–16.

19. Ibid., 11–19.

20. For an overview of the literature on this point, see Craig Ott and Stephen J. Strauss, *Encountering Theology of Mission: Biblical Foundations, Historical Developments, and Contemporary Issues*, with Timothy C. Tennent (Grand Rapids: Baker Academic, 2010), 97–104, esp. 102–3.

for this is the notion of "sending" in John's Gospel: "As the Father has sent me, so I send you" (John 20:21; cf. John 17:18). The significance of being sent into the world is noteworthy both in John's Gospel and for today's church. But it is a profound mistake to assume that John's Gospel makes the act of becoming incarnate a model for ministry. In John's Gospel, the uniqueness and unrepeatable character of the incarnation is a significant theme (see 1:14, 18; 3:14, 18). As Andreas Köstenberger points out, the use of terms such as "'coming into the world,' or 'descending' or 'ascending' is in the Fourth Gospel reserved for Jesus."[21] Thus, the way in which we are sent as the Son is sent is "not the way in which Jesus came into the world (i.e. the incarnation), but *the nature of Jesus' relationship with his sender* (i.e. one of obedience and utter dependence)."[22] Missional literature rightly points to this sending into the world, but the theme of sending in John provides no grounds for imitating the act of becoming incarnate. Instead, as the section "Participation Ministry as a Constructive Alternative to Incarnational Ministry" explores below, the Johannine theme of sending actually relates to union with Christ and to the way that those who belong to Christ bear witness to him. In sum, I affirm with the missional church literature on incarnational ministry that the church is sent as a community into the world to reflect the servanthood of Christ in our witness, and I affirm that we are to participate in *the Spirit's* work of indigenizing the gospel in different cultural contexts; but I deny that Christians are called to imitate the divine act of becoming incarnate.

Cross-Cultural Mission

Finally, we examine one of the most common examples of an incarnational approach, one that clearly takes the incarnation as a model for cross-cultural ministry. On a practical level, the incarnational analogy has been used to justify a missionary approach that moves missionaries from their isolated missionary compounds to a more relational position that takes the receiving culture very seriously. While there has certainly been a need for such a movement, it is curious

21. Andreas Köstenberger, *The Missions of Jesus and the Disciples according to the Fourth Gospel: With Implications for the Fourth Gospel's Purpose and Mission of the Contemporary Church* (Grand Rapids: Eerdmans, 1998), 216.
22. Ibid., 217, emphasis in original.

that the movement did not follow what would seem to be a much more direct precedent from 1 Corinthians 9, where Paul writes, "I have become all things to all people, that I might by all means save some" (v. 22). Rather than starting with this passage, which speaks quite directly about Paul's missionary strategy, many modern missiologists have looked to Philippians 2 for an incarnational model and then interpreted passages like 1 Corinthians 9 as examples of incarnational ministry.

In his widely used textbook *Ministering Cross-Culturally: An Incarnational Model for Personal Relationships*, Sherwood Lingenfelter argues that the incarnation has profound consequences for cross-cultural ministry. Specifically, the very act of incarnation—the Word becoming flesh—is set forth as an "example" for mission today.[23] Jesus came into the world as a "learner," needing to learn about Jewish language and culture. Like a careful anthropologist, he studied the culture of his people for thirty years before he began his ministry. Then, setting an example as a missionary, "he identified totally with those to whom he was sent," participating in their culture and lifestyle.[24] At the end of his book, Lingenfelter outlines a series of steps for missionaries to undergo in their own "incarnation process."[25] Key to Lingenfelter's rationale is his interpretation of Philippians 2:5–11. In his rendering, although Jesus Christ was "in very nature God," he identified with humanity and human culture, "taking the very nature of a servant, being made in human likeness" (Phil. 2:6–7 NIV). In fact, Jesus completely identified not only with humanity but with Jewish culture in particular. Thus Lingenfelter sees the incarnation as the model for incarnational ministry, for Jesus was "a 200 percent person"—"he was

23. Sherwood G. Lingenfelter and Marvin K. Mayers, *Ministering Cross-Culturally: An Incarnational Model for Personal Relationships*, 2nd ed. (Grand Rapids: Baker Academic, 2003), 16. Lingenfelter also uses the analogy in his book, coauthored with Judith Lingenfelter, *Teaching Cross-Culturally: An Incarnational Model for Teaching and Learning* (Grand Rapids: Baker Academic, 2003). While I focus on this widely used (and generally helpful) textbook as an example, there are similar claims made in many other sources, including other common textbooks, such as Paul Hiebert and Eloise Hiebert Meneses, *Incarnational Ministry: Planting Churches in Band, Tribal, Peasant, and Urban Societies* (Grand Rapids: Baker, 1995), chap. 10; and Ott and Strauss, *Encountering Theology of Mission*, 97–104. The Ott and Strauss volume not only summarizes approaches like the one described above but also contains some helpful qualifications about the limits of the notion of incarnational ministry.

24. Lingenfelter, *Ministering Cross-Culturally*, 17.

25. Ibid., 119–22.

100 percent God and 100 percent Jew."[26] Lingenfelter goes on to make an incarnational analogy with the work of missionaries, who should seek to become incarnate in another culture as Jesus became incarnate in history.[27] Indeed, Lingenfelter's account (along with other recent missiological accounts)[28] portrays Jesus as the model missionary-anthropologist who learns the language, participates in the culture, and embraces his cultural surroundings.[29] Thus missionaries should seek to be 150 percent persons, becoming less like persons of their own culture and more like persons of the culture they seek to minister to (so 75 percent of each culture).[30]

As I have noted, Lingenfelter has legitimate and pressing missiological concerns that underlie his use of the incarnational analogy. He has seen the tendency of Western missionaries to retreat to their safe missionary compounds rather than approach the receiving culture with humility and respect. He has seen how this action of distance rather than humble engagement distorts the message that Christian missionaries try to communicate. Yet his close analogy between the incarnation and cross-cultural ministry leads to intractable problems and depends on a questionable interpretation of Philippians 2 and a reduction of Christology to a problem of math. (How exactly is a "200 percent person" one person rather than "two sons," as the ancient heresy of Nestorianism claims?)[31]

For our present purposes, I will focus on a set of doctrinal observations and then on a concrete problem in practice. Lingenfelter's portrait of the incarnation tends to conflate the unique incarnation with our own process of learning about another culture. The deity of the Son is seen as a "culture," and humanity is seen as a second "culture" taken on in the incarnation.[32] In this paradigm, Jesus, as the pioneer of our faith, shows us how to take on a second culture as well. "If we are to follow the example of Christ, we must aim

26. Ibid., 17.

27. Ibid., 24–25.

28. See Darrell L. Whiteman, "Anthropology and Mission: The Incarnational Connection," *Missiology* 31, no. 4 (October 2003): 397–415, esp. 407–9.

29. Lingenfelter, *Ministering Cross-Culturally*, 16–17.

30. Ibid., 24–25.

31. For further analysis of the biblical and christological issues raised in proposals such as Lingenfelter's, see my article "'Incarnational Ministry': A Christological Evaluation and Proposal," *Missiology: An International Review* 32, no. 2 (April 2004): 187–201.

32. See Lingenfelter, *Ministering Cross-Culturally*, 17, 24–25.

at incarnation!" Lingenfelter writes.[33] But there are two doctrinal problems here: one with the analogy to Christ's humanity, the other with the analogy to Christ's deity. In his humanity, Jesus was not, in fact, the model anthropologist as portrayed by Lingenfelter. This would mean that Jesus was a "participant observer" in Jewish culture, going home each evening to make "field notes" on his cultural activity of the day. But ironically, this would make Jesus less than fully Jewish and less than fully human. A second problem is that the divine nature is not a "culture," and we cannot (and should not) see ourselves as analogous to the preincarnate Word that then takes on humanity. The deity of the Word won't fit into the box of "culture" because God is not a creature—and culture is a characteristic of creaturely existence. Instead, God is the transcendent and mysterious creator of the universe. The truth of the incarnation is that in the eternal Word, this same transcendent God takes on the flesh of human beings for the sake of our salvation.

This doctrinal conflation can lead to a significant concrete problem in practice: it can conflate the mission of Jesus with our own mission. While Lingenfelter certainly would not want to promote a messiah complex among missionaries, the close analogy between the incarnation as a culture-crossing action and our own culture-crossing action makes this a constant issue. I recall times when missionaries who had been schooled in incarnational ministry told me they were "cheating" from the model if they gave something away to persons in need or if they presented any ideas that were not already inherent in the culture of reception. While this may not sound like a "messianic" tendency, in its own way it was since behind this sense of cheating is the assumption that our identification with the culture is enough—this identification is our mission, and presumably, it is, in a mysterious way, redemptive. The necessity of the unique incarnation of the Word in Jesus Christ becomes displaced in this model by the apparent necessity of our own incarnation. While I agree that missionaries should seek to identify with and value the receiving culture, we need to be clear that our identification with that culture is not inherently redemptive. We should identify with the culture so that our words and lives offer a witness to the one redeemer of peoples from all cultures, Jesus Christ.

Instead of seeing the incarnation as a process we undergo, we should seek to be very clear about a central doctrinal point: the power

33. Ibid., 25.

of the incarnation is precisely in its uniqueness—that Jesus Christ
is God's incarnate one, and no other. Apart from the incarnation,
Christ's obedient life, death, resurrection, and ascension would be of
no use to us. Because of the incarnation, we know that it is none other
than *God* who has sought us out, cleansed us from our sins, and given
us new life by the Spirit. Since Christ is the Word incarnate and no
other, we know and have fellowship with God *in Christ*. If God and
humanity were not united in Jesus Christ, then being in Christ would
not be a locus of our communion with God. In terms of advocating
incarnational ministry for cross-cultural mission, there are aspects of
the incarnational ministry discussion that can be affirmed, such as the
need for self-sacrificial work in culture-learning and identifying with
the other culture as one seeks to "become all things to all people" for
the sake of the gospel (1 Cor. 9:19–23). Yet for both doctrinal and
practical reasons, the central claim that missionaries should imitate
God's act of becoming incarnate needs to be denied.

But advocates of incarnational ministry may ask, what about Philippians 2:5–8, as interpreted above? Doesn't this passage present the
incarnation as a model for our ministries to imitate? To its exegesis
we now turn.

What Should Be Imitated in Philippians 2:1–11?

We should keep in mind that Philippians 2:5–8 is a very difficult passage about which there is much disagreement in interpretation.[34] But
the fact that it is a difficult text doesn't mean that all interpretations
are equally valid or that interpreters disagree on all points of interpreting the passage. In focusing on Philippians 2:5–8 specifically, I am
seeking not to replace the vast commentary literature on this passage
but to consider the passage particularly in light of: (1) whether the
act of becoming incarnate should be "imitated," as claimed in many

---

34. Thus, it is remarkable that the otherwise strong account of Ott and Strauss
simply quotes Phil. 2:3–8 as obvious evidence for the incarnation as a model, without noting a single secondary source or commentary. This is immediately after Ott
and Strauss note the exegetical difficulty of interpreting John's "sending" theme as
grounds for the incarnation as a model. See Ott and Strauss, *Encountering Theology
of Mission*, 103–4. For an overview of modern interpretations of Phil. 2:5–11, see
Ralph P. Martin, *A Hymn of Christ: Philippians 2:5–11 in Recent Interpretation and
in the Setting of Early Christian Worship* (Downers Grove, IL: InterVarsity, 1997).

incarnational ministry approaches; and (2) how Philippians 2 fits into the overall matrix of Paul's theology of union with Christ. Let's begin by examining what most scholars consider to be the Christ-hymn (2:5–11) in light of the preceding verses (2:1–4).

[1] If then there is any encouragement in Christ, any consolation from love, any sharing in the Spirit, any compassion and sympathy, [2] make my joy complete: be of the same mind, having the same love, being in full accord and of one mind. [3] Do nothing from selfish ambition or conceit, but in humility regard others as better than yourselves. [4] Let each of you look not to your own interests, but to the interests of others. [5] Let the same mind be in you that was [or "that you have"] in Christ Jesus,

> [6] who, though he was in the form of God,
> did not regard equality with God
> as something to be exploited,
> [7] but emptied himself,
> taking the form of a slave,
> being born in human likeness.
> And being found in human form,
> [8] he humbled himself
> and became obedient to the point of death—
> even death on a cross.

> [9] Therefore God also highly exalted him
> and gave him the name
> that is above every name,
> [10] so that at the name of Jesus
> every knee should bend,
> in heaven and on earth and under the earth,
> [11] and every tongue should confess
> that Jesus Christ is Lord,
> to the glory of God the Father. (Phil. 2:1–11)

Before we focus on the key verses used to justify incarnational ministry (vv. 5–8), note the significance of the chapter's opening verses: Paul clearly sets the context in the familiar language of union with Christ, emphasizing the ethical implications of union with Christ. Readers are encouraged to avoid "selfish ambition," to act in "humility" toward each other, displaying the unity that comes in Christ. Indeed, the repeated admonition to be of "the same mind" is a reference to living into the oneness of the new identity in Christ.

In translating and interpreting verse 5, we reach a dividing point in the scholarship on this passage. The NRSV preferred translation of verse 5 is an imperative to "let the same mind be in you that was in Christ Jesus." This fits with a school of thought known as the "ethical approach," which has been widespread in both precritical exegesis (with variations) and modern scholarship. In this broad group of approaches, the ethical context of the passage—framed in the language of union with Christ—means that Jesus Christ himself is set forth as the servant to be imitated.

The second approach is called the "kerygmatic approach" (from the Greek *kerygma*, meaning "proclamation" or "preaching") and also recognizes the prominence of union with Christ language. But while advocates of this approach can still claim that the christological hymn has some ethical significance,[35] the accent in verse 5 is somewhat different. The alternate reading in the NRSV follows the kerygmatic approach by changing a few key words in the translation: "Let the same mind be in you *that you have* in Christ Jesus," instead of *"that was* in Christ Jesus."[36] Thus, Jesus Christ, and his activity in the hymn of 2:5–11, is not directly set forth as the example for our "minds" to follow. Rather, verse 5 has the following sense in the kerygmatic approach: "Think this way in your community which you also think in your union with Christ."[37] Clearly, union with Christ is still central, and there is an ethical imperative. Yet with this kerygmatic approach, the emphasis of the Christ-hymn is on making a doxological statement to worship Christ rather than setting Christ himself as a direct example for Christians to follow. With this approach, "Paul does not use the hymn to set forth a series of steps to follow in the imitation of Christ," yet the Christ-hymn, which sets forth the gospel message, still calls readers to "humble Christian service."[38] In this approach, while "the narration of the unique events of the Incarnation, crucifixion, exaltation, and universal worship of Christ does not provide a step-by-step pattern to be imitated," qualities like the humility and obedience of Christ can still be set forth as "precedent" in calling Christians to imitate "the self-humbling obedience of Christ."[39]

---

35. See, for example, Walter Hansen, *The Letter to the Philippians* (Grand Rapids: Eerdmans, 2009), 121–22.
36. Emphasis added.
37. Hansen, *Letter to the Philippians*, 121.
38. Ibid.
39. Ibid., 155–56.

One argument of the kerygmatic school has particular relevance for the incarnational ministry discussion. It notes that if one reads the entire hymn—from incarnation to glorification—as presenting a model to be imitated, then Christians should somehow imitate Christ's exaltation in 2:9–11. Curiously, advocates of incarnational ministry quite uniformly omit these last three verses of the Christ-hymn, presumably because of the difficulty of such an idea. Yet if one is to exclude the exaltation from imitation, it is unclear why one would not exclude another unique act in the Christ-hymn—the divine act of becoming incarnate.

At this point, for our purposes we should make a few observations. First, both major strands of interpretation have an ethical dimension, and both make a prominent place for Paul's theology of union with Christ as a key to understanding the significance of 2:5–11 in Paul's letter to the Philippians. Second, the Christian activity of imitating the incarnation is categorically counted out by the kerygmatic approach. The incarnation is mentioned as part of this early Christian summary of the kerygma, but there is no direct or indirect sense in which the act of becoming incarnate is commended as a model for ministry. Thus, for those who follow the kerygmatic view, the use of Philippians 2 to justify the incarnational ministry analogy is not only suspect, but categorically mistaken.

We should also briefly note a third trajectory of interpretation advocated by scholars such as James Dunn—briefly, not because its conclusions are mistaken but because its implications for incarnational ministry are very clear. Some scholars understand the hymn to be portraying Christ as the new Adam, living in an obedient way in contrast to the first. For Dunn, being "in the form of God" does not refer to the preexistent Christ but is a way to speak of Christ, like Adam, as being in the "image of God."[40] Thus, the entire Christ-hymn speaks about how Jesus lived his life and makes no reference to the incarnation. While scholars debate the plausibility of this interpretation,[41] its implications for seeing the incarnation as something to be imitated

40. See James Dunn, *Christology in the Making: A New Testament Inquiry into the Origins of the Doctrine of the Incarnation* (Grand Rapids: Eerdmans, 1996), 119–20. For a similar account, see Colin Brown, "Ernst Lohmeyer's *Kyrios Jesus*," in *Where Christology Began*, ed. Ralph P. Martin and Brian J. Dodd (Louisville: Westminster John Knox, 1998), 27–28.

41. For a circumspect recent assessment, see Hansen, *Letter to the Philippians*, 139–42.

are obvious: if Philippians 2:5–11 does not even include a reference to the incarnation, then it is impossible for the passage to call Christians to emulate the act of becoming incarnate.

Returning, then, to the so-called ethical approach to Philippians 2:5–11, does this approach involve affirming that Christ's act of becoming incarnate is a model for ministry? Whether one looks to contemporary critical commentators or to historic interpretive approaches in the church fathers or the Reformation, the overall answer appears to be no.[42] Let's explore why, starting with the perspectives of recent scholars who align with this school of thought.

Peter O'Brien clearly identifies with the ethical school of thought, which he considers to be the standard scholarly interpretation from the time of the Reformation until the middle of the twentieth century.[43] O'Brien, differing from the kerygmatic interpretation, makes a direct link between the ethical emphasis of Paul's language of union with Christ in 2:1–4 and the person of Jesus presented in his humiliation in 2:5–8. "The Christ-hymn presents Jesus as the ultimate model for Christian behavior and action, the supreme example of the humble, self-sacrificing, self-giving service that Paul has just been urging the Philippians to practice in their relations toward one another (vv. 1–4)."[44] Yet even here there is no imperative to imitate the process of becoming incarnate. Other ethical interpreters such as Gordon Fee, Stephen Fowl, and Gerald Hawthorne concur, describing what should be imitated in terms of humility, self-giving for the sake of others, servanthood, and obedience. Indeed, while there are in this school of thought various translations of *kenosis* as self-emptying, these commentators emphasize how it expresses the loving nature of God to take on the form of a servant (Phil. 2:7). In a sense, we can emulate that loving nature, but we cannot and are not called to imitate the preincarnate Christ in the act of becoming incarnate. Why can't we imitate the act of becoming incarnate? In the words of Hawthorne, "it becomes a virtual impossibility to see how Christians can be said to imitate him [the preincarnate Christ]" because "he alone enjoyed

---

42. Most patristic and Reformational interpretations tend to focus on doctrinal issues in Christology, though there is usually an ethical dimension to their exegesis as well. On patristic exegesis, see *Galatians, Ephesians, Philippians*, Ancient Christian Commentary on Scripture NT 8 (Downers Grove, IL: InterVarsity, 1999), 236–54.

43. Peter O'Brien, *The Epistle to the Philippians*, New International Greek Testament Commentary (Grand Rapids: Eerdmans, 1991), 256, 262.

44. Ibid., 262.

his being in the form of the divine, just as he received the unique name 'Lord'" (cf. Phil. 2:11).[45] Thus, it is best to say that the overall passage presents the life and death of Jesus as "a pattern for Christians to follow," like numerous other New Testament passages.[46] For the "conduct of a heavenly being who does something unique cannot, in all logic, be mimicked or made the model for replication."[47] The act of incarnation is a divine act, not a human act that can be imitated.

O'Brien's account gives a further hint as to why the incarnation is not to be imitated. He argues that while "the Christ-hymn presents Jesus as the supreme example of the humble, self-sacrificing, self-giving service," it is best to speak of "'conformity' to Christ's likeness rather than an 'imitation.'"[48] This framing has the advantage of setting the Christ-hymn in a distinctly "union with Christ" context, which fits with Paul's language. Moreover, it explains why the incarnation is excluded from the "example" of Christ: Paul is using the hymn to speak about how Christians should grow in conformity to Christ the servant—who was revealed in his earthly ministry but who is still alive and active as the Head of the church. Growing in conformity to Christ does not mean growing in one's ability to imitate the preincarnate Christ or deciding to become incarnate—especially since Paul's readers are already "in Christ," the living Christ to whom the Spirit is conforming them. Christ is *alive*; thus we are incorporated into him. Certainly Philippians 2:1–11 suggests that the identity of the living, exalted Christ is revealed in his earthly ministry of taking the form of a servant. But in the New Testament and orthodox Christian theology, participating in Christ or growing in conformity to Christ simply does not mean imitating the preincarnate Christ's divine act of becoming incarnate.

Commentators associated with the ethical school come closest to seeing the incarnation in Philippians 2:6–7 as something to be emulated when they note how the extravagant love of God is revealed in the act of becoming incarnate. "Christ serves as pattern, to be sure," Gordon Fee says, "but he does so as the one who most truly expresses God's nature. . . . As God, Christ poured himself out, not seeking his

45. Gerald F. Hawthorne, *Philippians*, rev. ed., with Ralph P. Martin, Word Biblical Commentary (Dallas: Word, 2004), 105.

46. Hawthorne (ibid.) lists Rom. 15:1–7, esp. v. 5; 1 Cor. 10:31–11:1; 2 Cor. 8:6–9; 1 Thess. 1:6; and 1 Pet. 2:20–21; 3:17–18.

47. Ibid.

48. O'Brien, *Epistle to the Philippians*, 262.

own advantage."[49] Thus Christians are called to emulate the love of God, but the key point is missed if one seeks to emulate the process of incarnation. For "the Philippians—and we ourselves—are not called upon to simply 'imitate God' by what we do, but to have this very mind, the minds of Christ, developed in us."[50] It is precisely the humble, obedient, cruciform life and death of Jesus Christ that is a perfect expression of God's nature and serves as a pattern for believers. In the words of Stephen Fowl, "Self-emptying does not primarily represent a decision on the part of the preexistent Christ prior to the Incarnation" that could then be imitated by Christians; rather, "it displays something crucial about the character of God."[51] The pattern that Paul highlights as the shape of the Christian life is not the process of becoming incarnate but is the life and death of Christ, which is made God's own (reflective of God's character) through the incarnation. But to emulate the great love of God displayed in the incarnation, we can look only to the person and pattern of the incarnate Christ himself.

The account of Fee and Fowl, which says that the thing to be imitated is not the incarnation but rather the expression of God's love that is *made known* through the cruciform life and death of Christ, introduces a theme that we will develop further below by examining the thought of Barth and Calvin.[52] According to Philippians 2:5–11, the act of becoming incarnate is a unique saving action that shows God's love. But precisely because we are not the preincarnate Christ with his redeeming power, it is not a process to be imitated. Rather, it is God's utterly unique action in Jesus Christ that provides the grounds for a new life of humility and service: in Jesus Christ not only do we see a pattern to be imitated, but we also see *the pattern* of the God-human that Christians are to be conformed to by way of union with Christ—namely, the pattern of Christ's cruciform life. The

49. Gordon D. Fee, *Paul's Letter to the Philippians*, New International Commentary on the New Testament (Grand Rapids: Eerdmans, 1995), 228.

50. Ibid., 229.

51. Stephen E. Fowl, *Philippians*, Two Horizons New Testament Commentary (Grand Rapids: Eerdmans, 2005), 96.

52. In this chapter I use the term "cruciform" to express how the cross represents the culmination of Christ's life of service—his living in the way of the cross was not just something occurring at the end of his life. As Ronald Wallace says in summary of Calvin's reflection on the matter, "The life of Jesus from His infancy was marked by cross-bearing." Wallace, *Calvin's Doctrine of the Christian Life* (Grand Rapids: Eerdmans, 1959), 43.

uniqueness of the incarnation confirms that this pattern of Christ's cruciform life is not just a good idea or a way to be virtuous, but it is the very pattern appropriated by God. To live into who we are in Christ means to grow deeper into this identity of servanthood displayed in the life and death of Christ, not to see the act of becoming incarnate as a model to be copied.

Those who support the notion of incarnational ministry claim as their exegetical basis Philippians 2:5–11, using this passage as a key to seeing incarnational ministry in other New Testament passages. Yet as we have seen, their interpretation of Philippians 2:5–11 is highly dubious because it fails to see the significance in the text itself of Paul's ethical theology of union with Christ within the overall context—a theology that is portrayed in Paul's writings as entailing conformity to Christ's cruciform life and death, rather than the act of becoming incarnate. The fact that Paul does *not* ask us to imitate the unique divine act of becoming incarnate is not lost upon past interpreters in the history of the church or any major stream of critical scholarship on Philippians 2 today.

What alternative, then, is there to seeing ourselves as the ones becoming incarnate? In the next section, we explore how the genuine insights of incarnational ministry can be refined within the richer theological framework of union with Christ.

A Theology of Ministry in Union with Christ the Servant

For some Christians, the notion of the incarnation as a model for ministry has become so central that it may be difficult to imagine the shape of ministry without it. Am I suggesting that we should move toward the things that incarnational ministry stands so firmly against, such as a program-oriented approach to ministry, an ethnocentric approach to mission, or a gnostic-tending view of the Christian life? Of course not. As I noted in the first section of this chapter, incarnational ministry has made valuable and valid claims. However, in order to retain these genuine insights, it is not necessary to claim that we should imitate the divine act of becoming incarnate, as advocates of incarnational ministry have claimed. Indeed, if one is looking for an approach to ministry that is relational and embodied, willing to "relocate" to meet those in need, as well as seeking to be "all things to all people" for the sake of Jesus Christ, one simply needs to dig deeper into the reality of union with Christ, a theological reality testified to in numerous New Testament texts.

For example, instead of seeing the incarnation as a model for cross-cultural ministry—and using it as a hermeneutical key to interpret passages such as 1 Corinthians 9—the notion of union with Christ is a much more organic and fruitful lens through which to see the passage. Although it needs to be read in light of the controversial issues around Jewish dietary laws in Corinth rather than as an abstract missionary credo, 1 Corinthians 9 still provides a substantial passage that addresses missiological concerns.

> For though I am free with respect to all, I have made myself a slave to all, so that I might win more of them. To the Jews I became as a Jew, in order to win Jews. To those under the law I became as one under the law (though I myself am not under the law) so that I might win those under the law. To those outside the law I became as one outside the law (though I am not free from God's law but am under Christ's law) so that I might win those outside the law. To the weak I became weak, so that I might win the weak. I have become all things to all people, that I might by all means save some. I do it all for the sake of the gospel, so that I may share in its blessings. (vv. 19–23)

As tempting as it may be to see the language of becoming "one" with those under the law or outside the law (9:20–21) as "incarnational," there is no textual indication that Paul thinks he is imitating the eternal Son's action of becoming one with humanity. Rather, particularly in light of Paul's reference to being "under Christ's law" (9:21) even as he has solidarity with those "under the law" or "outside the law," one can see how the norm is oriented by union with Jesus Christ. Specifically, in the words of Richard Hays, Paul "is asserting that the pattern of Christ's self-sacrificial death on a cross has now become the normative pattern for his own life."[53] Thus, as we saw with Philippians 2, it is the cruciform life of Christ culminating in "the pattern of Christ's self-sacrificial death" that is the decisive pattern for Paul to follow; in the case of 1 Corinthians, following this cruciform pattern of Christ connects with Paul's willingness to have solidarity with the

---

53. Richard Hays, *First Corinthians*, Interpretation (Louisville: Westminster John Knox, 1997), 154. See also Anthony C. Thiselton, *The First Epistle to the Corinthians*, New International Greek Testament Commentary (Grand Rapids: Eerdmans, 2000), 704.

"weak" or "foolish." In his exposition of the scandal of the cross in the opening chapter, Paul writes that "God chose what is foolish in the world to shame the wise; God chose what is weak in the world to shame the strong" (1 Cor. 1:27). It is precisely because believers are "members of Christ" (1 Cor. 6:15) and united to Christ that they can share in "his sufferings by becoming like him in his death" (Phil. 3:10). Because "Jesus himself is the paradigm for such servanthood,"[54] as 1 Corinthians 9 speaks of, Paul can rightly say, "I have made myself a slave to all" (9:19).

One implication of adopting an approach favoring the notion of union with Christ the servant over that of incarnational ministry is that union with Christ puts more emphasis on the specific, concrete ministry and life of Jesus Christ. For incarnational ministry, the pattern of becoming incarnate functions as an abstract pattern—a model promoting immersion into a culture. But for Paul and for a Christian theology of union with Christ it is more concrete: precisely because God has revealed himself in the particularity and uniqueness of the obedient servant, Jesus Christ, Christians are called to reflect this humble service in ministry, as Paul does in 1 Corinthians 9:19–23.

Revealing God's Lavish Love: The Lord Who Is a Servant in Jesus Christ

Instead of just giving us the abstract "pattern" of incarnation as a model for ministry, God unites us to Jesus Christ, a servant in a concrete and particular way, who shows us the very character of God. Karl Barth develops this point with helpful thoughts on the significance of Christ the servant's cruciform life for the doctrine of God. In *Church Dogmatics* 4/1, Barth discusses the significance of the eternal Word not simply taking on human flesh in general but taking on Jewish flesh as a suffering servant who fulfills the role of covenant servant to his Father. Moreover, the "flesh" that was assumed by the Word stands in the place of sinners. "The Son of Man from heaven had to be the friend of publicans and sinners, and die between two thieves. He had to, because God was also the God who loved His enemies, who 'endured such contradiction of sinners

---

54. Gordon Fee, *The First Epistle to the Corinthians*, New International Commentary on the New Testament (Grand Rapids: Eerdmans, 1987), 426.

against himself'" (Heb. 12:3).[55] This is the particular, concrete life that God has united himself to in the incarnation, thus revealing God's lavish love. "That God as God is able and willing and ready to condescend, to humble Himself in this way is the mystery of the 'deity of Christ.'"[56] More radical than a general paradigm of someone who simply identifies with another culture in order to communicate with members of that culture, in Jesus Christ God takes on the suffering, Jewish humanity of a servant, identifying with sinners in his cruciform life and death.

For Barth, the mystery of Christ's deity shows us God's free and sacrificial love toward humanity (as Fee also emphasized in his interpretation of Phil. 2:5–8, discussed above). But note that Christ's *deity* is at issue here, something Christians do not have, even in an analogous sense. Barth insisted on this point, over and against those in his day who said that the preexistent Christ "self-emptied" aspects of his divinity (an interpretation of *kenosis* in Phil. 2:7): For "if in Christ—even in the humiliated Christ born in a manger at Bethlehem and crucified on the cross of Golgotha—God is not unchanged and wholly God, then everything that we may say about reconciliation of the world made by God in this humiliated One is left hanging in the air."[57] Precisely because "in Christ God was reconciling the world to himself" (2 Cor. 5:19), there cannot be a general pattern of incarnation that we imitate. And precisely because we follow the cruciform life of Jesus (rather than a general model of ministry as "incarnation"), we should open ourselves—and our ties to our home culture—to be transformed and changed as we seek to reach others.

The need for missionaries to be open to transformation in their cultural encounter is a major point in Lingenfelter's *Ministering Cross-Culturally*.[58] "Following the example of Christ, that of incarnation," he says, "means undergoing drastic personal and social reorientation."[59] Lingenfelter is right to speak about the reorientation and transformation needed for cross-cultural ministry. But his attempt to ground this in imitating the act of incarnation pushes in the other direction; since in the incarnation God remains God, the divine nature is not given up, modified, or transformed. For those searching for a minis-

55. CD 4/1, 172.
56. CD 4/1, 177.
57. CD 4/1, 183.
58. See esp. chap. 9.
59. Lingenfelter, *Ministering Cross-Culturally*, 117.

try model in which ethnocentric tendencies are surrendered, union with Christ the servant is not only more faithful to the gospel but is better missiology as well. As Barth says, "God is always God even in His humiliation."[60] God's identity does not need surrendering. If we want a biblical or theological analogy that transforms the subject in question, we should not use a general paradigm of incarnation as a model. Rather, we should follow the New Testament and look at our lives in light of having been united to Jesus Christ yet also as those called to "put on Christ." God is not in need of formation. But those who are in Christ *are* in the process of formation. They are on a journey, moving from the prideful, ethnocentric "old self" to the new humanity in Christ.

On the other hand, in Barth's view, affirming that God is God in his humiliation does not mean we should think of God as "far removed from any lowliness and quite alien to it."[61] No. A key aspect of the incarnation is that God has united himself to this way of lowliness displayed in Jesus Christ, "making His own both its form, the *forma servi* ["form of a servant" from Phil. 2:7], and also its cause."[62] It is none other than God who has shown his power by assuming and making his own the form of a suffering servant.

For Barth, the reality that God reveals his nature by taking the form of a servant in Jesus Christ is at the core of New Testament ethics.[63] It is *not* that Christians are continually called to imitate the act of becoming incarnate, but they are continually called to imitate—or better, to participate in the life and way of—the suffering servant, Jesus Christ. In New Testament ethics there is a "radical downward trend" toward a life of humble service and weakness.[64] When the Lord does not remove Paul's thorn in the flesh, Paul is told, "My grace is sufficient for you, for power is made perfect in weakness." So, Paul says, "I will boast all the more gladly of my weaknesses, so that the power of Christ may dwell in me" (2 Cor. 12:9). What is the context, then, for this power of Christ dwelling in Paul? Is it success in ministry or a smooth path for his life? No. It is the way of lowliness that he shares with Jesus Christ, who embodied this way. "Therefore I am content with weaknesses, insults, hardships, persecutions, and

60. *CD* 4/1, 179.
61. *CD* 4/1, 191.
62. *CD* 4/1, 187.
63. See *CD* 4/1, 188–92.
64. *CD* 4/1, 189.

calamities for the sake of Christ; for whenever I am weak, then I am strong" (2 Cor. 12:10).

According to Barth, this downward movement in New Testament ethics is not a matter of pessimism, but it has everything to do with "the way and example of Jesus Christ," which God claims as his own in the incarnation.[65] In Jesus Christ, we see that God has made his own the form of a servant. If we want to see what that form of a true servant looks like—the true covenant partner, the true human—we should look to Jesus Christ.

United to Christ the Servant: The Similarity and Difference between Christ and Those Who Belong to Christ

As explored above, our participation in Jesus Christ entails nothing less than entering into an ethic of humble service that reflects the obedient servanthood of Christ. Yet this does not mean that our own action is inherently redemptive. In a theology of union with Christ, there is a fundamental asymmetry between Christ and his people, between the Head and the body, between Christ's redemptive work on the cross and the Christian's carrying of the cross, which does not redeem others.

Both Calvin and Barth provide helpful clarifications concerning both the union with Christ and the ongoing difference between Jesus Christ and those who belong to him. Although Barth differs from Calvin and the early Reformation in certain aspects of his theology of union with Christ,[66] he repeatedly draws on Calvin and the Heidelberg Catechism in his account of the cross in the Christian life, speaking

65. CD 4/1, 190.

66. On Barth's theology of participation in Christ, see the instructive monograph by Adam Neder, *Participation in Christ: An Entry into Karl Barth's* Church Dogmatics (Louisville: Westminster John Knox, 2009). While Barth draws on both the Reformation and the church fathers in his formulation, Neder is helpful in pointing out the ways that he differs from both, particularly because of his novel account of both election and Christology, formulated in light of his actualistic ontology. In terms of participation in Christ, his actualistic ontology puts emphasis on participation in Christ being about the correspondence of the *action* of the Christian with the action of Jesus Christ. In this account, Jesus Christ's action is primary, and the Christian's action is derivative and subordinate. For an evaluation of Neder's book and a brief critical engagement with Barth's theology of union with Christ, see my review in *Theology Today* 68, no. 2 (July 2011): 195–97.

about how "Calvin was at his best in this context."[67] Barth writes that "between Christ and the Christian, His cross and ours, it is a matter of similarity in great dissimilarity."[68] On the one hand, "the special fellowship of the Christian with Christ involves participation in the passion of His cross."[69] Christians follow in the steps of Christ the humble servant, enduring suffering on behalf of their identification with Christ, particularly in the form of persecution.[70] While there is a necessary connection between Christians and the cross—particularly in the call to humble obedience and service, in self-denial (putting to death the old self)—there is also a profound difference between the two. Christians do not bear the cross on behalf of the sin of human-ity—their cross reconciles no one to God.[71] Only Christ's life and work is inherently redemptive. Moreover, "self-sought suffering has nothing whatever to do with participation in the passion of Jesus Christ, and therefore with man's sanctification."[72] Not only is suffering not an end in itself, but the cross that a Christian bears also points beyond itself. "Borne in participation in the suffering of Jesus, it will cease at the very point to which the suffering of Jesus points in the power of His resurrection, and therefore to which our suffering also points in company with His." Even in the midst of carrying our cross, there is "a foretaste of joy" in the resurrection reality opened up by the cross of Jesus Christ.[73]

For Barth, the key word that expresses this asymmetry between Christ and the Christian is "witness." For the Christian, "he and his service, his very existence, are the appointed sign of the living Word of God" through the Holy Spirit.[74] Since the risen Christ declares that "you will be my witnesses" (Acts 1:8), this identity encompasses the whole Christian life: "in all circumstances and with his whole existence he is a responsible witness of the Word of God."[75] Indeed, since the notion of witness presupposes a priority of Christ and his work over those who are in Christ, the church "can exist only as it points beyond

67. CD 4/2, 606. The overall section is part of Barth's theology of sanctification, called "The Dignity of the Cross" (598–613).
68. CD 4/2, 605.
69. CD 4/2, 604.
70. See CD 4/2, 599, 609–11.
71. CD 4/2, 600.
72. CD 4/2, 613.
73. CD 4/2, 613.
74. CD 4/3/2, 610.
75. CD 4/3/2, 609.

itself."[76] The Christian's action as witness "is wholly dependent on the truth and reality of what he attests." For "as we remember from the exemplary figure of John the Baptist, he cannot come and speak among them as a second Christ."[77] As witness, the Christian recognizes the uniqueness of God's Word in Jesus Christ and bears witness to him.

Calvin likewise holds together a theology of union with Christ the servant with the asymmetry between Christ and the Christian. For Calvin, at the center of the Christian life is the denial of ourselves, which involves bearing our cross for Christ's sake. Christians are called to follow Jesus, "whose pattern we ought to express in our life."[78] For Calvin, this is not simply a moral call but a deep issue of identity, of coming to terms with the fact that we are not our own but belong to God in Jesus Christ:

> We are not our own: let not our reason nor our will, therefore, sway our plans and deeds. We are not our own: let us therefore not set it as our goal to seek what is expedient for us according to the flesh. We are not our own: in so far as we can, let us therefore forget ourselves and all that is ours.
>
> Conversely, we are God's: let us therefore live for him and die for him. We are God's: let his wisdom and will therefore rule all our actions. We are God's: let all the parts of our life accordingly strive toward him as our only lawful goal.[79]

What identity is expressed in this life of humble self-denial and self-offering, of living for God? Its shape is that of participation in Christ, of living into our adopted identities as children of God. Expressing the pattern of Christ is connected to a new identity in Christ: "For we have been adopted as sons by the Lord with this one condition: that our life express Christ, the bond of our adoption."[80] We have been adopted, and our lives are to express Christ. The "condition" here is not something to be earned but is Calvin's way of speaking about our new life as an inseparable consequence of our new identity. As we explored in the opening chapter, salvation as adoption means that both justification and sanctification are received in Christ as gifts,

76. CD 4/2, 623.
77. CD 4/3/2, 629.
78. *Inst.* 3.6.3.
79. *Inst.* 3.7.1.
80. *Inst.* 3.6.3.

distinct yet inseparable from each other. Here, Christ's work for us necessarily leads to Christ's work in us that "express(es) Christ." In union with Christ, Calvin claims, Christ lives in the Christian—the same Jesus Christ who shows us what it means to be humble, obedient servants before God.

Drawing on Paul, Calvin asserts that Christ does indeed live within believers, but he is sensitive to the way Paul connects this with obedient living in Christ and participating in his death. As Paul says, "I have been crucified with Christ; and it is no longer I who live, but it is Christ who lives in me" (Gal. 2:19–20). Commenting on Paul's phrase that "it is Christ who lives in me," Calvin writes, "Christ lives in us in two ways. The one life consists in governing us by his Spirit, and directing all our actions; the other, in making us partakers of his righteousness; so that, while we can do nothing of ourselves, we are accepted in the sight of God."[81] By participating in Christ's righteousness, believers receive forgiveness of their sins, and as they continue to participate in Christ, the Spirit directs their lives and actions after the pattern of Christ.[82]

Thus, for Calvin, the specific, concrete cruciform pattern of the obedient life and teaching of Jesus is decisive. We do not imitate the act of becoming incarnate but are conformed to Jesus Christ, the incarnate one. Christian identity is derived from the pattern of Jesus's life: self-denial and obedient service toward God and love toward neighbor. Moreover, since believers have actually been united to Jesus Christ, the way of service is not an abstract "model" for ministry, which would make Christ an "example" to follow at a distance. According to Calvin, Paul says we have been united to Christ, "not only a conformity of example, but a secret union, by which we are joined to him."[83]

But on the other hand, Christians are "far from being equal to Christ" as they follow him. Christian action is always derivative and subordinate, even as the call to discipleship is real—"for though we do not overtake him," it is right that "we should follow his steps."[84] Precisely because Christ is the "King and High Priest" and we are not, there will be ways that Christians need to act differently than Christ even as we are called to carry our crosses in following him.[85]

81. Comm. on Gal. 2:20, CTS.
82. In his Comm. on Gal. 2:20, CTS, Calvin explicitly connects these two dimensions of "Christ who lives in me" with justification and sanctification.
83. Comm. on Rom. 6:5, CTS.
84. Comm. on 1 John 3:16, CTS.
85. Comm. on Matt. 12:21 (*Harmony of the Gospels*, vol. 3), CTS.

Building on these insights from Calvin and Barth, we now move to give a broad constructive portrait of what I will refer to as "participation ministry" (ministry flowing from our participation in Christ), which provides a compelling alternative to incarnational ministry.

Participation Ministry as a Constructive Alternative to Incarnational Ministry

United to Christ the Servant: Christian Witness to Jesus Christ in Both Word and Life

As explored in the previous section on Calvin and Barth, participation ministry maintains a clear distinction between Christ and those who belong to him in union with him. Christians are indeed united to Christ the servant by the Spirit and are called to a way of humble service in conformity to Christ. Indeed, as Calvin says, our lives should "express Christ, the bond of our adoption."[86] Yet we are not Christ, and our cross is not redemptive. Thus, rather than imitating the act of becoming incarnate as a model for ministry, Christians are called to witness to God's unique Word, Jesus Christ, in a way that reflects conformity to his life of obedient servanthood.

Union with Christ and Culture-Crossing Witness: Sent and Gathered to Share in the Spirit's Work of Creating a New Humanity in Christ

How should Christians bear witness to Christ in a way that crosses barriers, such as the barriers between radically different cultures, or between adult culture and youth culture, or between suburban culture and urban culture? Incarnational ministry has provided a strategy for seeking to transcend these barriers by the metaphor of "becoming incarnate" in the second culture. But there is a better way—that of being sent as witnesses to Christ who discover the Spirit's creation of a new humanity in Christ as one identifies with people of a different culture.

In the high priestly prayer, Jesus prays for the church, "As you have sent me into the world, so I have sent them into the world" (John

86. *Inst.* 3.6.3.

17:18). The church is not to be a social club that simply markets itself or advertises in order to find new members. As noted above in the section on the missional church, the church is indeed a community sent by Jesus Christ into the world. Yet according to the overall passage in John 17, the sent church is not able on its own to bear witness to Christ. It bears witness not by trying to copy the act of incarnation but by Christ's own dwelling in the church through union with Christ. "I in them, and you in me, that they may become completely one, so that the world may know that you have sent me and have loved them even as you have loved me" (17:23). In this way, Christ promises to unite himself to the church, to be one with it. But note the way that the church testifies to the world: through displaying the "oneness" of the people united to Christ. This approach in John 17 is not at all antithetical to preaching the gospel to unbelievers. Indeed, John's Gospel tells the story of Jesus in a way that invites faith, since "whoever believes in him may have eternal life" (John 3:15). But integral to the witness to Christ is also the disclosure of an astonishing reconciled oneness of the people of God—what Paul calls the "new humanity" in Christ.

Thus, in identifying with people of diverse cultures, becoming "all things to all people," there is not only an ethical dimension of conformity to Christ the servant (noted above in "A Theology of Ministry in Union with Christ the Servant") but an eschatological dimension as well: discovering the new humanity in union with Christ. On the one hand, the eschatological reality that scripture testifies to is that peoples from all tribes and cultures will worship Jesus Christ. In the words of Revelation, "They sing a new song: 'You are worthy to take the scroll and to open its seals, for you were slaughtered and by your blood you ransomed for God saints from every tribe and language and people and nation'" (Rev. 5:9). But on the other hand, this eschatological reality is not relegated exclusively to the future. In Ephesians 2:13–18, Paul indicates that the present reality of union with Christ anticipates the final oneness of God's people by breaking down the dividing walls between people groups. For "in Christ Jesus you who once were far off have been brought near by the blood of Christ." Given this key context of being "in Christ Jesus," Paul continues.

> For he is our peace; in his flesh he has made both groups into one and has broken down the dividing wall, that is, the hostility between us. He has abolished the law with its commandments and ordinances, that he might create in himself one new humanity in place of the two, thus

making peace, and might reconcile both groups to God in one body through the cross, thus putting to death that hostility through it. So he came and proclaimed peace to you who were far off and peace to those who were near; for through him both of us have access in one Spirit to the Father.

All of these dynamics—Christ being the peace that breaks down the dividing walls between hostile groups, reconciliation into one body through the cross, and the gathering of those far and near by one Spirit to serve the Father—are dynamics that take place in union with Christ. This is what the corporate dimension of adoption looks like: being adopted by God into a new family, a new humanity, in which dividing walls are broken down.

Is this new family a human creation or the work of the Spirit? The book of Acts, in particular, makes it clear that it is the Spirit's work that unites Jew and Gentile together into one new family in Christ. In the New Testament church's first major cross-cultural challenge, it did not draw upon a theology of "incarnational ministry," but responded to the Spirit's work in creating a new people that overcame cultural divisions. This began at Pentecost, where the Spirit came upon the followers of Jesus and "gave them ability" to speak "about God's deeds of power" in the languages of the Jews gathered there "from every nation under heaven living in Jerusalem" (Acts 2:4–5, 11). But not only does the Spirit overcome linguistic divisions among the Jews; this same Spirit gives visions to both Peter and Cornelius, a Gentile—visions that lead to their meeting and the disclosure that the good news is for Gentiles as well as Jews (Acts 10:1–33). In Peter's words, "I truly understand that God shows no partiality, but in every nation anyone who fears him and does what is right is acceptable to him" (Acts 10:34–35). In Peter's account to the church in Jerusalem, this movement for God to include the Gentiles is repeatedly attributed to the Spirit (Acts 11:1–18); likewise, at the council of Jerusalem, Peter points to God's "giving them the Holy Spirit, just as he did to us," for in this God "has made no distinction between them and us" (Acts 15:8–9). It is in light of the Spirit's work that the council of Jerusalem makes significant cultural concessions to Gentiles to allow for the united fellowship of Jew and Gentile together in Christ (Acts 15:22–29).

Given this, it is not surprising that God's work in creating a new family, a new humanity, is central to Paul as an apostle to the Gentiles.

As Paul speaks about in Galatians 3:26–29, the overcoming of cultural divisions is the corporate dimension of the "in Christ" reality: "For in Christ Jesus you are all children of God through faith." Paul continues, describing the consequence of all those who are "in Christ" being children of God: "As many of you as were baptized into Christ have clothed yourselves with Christ. There is no longer Jew or Greek, there is no longer slave or free, there is no longer male and female; for all of you are one in Christ Jesus. And if you belong to Christ, then you are Abraham's offspring, heirs according to the promise." As I noted in the first chapter, the Christian's "in Christ" identity has an eschatological character that comes forth from the future. It is the Christian's true identity to be lived into by the Spirit's power, so that Christians are called to act in accordance with their new adopted identity. In Galatians 3, we see specific features of that identity coming forth from the future, a future in which there is "no longer Jew or Greek . . . slave or free . . . male and female." Paul does not seem to be suggesting that these differences no longer matter but rather that they are made penultimate because of the eschatological identity of Jew and Greek—indeed, of all tribes and nations—being part of one new humanity in Christ.

Is the possibility of sharing in the Spirit's work of creating a new humanity—a multicultural family in Christ—sufficient motivation for a cross-cultural ministry of witness? If Paul's response is any indication, then yes, it is sufficient. Rather than God's work being dependent on our prior work of "becoming incarnate" or "making Christ incarnate" in a culture, it depends on the work that the Spirit is already doing, for "in him [Christ] the whole structure is joined together and grows into a holy temple in the Lord" (Eph. 2:21). In reference to the fact that the Spirit has united together a new family to be "members of the household of God" (Eph. 2:19) and "a holy temple in the Lord," Paul says, "This is the reason that I Paul am a prisoner for Christ Jesus for the sake of you Gentiles" (Eph. 3:1).[87] Precisely because of God's amazing reconciling work in creating a new adoptive humanity, Paul is a slave or servant for Jesus Christ, bearing witness to the gospel: for "Gentiles have become fellow heirs, members of the same body, and sharers in the promise in Christ Jesus through the gospel" (Eph. 3:6).

---

87. See Andrew T. Lincoln, *Ephesians*, Word Biblical Commentary (Dallas: Word, 2002), 167.

What are the implications of being sent to bear witness to Christ in order to discover this new humanity in Christ that is made possible by the Spirit? It means that while evangelism is essential, it cannot simply be done by delivering a message from a distant missionary compound or by setting up a new "program" at church for youth. It means that we are sent into the world to bear witness to Christ in a way that allows the new humanity to be disclosed—a new humanity that does not mirror our own culture but that finds oneness in Christ from different cultural locations. Thus, identifying with and respecting the culture one is sent to is essential. We cannot pretend to inhabit or to "incarnate" into that culture. At the same time, because we seek to participate in the Spirit's work of creating a new humanity of people from all tribes and nations, we cannot say, "Follow my cultural manifestation of Christianity." No. Precisely because of the differentiated oneness of Christ's body, the new adopted humanity, we are called to honor this cultural difference as we bear witness to Jesus Christ.

But the church is a people who are not only sent but also gathered by the Spirit. This is a weakness of many "incarnational ministries": practitioners go out to the youth or to persons in the city, or they reach across other cultural boundaries, but because the metaphor of incarnation is about sending, there is little emphasis on gathering. Many youth reached through incarnational ministry do not join a community in worship; indeed, some advocates of incarnational ministry treat corporate worship as a distraction from true ministry, which is simply about identifying with the other. While this relational emphasis has value, focusing only on the dispersed church ends up promoting individualism and devaluing the ways that Jesus has promised to present himself by the Spirit (as Reformational theology points out): in word and sacrament in corporate worship.

The eschatological image in Revelation 5:9 is of the new humanity *in corporate worship*. This fits with Paul's teaching that the Spirit unites peoples of many cultures and tribes precisely so that they might "have access in one Spirit to the Father" (Eph. 2:18). Worship is central to this adoptive reality, for the Spirit cries, "Abba! Father!" in God's children, and the Spirit "intercedes with sighs too deep for words" for those who are in Christ (Rom. 8:15, 26). Gathering as a people made one in Christ displays the church's reconciled yet differentiated oneness, bearing witness to the world as Jesus prays in John's Gospel (17:23).

The Indicative and the Imperative in Christ: Living by the Spirit in Gratitude

Let me now consider an objection to my account. Given the reality of Christian division, how can discoveringing the oneness of Christ's body as the new humanity be a motivation for ministry? Doesn't the embarrassing fact that there are many denominations and Christian divisions make void this desire to see oneness?

At this point Reformation voices like Calvin's can be quite helpful. Calvin took very seriously the language about the oneness of the church noted in the passages above. He also knew the pain of Christian division, as refugees fleeing religious persecution flooded into Geneva. In noting why the church is called "catholic," Calvin writes,

> The church is called "catholic," or "universal," because there could not be two or three churches unless Christ be torn asunder (cf. 1 Cor. 1:13)—which cannot happen! But all the elect are so united in Christ (cf. Eph. 1:22–23) that as they are dependent on one Head, they also grow together into one body, being joined and knit together (cf. Eph. 4:16) as are the limbs of a body (Rom. 12:5; 1 Cor. 10:17; 12:12, 27). They are made truly one since they live together in one faith, hope, and love, and in the same Spirit of God. For they have been called not only into the same inheritance of eternal life but also to participate in one God and Christ (Eph. 5:30).[88]

The oneness of the church is a gift. The church is not one because of an achievement but because of the oneness of Jesus Christ himself. Because Christ is one, all who are in Christ are one—given one inheritance and one Spirit who enables Christians to grow in this unity in Christ. The indicative "you are one in Christ" leads to the imperative to "live into that oneness" by walking by the Spirit, practicing love and forgiveness in the body of Christ, and bearing witness to Christ the Head, the source of unity. Christian division is indeed a painful reality. But there are also signs of the kingdom around us, ways that the dividing walls between adults and youth, urbanites and suburbanites, black and white, have begun to be overcome in Christ. The way toward unity is not in manufacturing it ourselves but in seeking in concrete ways to recognize and live into the oneness in Christ,

88. *Inst.* 4.1.2.

participating in the ways that the Spirit is already at work creating a new humanity in Christ.

Thus the overall character of participation ministry is that of gift. As explored in chapter 1, because those in Christ know the Father's pardon in justification, they can live into the imperatives of walking by the Spirit in a way that is freed from the "severe requirement" of the law.[89] As adopted children, they can "hear themselves called with fatherly gentleness by God, [and so] they will cheerfully and with great eagerness answer, and follow his leading."[90] Both justification and sanctification in Christ are gifts—they constitute a "double grace." Along with this, the oneness in the body of Christ is a gift that those who are in Christ can live into both through seeking to live in harmony as the church *and* in being sent to discover the Spirit's work of continuing to create this oneness in Christ across cultural divisions. The good news of the gospel is Jesus Christ and union with him. That is why Calvin so clearly distinguishes between the transcendent Christ (to whom we are united by the Spirit) and our own lives, in which we are called to follow and "express Christ" the servant. Our reflection of Christ is not the good news itself; it is testimony to Jesus Christ and to the gifts of the double grace received in him.[91]

Yet when one's model for ministry is that of "imitating" the process of becoming incarnate, that distinction tends to be compromised in practice, as we have seen above. We need to hold together two truths: As those who belong to Christ, we *are* called to "express Christ," to be a sign of the kingdom, a sign of God's reign in the new humanity in Christ. But a sign also points beyond itself—in this case, to Jesus Christ, the King, just as John the Baptist pointed to Christ. Instead of making the incarnation into an abstract principle that places our own action at the center, we need to realize that we are participants and sharers in Jesus Christ, the one redeemer, by the power of the Spirit. As Andrew Purves notes, "Making the incarnation something that we do can easily assume that the living Christ is not present and active."[92] Indeed, speaking of the incarnation as repeatable can

---

89. *Inst.* 3.19.4.

90. *Inst.* 3.19.5.

91. On the importance of this distinction in Calvin's thought, see Ronald Wallace, *Calvin's Doctrine of the Christian Life* (Grand Rapids: Eerdmans, 1959), 42–43.

92. Andrew Purves, *The Crucifixion of Ministry: Surrendering Our Ambitions to the Service of Christ* (Downers Grove, IL: InterVarsity, 2007), 57.

leave us with an abstract "Christ-principle" rather than the living Christ who acts in the world.[93] It conceals the fundamental reality of ministry that "it is *his* ministry that is primary, for his ministry alone is redemptive."[94] Rather than making our own action primary, participation ministry has the character of receiving a gift that leads to participation in God's ongoing work—receiving a new identity of oneness in Christ and gratefully sharing in the Spirit's work of creating a new humanity in Christ.

In sum, in addition to having a much richer biblical and theological warrant, there are several practical ways that participation ministry overcomes the deficiencies of incarnational ministry.

(1) Realism about cultural difference. Incarnational ministry gives us an objective that is inherently impossible to achieve—that of truly becoming "one" with another culture. This can lead to continual frustration on the one hand or to self-deception on the other. Participation ministry maintains a realism about cultural difference, even while encouraging the crossing of cultural boundaries in ministry. How? Participation ministry means that those in Christ are sent into the world to bear witness to Jesus Christ in a way that reflects Christ's way of servanthood and humility, living into the Spirit's work of creating a new humanity in Christ. This reconciled oneness in Christ created by the Spirit comes about not through encouraging cultural homogeneity, but rather through the gathering of a diverse people into the one body of Christ united to worship the Father.

(2) Service that is rooted in grateful reliance upon the Spirit. In many instances, incarnational ministry gives practitioners the arduous task of repeating the act of incarnation through cultural identification, which is assumed to make Christ present. But in New Testament and also Reformational terms, it is the Spirit who makes Christ present. "Christ does not otherwise dwell in us than through his Spirit, nor in any other way communicate himself to us than through the same Spirit," Calvin says.[95] Primary to the Spirit's work is the act of uniting

---

93. "Even the appeal to an implicit Christ (for the word *incarnation* has only one subject, referring to a specific event in history) becomes the appeal to a spiritual or ethical Christ-principle." Andrew Purves, *Reconstructing Pastoral Theology: A Christological Foundation* (Louisville: Westminster John Knox, 2004), 179.

94. Purves, *Crucifixion of Ministry,* 57, emphasis added.

95. John Calvin, "Summary of Doctrine concerning the Ministry of Word and Sacrament," in *Calvin: Theological Treatises,* ed. J. K. S. Reid (Philadelphia: Westminster, 1964), 172.

people to Jesus Christ and his body, of giving the gift of free pardon and new life in Christ so that conformity to Christ the servant is an action of grateful adopted children rather than of achievers trying to make ministry happen on their own. This emphasis on the Spirit's mediation of Christ also gives an important place to gathering as Christ's body for corporate worship, thus living into the Spirit's work of gathering a people to worship Jesus Christ, the Head. In this, worshipers encounter the living Christ through word and sacrament by the Spirit's power and then are sent again into the world as Christ's witnesses.

(3) Witness to the transcendent Christ. Finally, incarnational ministry asks us to imitate what the New Testament does not ask us to imitate (the unique incarnation of the Word), while participation ministry is first and foremost about *witness* to the unique Christ in word and deed, a pervasive theme in the New Testament. One bears witness to Jesus Christ in light of the indicative: since the Spirit has already united us to Christ the obedient servant, the expression of this life will live into the "imperative" of putting on Jesus Christ, displaying our union with him and seeking to reflect his life of humble service by following his example and his teaching. Ultimately, our lives are not the good news, and we ourselves are not the good news. Instead, in participation ministry we bear witness in word and deed to Jesus Christ, the one who is the good news, as ones united to him by the Spirit.

Excursus: Ursinus on Participation in the
One True Prophet, Priest, and King

While the preceding chapter drew upon the thought of Calvin as a theologian of the Reformation, there is much more to be retrieved from the Reformation in formulating a theology of ministry that is an alternative to incarnational ministry. This excursus gives a Reformational retrieval that helps, in a concrete way, to address a question that arises for a framework of ministry that is rooted in union with Christ: what does it mean to participate in the unique Christ—in the power and expansiveness of his life and ministry by the Spirit—yet recognize that we are not Christ but ones who belong to Christ?

We find helpful reflections on this in the third generation of the Reformation in Ursinus and the Heidelberg Catechism, of which Ursinus was the primary author. His approach is both simple and profound. The concept of the "three offices" is one of the most deeply biblical and broadly comprehensive ways to speak about Christ's person and work in brief terms. Ursinus takes the three offices and considers them in terms of what it means to participate in Christ.

Question 31. Why is he called "Christ," meaning anointed?

Answer. Because he has been ordained by God the Father and has been anointed with the Holy Spirit to be our chief prophet and teacher who perfectly reveals to us the secret counsel and will of God for our redemption; our only high priest who has redeemed us by the one sacrifice of his body, and who continually pleads our cause with the Father; and our eternal king who governs us by his Word and Spirit, and who guards us and keeps us in the redemption he has won for us.

Question 32. But why are you called a Christian?

Answer. Because by faith I am a member of Christ and so I share in his anointing. I am anointed to confess his name, to present myself to him as a living sacrifice of thanks, to strive with a good conscience against sin and the devil in this life, and afterward to reign with Christ over all creation for all eternity.[96]

Note how the Heidelberg Catechism does two things simultaneously. First, it speaks about a profound union between believers and Jesus Christ. "I am a member of Christ and so I share in his anointing." Its language is strong and unequivocal on this sharing in Christ. But second, note how our "membership" in Christ and "sharing" in his anointing are derivative and subordinate to Jesus Christ. Christ alone is the "chief prophet and teacher," our "only high priest," and our intercessor to the Father. In ourselves, we can do none of these things. Indeed, not even our ministries can act as prophet, priest, or king to the people we serve apart from the activity of the living Christ.

Nevertheless, as Ursinus explains in his commentary, it is an extraordinary gift given to all who share Christ's anointing—all Christians—to participate in Christ as the true prophet, priest, and king. For through faith Christians are "engrafted

---

96. In *Ecumenical Creeds and Reformed Confessions* (Grand Rapids: CRC Publications, 1987), 25.

into Christ as members to the head, that we may be continu-
ously sustained, governed and quickened by him; and because he
makes us prophets, priests and kings unto God and his Father,
by making us partakers of his anointing."[97] This new identity
conferred upon Christians is an "unspeakable dignity," a new
identity that calls forth a response in action. For in this new,
anointed identity is "a participation in all of the gifts of Christ"
through our participation in the three offices.[98]

What, specifically, does it look like to *live into* the new identity
as "members of Christ," who is the prophet, priest, and king?
As prophets, Christians are anointed to "confess his name,"[99] to
participate in the teacher who is the truth through "understanding, acknowledgement and confession" of "the true doctrine of
God necessary for salvation." All who participate in Christ are
called to both "know" and "confess" the truth about God in
Christ, so that Christ's truth can be "revealed in its living force
and power."[100] In his commentary on the Heidelberg Catechism,
Ursinus carefully holds together two concerns as he approaches
this office. On the one hand, we look to Christ (and not ourselves) as the prophet, the one who teaches the truth. For Christ
is the head of the church, thus "just as a head is placed highest,
and is, therefore, deserving of the greatest honor, and is the
fountain of all life, so Christ has the highest place in the church,
for in him the Spirit is without measure, and from his fullness
we receive all of the gifts we enjoy."[101] Christians share only in "a
certain measure" of Christ's gifts.[102] Christ is the true prophet, the
great teacher of the truth, while Christians are not. Yet, on the
other hand, this sharing in Christ is real—for we are members
of Christ's body, which means there is "a close and indissoluble

---

97. *HC Comm.* 180. For an articulate account of how Ursinus on the three offices
can counter misconceptions about the Reformed confessional tradition expressed by
parts of the missional church movement, see Renee S. House, "Becoming a 'Missional'
Denomination for the Twenty-first Century: A Constructive Analysis of Theology
and Specific Practices in the Reformed Church in America" (PhD diss., Princeton
Theological Seminary, 2008), 215–324.

98. *HC Comm.* 180.

99. Heidelberg Catechism, question 32, in *Ecumenical Creeds and Reformed
Confessions*, 25.

100. *HC Comm.* 179.

101. *HC Comm.* 177.

102. *HC Comm.* 178.

union between Christ and us."[103] Christ is the "living head," and members of his body have the Spirit dwelling in them, enabling a sharing in the gifts and offices of Christ.[104] Thus, while Christians are not masters of the truth or prophets in themselves, they are to know and confess the truth in Christ as the Spirit enables them to have fellowship with Christ the Prophet.

But Christians are not just called to know the truth in their minds and confess the truth with their mouths. As ones who share in Christ's priesthood, Christians are called to intentionally "show and communicate" this truth to others with their lives. This involves no less than dying to the "old man" and giving one's whole self as an instrument "of righteousness unto God." This death with Christ to the old self will involve "cheerful and patient endurance of the cross."[105] Simultaneously, Christians as priests are called to pray and intercede for those around them, to offer alms to those in need, and to offer grateful worship to God.[106] Thus, in contrast to some forms of incarnational ministry that downplay the significance of corporate worship, for Ursinus it has a key role: corporate worship is essential both for the edification of the body and for its ministry in and to the world; it is essential to the calling of all who share in Christ's anointing as priest.

Moreover, extrapolating from Ursinus's commentary, we can say that all of this action as priests on behalf of others reflects the way that Christians participate in Christ, the high priest who could sympathize with the weaknesses of those he served (Heb. 4:15; 5:2). Whether in urban, youth, or cross-cultural ministry, Christians as priests are called to "show and communicate" the good news in a way that is in "sympathy" with the hearers, while also reflecting the cruciform way of service seen in Jesus Christ. This involves living lives of self-giving, but since Jesus Christ is the true prophet and priest, rather than us, it also involves "confessing" the gospel before others (Matt. 10:32).[107] In order to be a coherent witness and truly "show and communicate" the truth of the gospel—with word and deed

---

103. *HC Comm.* 177.
104. *HC Comm.* 177–78.
105. *HC Comm.* 179.
106. See *HC Comm.* 179.
107. *HC Comm.* 179.

held together—one must seek to reflect the humility and love of Christ the servant and priest. However, lest we think that our own presence is inherently redemptive, Ursinus's commentary insists that "Christ offered up a sacrifice of thanksgiving and propitiation, [while] at the same time, we offer only sacrifices of thanksgiving."[108] Unlike Christ's sacrifice, our sacrifice of thanksgiving (in our lives of grateful service) does not forgive sins; it is not perfect, nor is it redemptive. We share in Christ's priestly anointing, but we are not Christ.

Moving on to Christ's office of king, Ursinus continues his careful balance. On the one hand, since we share in Christ's anointing, we share in Christ's kingship and victory. Thus, Christians inherit the kingdom of God as adopted children.[109] In this way, Ursinus integrates Christ's teaching about the kingdom in the Gospels with Paul's theme of union with Christ: as those who share in Christ the King's anointing, we inherit the kingdom.[110] In addition, Christians share in Christ's victory as king over that which opposes God—for "through faith, the devil, the world, and all our enemies" are overcome, making reference to 1 Corinthians 15:57 in which God "gives us the victory through our Lord Jesus Christ."[111] Yet on the other hand, Ursinus insists that Christ is the true king and we are not. Only Christ is the natural king, while we share in his kingship by adoption. For "Christ conquers his enemies by his own power," while "we overcome our foes in and through him—by his grace and assistance." Moreover, Christ alone rules the world by "his word and Spirit"; Christ alone is the redeemer who gives the Spirit and brings salvation.[112] It is a great privilege and calling to participate in Christ's kingdom reign—opposing by faith the spiritual enemies that oppose Christ's lordship, and sharing in Christ's victory. But Ursinus remains very clear that Christ alone is the true king who brings victory and salvation.

In sum, there is a profound balance in Ursinus's theology of participating in Christ the Prophet, Priest, and King. There is a great "dignity" in this sharing in Christ, in his anointing,

---

108. HC Comm. 179.
109. HC Comm. 180.
110. HC Comm. 179–80.
111. HC Comm. 179-80.
112. HC Comm. 180.

in his offices.[113] We have the great privilege of testifying to the truth in Christ as prophets; of worshipfully offering our lives to God as priests in a way that can "show and communicate" the gospel; of opposing the sinful ways of the world that resist Christ's lordship, knowing that we share in Christ's kingly victory. But it is always Jesus Christ alone who is the redeemer—Jesus Christ who is the true prophet, priest, and king. While we should seek for our ministries—whether to youth or to people in urban or cross-cultural settings—to be relational, full of a servanthood that meets people where they are at, we can never be the true prophet, priest, or king to those around us. It is only by "participation" that we can act in these roles—derivatively, subordinately, as witnesses to the true redeemer, Jesus Christ.

113. *HC Comm.* 180.

Conclusion

y hope is that the preceding chapters present a theological vision that is strange to modern eyes. This vision explores the significance of biblical and theological language that has often become dulled in contemporary Western churches. It has been colonized by the dualisms and individualism of our age. Our eyesight has become so colored by the idols of modernity that scripture's language of union with Christ can be reduced to self-help strategies to make us feel good about ourselves; thus, loving communion with God can be trivialized, evacuated of either a sense of God's majestic transcendence, at one extreme, or the startling closeness of God that calls for our whole identity, at the other. In this dualism emerging from modernity, the biblical call to justice in Christ becomes either a way to talk about our own heroic action or an optional "extra" for super-Christians. Even when we seek to claim a central doctrine of the Christian faith for our ministry—the incarnation—it tends to be received in a way that makes it into an abstracted model for ministry, conforming Jesus into *our* ideal of the missionary-anthropologist rather than conforming our own identity to that of Jesus Christ, the wholly unique, obedient servant.

In light of this cultural captivity, we do not need simply to cognize a new set of propositions. We need new eyes, new vision, a way to begin to sense our cultural captivity and receive the Spirit's word to the church through scripture. As noted in the introduction, this book utilizes a theology of retrieval as a strategy to address our cultural captivity. Like a cross-cultural encounter, we begin to see "with new eyes" when we encounter the Spirit's work in the Christian past. It should strike us as strange at points. It should shake up our modern categories. But it should also seem strangely familiar, for it orients us to conformity to the same Jesus Christ to whom Christians have already been united by the Spirit.

John Webster likewise describes theologies of retrieval in terms of a renewal of vision, for their posture is "to stand with the Christian past which, precisely because it is foreign to contemporary conventions, can function as an instrument for the enlargement of vision."[1] Theologians of retrieval return to classical, particularly premodern, sources so that these sources can help enlarge their vision and "exceed the possibilities of the present." For while systematic theologians often engage in a rereading of the tradition, "what distinguishes theologies of retrieval is that its practitioners do not regard these classics as only one element, however authoritative, in a process of correlation or negotiation between the Christian past and modernity. Classics come first; they exceed the possibilities of the present and have the capacity to expose and pass beyond its limitations."[2] Stated differently, theologies of retrieval simultaneously challenge the modern categories that squeeze the gospel into its own mold and renew the theological imagination, shedding new light on the scriptural witness.

Theologies of retrieval do not describe the logic of early theologies in order to simply reify or repristinate those earlier theologies. Indeed, such a view violates the critical dimensions of retrieval that were outlined in the introduction, as well as many of the (retrievable!) insights of our present theology of pilgrimage, outlined in chapter 3. Instead, theologies of retrieval begin to give us new eyes toward scripture and toward our present context, as well as toward the Christian past. For this book in particular, seeing with new eyes does not point to an end of the conversation but to a change in the theological conversation. Thus, in this conclusion I end with some brief observations about how the act of retrieval in this book can change today's theological conversation.

The opening chapter focused on the countercultural character of a key yet neglected image for salvation: adoption by the Triune God.

1. John Webster, "Theologies of Retrieval," in *Oxford Handbook of Systematic Theology*, ed. John Webster, Kathryn Tanner, and Iain Torrance (Oxford: Oxford University Press, 2007), 590.
2. Ibid.

In this vision of salvation, believers are conferred a new identity in union with Christ and are called to live into this identity by the Spirit. Calvin's use of this biblical image in his theology of the double grace of union with Christ leads to astonishing results. Salvation is not just about maintaining a faith commitment or being "good and nice," as the functional deism of Western culture assumes. Salvation is nothing less than a new identity, received as a gift. In union with Christ, believers receive both forgiveness of sins and new life by the Spirit, as children of the Most High. Salvation is about nothing less than this gift of a new, adopted identity in which God's good creation is restored. Rather than placing our own action at the center of the drama and seeing religion as a decision-making rule book that makes us feel good about ourselves (as in moralistic therapeutic deism), we find our true identities in Jesus Christ as part of a drama in which the Triune God is the central actor: united to Jesus Christ by the Spirit, this same Spirit enacts our adopted identity in and through us, calling out to God as Abba, Father. In activities such as prayer and the Lord's Supper, our capacities are activated by the Spirit to be who we were created to be—children of God, loving God and neighbor in gratitude, as co-heirs with Christ. In this new identity in Christ, we not only move beyond the distant yet convenient God of MTD, but we also overcome our modern aversion toward commitment and witness in a pluralistic society. Because Jesus Christ is the Alpha and Omega, we can be confident that he is unsurpassable. He is, in fact, the ultimate "progressive" person; bearing witness to Jesus Christ as the way, the truth, and the life (rather than to ourselves as the way, the truth, and the life) means that we can be clear about our testimony to Jesus Christ without turning it into an act of arrogant conceit. For our true identity—the future that we are living into—is in Jesus Christ. We do not own the future, but Jesus Christ does. Thus we are freed to witness to him with humility and love in our pluralistic world.

Chapter 1 changes the conversation on various levels. When we recognize the functional MTD present in much Western Christianity, we can see more clearly the radical character of the gospel as the double grace of union with Christ—the gospel of salvation as adoption. The common theological move of accepting a functional deism, which pushes the Trinity and union with Christ out of view, is challenged. In addition, our own ideals about owning the future and being "progressive" are unveiled as we recognize Jesus Christ as the Lord of the future, freeing us to live into our identity in Christ. This leaves us with a newly framed conversation, one that focuses on discerning the nature of Christian identity *in Jesus Christ* rather than treating Christianity as a generic religion that needs to be reworked from the outside in a pluralistic context. Jesus Christ is the origin and goal of history. This conviction frees us, as finite, limited human beings, to witness to him rather than ourselves.

In chapter 2, I begin with the observation that the New Testament's strongest language about sin—as slavery, death, and the ability to do "nothing"—represents one side of the coin that corresponds to a soteriology of communion: communion with God through union with Christ, abiding in Christ, participating in Christ. In this context, the affirmation of "total depravity"—the inability of a fallen sinner to perform any good for the sake of salvation—goes hand in hand with a profound soteriology in which humans are created for communion with God; and in redemption this communion is restored in Christ by the Spirit. Seen in light of Augustine's meditation on the incarnation, true humanity exists in harmony and communion with God, in response to divine initiative. The humanity of Christ did not take an autonomous first step toward God. Likewise, it is a contradiction in terms for our own humanity to move toward God "in itself," autonomously, because salvation is communion with God, not autonomy. "Total communion" is a soteriology that recognizes that humans cannot move toward God apart from communion with God. Salvation is not partial communion with God and partial autonomy from God; insofar as it is salvation, it is divinely initiated communion with God all the way down. The chapter continues by articulating the way that the "bound will" is still free, in certain senses, highlighting developments in Reformed scholasticism that are usually neglected or caricatured but that actually build on the positive insights of Augustine and Calvin explored in earlier parts of the chapter.

The material in chapter 2 involves such a change of the conversation that many who heard the lecture version of the chapter were simply astonished. Calvinists who defined their theological core by the TULIP acronym were challenged to see total depravity in a completely different context—in light of the broad themes of the incarnation, union with Christ, and the gracious work of the Spirit, which activates human capacities. On the other hand, many who used TULIP as obvious evidence of the absurdity and fatalism of Reformed teaching found themselves in a new world: why hadn't anyone pointed out these connections to "total communion" before? The account of total depravity and total communion will not convince all, but it is an utterly different conversation than conventional modern debates about TULIP. It opens up a new world for the conversation.

Chapter 3 focuses on the profound way that divine mystery and communion are held together in Calvin, Junius, and Bavinck. Between these figures, I explore an area where Calvin's theology of accommodation and divine mystery could have been more consistent: his account of the beatific vision. Earlier studies of Calvin on accommodation have not noted the potentially problematic character of his account, particularly his ambiguity about whether all human knowledge is, in the end, accommodated. In order to provide a supplement that extends the positive insights of his theology of accommodation yet upholds it more consistently, I draw upon Junius and Bavinck, particularly in their use of the distinction between archetypal and ectypal knowledge of God. In the end, all three figures give an account of divine mystery and communion that overcomes modern polarities between immanence and transcendence, knowledge and mystery. By engaging these figures, we can see with new eyes: one does not have to choose between emphasizing God's immanence or God's transcendence. Indeed, a strong account of divine transcendence is precisely what makes intimate communion with God possible. Negative theology, which openly confesses the incomprehensibility of God, is a necessary presupposition for a theology of communion with God in union with Christ.

In addition, in this account, emphasizing the mystery of God does *not* downplay God's self-disclosure in revelation. We are not left with simply our own projections about God. Instead, although all of our knowledge of God is accommodated—in Bavinck's words, "inadequate, finite, and limited"—our knowledge of God is sufficient for its purpose: providing a relational way to know God, to be in fellowship with the Triune God in Christ. Indeed, as Junius eloquently argues, all of our knowledge of God, although accommodated, is a feature of our union with and sharing in Jesus Christ and his human knowledge of the Father. In all of this, a false either-or of modernity—with one side focusing on divine mystery and human finitude and the other side on the divine origin of revelation—is overcome. The theology of Calvin, Junius, and Bavinck holds together mystery and knowledge, finitude and the Triune God's loving, accommodating action in Christ in ways that can be instructive for both the theological left and the theological right of modernity.

Chapter 4, which deals with the Lord's Supper, union with Christ, and justice, also gives us new eyes to see, allowing us to move beyond persistent modern dualisms related to the gospel and justice. On the ecclesial left, the gospel tends to be collapsed into nothing more than a call to justice; the good news comes to be about our own heroic actions rather than being centered in the action of the Triune God in and through Jesus Christ. On the other side, evangelical congregations often consider justice to be an optional extra for Christians; some evangelicals have rediscovered its importance, but there is still a lack of clarity about how justice relates to the gospel of Jesus Christ.

By analyzing a historical example of racial injustice in the Dutch Reformed Church in South Africa, this chapter shows the close lines of connection between the Lord's Supper, union with Christ, and the church's call to unity, reconciliation, and justice. In light of the response of the Belhar Confession to this tragic history, I give a constructive retrieval of Calvin's theology of the Lord's Supper and justice, which roots both in Jesus Christ. In the process, I show how justice is not an optional extra for Christians, nor is it meant to be about our own heroic actions. Instead, the gospel is Jesus Christ and our union with him. In this union with Christ we receive both forgiveness and new life as gifts of the Spirit—new life that is *inseparable* from the call to love our neighbor and act with justice. Specifically, the Lord's Supper is a site where the close connection between the gospel and justice is seen, for in the Supper we participate in Jesus Christ and in the church as the body of Christ; as we do so, we also offer ourselves as "a sacrifice of praise" to love our neighbor—especially the neighbor in need, the wounded body. Thus, in the Supper we are brought into communion with three distinct and yet inseparable bodies: the body and blood of Christ, the body of the church, and the wounded body of the neighbor. This chapter changes the conversation not only by overcoming false modern polarities between the gospel and justice, but also by showing how Christ-focused worship is absolutely key for living into the connection between the gospel and justice. The substance of this connection is union with Christ by the power of the Spirit.

The final chapter provides an appreciative critique of incarnational ministry and an alternative theology of ministry through union with Christ—participation ministry. This is quite clearly a conversation changer. Indeed, in writing this chapter, it was clear that the conversation about this topic is broken. Biblical scholars and systematic theologians generally dismiss a key assumption of incarnational ministry—namely, that we should attempt to imitate the act of the Word becoming incarnate. Yet the notion of incarnational ministry is a powerful motivator for culture-crossing ministry that has become very widespread even as the concerns of biblical scholars and systematic theologians remain unaddressed. A theology of union with Christ offers a way for the conversation to move forward once again.

Rather than dismissing everything that advocates of incarnational ministry claim, I sort out the basic strands of thought in my typology of various streams of the movement. There is much to affirm in the thought of incarnational ministry, and those insights can be both retained and refined when the key "proof texts" for incarnational ministry are seen in light of union with Christ. Rather than imitating the abstract model of becoming incarnate, we are united to Christ, the humble servant, and are being conformed to his image by the Spirit. Drawing upon Calvin, Barth, and Ursinus in the excursus, I show how viewing ministry as union with and participation in Christ holds promise by providing both a Christ-centered way to speak about the humility and service that Christians are called to and strong grounds for "becoming all things to all people," taking cultural identification very seriously. Indeed, we are sent to witness to Jesus Christ in word and deed in a way that participates in the Spirit's work of creating a new humanity; this new humanity in Christ overcomes the dividing walls between cultures, even as it displays a culturally diverse oneness in Christ. Incarnational ministry, in its analogy between us and the divine Word that takes on flesh, tends to assume on a practical level that our cultural identification is inherently redemptive. But ministry as participation in Christ holds together the reality of our union with Christ and the fact that Christ himself is the redeemer. We point not to ourselves but to Christ, like John the Baptist.

In all these chapters, we see how a theology of union with Christ can give us new eyes, changing not only the theological conversation but the way that we live into the Christian life and ministry. It is no accident that various chapters exposit union with Christ in terms of prayer, the sacraments, the reception of God's word, a life of justice, and culture-crossing ministry. Retrieving a Reformational theology of union with Christ should not just focus on reviving debates about justification, as important as those debates are. Union with Christ is a biblical, catholic, and Reformational theme that has astonishing implications for our identity. It impacts the way we conceive of our identity as ones who belong to Christ, members of Christ's body called to love those with wounded bodies in the world. It reorients our desires, our view of God's kingdom as we are united to Jesus Christ, the King, as his children. It cuts through our self-centered ideologies, putting the action of the Triune God in Christ at the center. Yet as it does so, we are not left behind but are brought into an exciting new world, one in which we are united to Christ and filled with the Spirit who prays to God as Abba, Father, in and through us. This new world—coming forth to us from the future—reveals our true identity as ones created for communion with God. As adopted children, we are freed to act with gratitude, to love God and neighbor as ones who have been forgiven of sin and given new life in Christ.

Index